CW00631420

Technician Unit 19

Preparing Personal Taxation Computations (FA 2004)

For exams in June 2005
and December 2005

Combined Text and Kit

In this August 2004 edition

- Combined Text and Revision Kit written in a clear straightforward way
- Numerous new examples and activities
- Activities checklist to tie in each activity to specific knowledge and understanding, performance criteria and/or range statement
- December 2003 paper included as a practice exam
- Thorough reliable updating of material to FA 2004

FOR EXAM BASED ASSESSMENTS IN JUNE 2005 AND DECEMBER 2005 UNDER THE FINANCE ACT 2004 TAX LEGISLATION

PROFESSIONAL EDUCATION

First edition August 2003
Second edition August 2004

ISBN 0 7517 1723 1

British Library Cataloguing-in-Publication Data
A catalogue record for this book
is available from the British Library

Published by

BPP Professional Education
Aldine House, Aldine Place
London W12 8AW

www.bpp.com

Printed in Great Britain by WM Print
Frederick Street
Walsall
West Midlands
WS2 9NE

We are grateful to the Lead Body for Accounting for
permission to reproduce extracts from the Standards
of Competence for Accounting, and to the AAT for
permission to reproduce extracts from the mapping
and Guidance Notes.

Contents

Introduction

How to use this Combined Text and Kit – Technician qualification structure –
Unit 19 Standards of competence – Exam based assessment technique – Assessment
strategy – Tax rates and allowances

		Page	Answers to activities

Order form

Review form & free prize draw

Introduction

How to use this Combined Text and Kit

Aims of this Combined Text and Kit

To provide the knowledge and practice to help you succeed in the examination for Technician Unit 19 *Preparing Personal Tax Computations*.

To pass the examination successfully you need a thorough understanding in all areas covered by the standards of competence.

To tie in with the other components of the BPP Effective Study Package to ensure you have the best possible chance of success.

Combined Text and Kit

Parts A to C covers all you need to know for the exam based assessment for Unit 19 *Preparing Personal Tax Computations*. Numerous activities throughout the text help you practise what you have just learnt.

When you have understood and practised the material in Parts A to C and reviewed the answers to activities in Part D, you will have the knowledge and experience to tackle Parts E and F of this Combined Text and Kit for Unit 19 *Preparing Personal Tax Computations*. These parts aim to get you through the exam by providing you with plenty of activities to practise and also some full exam based assessments.

Passcards

These short memorable notes are focused on key topics for the technician units, designed to remind you of what the Combined Text and Kit has taught you.

Recommended approach to this Combined Text and Kit

(a) To achieve competence in Unit 19 (and all the other units) you need to be able to do **everything** specified by the standards. Study Parts A to C carefully and do not skip any of it.

(b) Learning is an **active** process. Do **all** the activities as you work through Parts A to C so you can be sure you really understand what you have read.

(c) Before you work through Parts E and F of this Combined Text and Kit, check that you still remember the material using the following revision plan for each of the chapters in Parts A to C.

    (i) Read and learn the **key learning points**, which are a summary of the chapter. This includes key terms and shows the sort of things likely to come up in the exam. Are there any gaps in your knowledge? If so, study the section again.

    (ii) Do the **quick quiz** again. If you know what you're doing, it shouldn't take long.

(d) Once you have completed your quick revision plan for each chapter, you are ready to tackle Parts E and F of this Combined Text and Kit.

    (i) Try the **Practice Activities**. These are short activities, linked to the Standards of Competences, to reinforce your learning and consolidate the practice that you have had doing the activities in parts A to C of this Combined Text and Kit.

    (ii) **Attempt the Exam Based Assessments**. These will help you develop techniques in approaching the assessments and allocating time correctly. For guidance on this, please see Exam Based Assessment Technique on page (xvii)

(e) Go through the **Passcards** as often as you can in the weeks leading up to your examination.

This approach is only a suggestion. You or your college may well adapt it to suit your needs.

Remember this is a **practical** course.

(a) Try to relate the material to your experience in the workplace or any other work experience you may have had.

(b) Try to make as many links as you can to your study of the other Units at Technician level.

(c) Keep this text, (hopefully) you will find it invaluable in your everyday work too!

Lecturers' Resource Pack Activities

Part G of this Combined Text and Kit includes a number of chapter-linked activities without answers. We have also included one exam based assessment without answers. The answers for this section are in the BPP Lecturers' Resource Pack for this Unit.

Tax forms

In your exam you are likely to have take information from Forms P60 and P11D. We have included the applicable forms within this text for illustrative purposes. You will practice using these forms when you try the Practice Examinations in Parts F.

In addition you may have to complete the following supplementary pages to the tax return form:

(i) Employment income
(ii) Property income.

You can practice using these forms when you try the activities in Parts E and F of this combined text and kit.

Please note that at the time this Text was printed 2004/05 versions of these pages were not available. We have therefore updated the 2003/04 versions of the forms and amended them where necessary to fit in with Finance Act 2004/05 tax legislation. This necessarily involves us in making 'guesses' about how the 2004/05 forms will change. Although, it is unlikely that the 2004/05 versions of the forms will differ significantly from what we have included here, it is important that you contact the Revenue for updated copies before you sit your examination.

If you have internet access you should be able to find the 2004/05 forms on the Revenue's website (www.inlandrevenue.gov.UK).

Technician qualification structure

The competence-based Education and Training Scheme of the Association of Accounting Technicians is based on an analysis of the work of accounting staff in a wide range of industries and types of organisation. The Standards of Competence for Accounting which students are expected to meet are based on this analysis.

The AAT issued new standards of competence in 2002, which took effect from 1 July 2003. This Text reflects the **new standards.**

The Standards identify the key purpose of the accounting occupation, which is to operate, maintain and improve systems to record, plan, monitor and report on the financial activities of an organisation, and a number of key roles of the occupation. Each key role is subdivided into units of competence, which are further divided into elements of competences. By successfully completing assessments in specified units of competence, students can gain qualifications at NVQ/SVQ levels 2, 3 and 4, which correspond to the AAT Foundation, Intermediate and Technician stages of competence respectively.

Whether you are competent in a Unit is demonstrated by means of:

- *Either* an Exam Based Assessment (set and marked by AAT assessors)
- *Or* a Skills Based Assessment (where competence is judged by an Approved Assessment Centre to whom responsibility for this is devolved)

Below we set out the overall structure of the Technician (NVQ/SVQ Level 4) stage. In the next section there is more detail about the Exam Based Assessment for Unit 19.

NVQ/SVQ Level 4

Group 1 Core Units – All units are mandatory.

| Unit 8 Contributing to the Management of Performance and the Enhancement of Value | Element 8.1 | Collect, analyse and disseminate information about costs |
| | Element 8.2 | Make recommendations and make recommendations to enhance value |

Unit 9 Contributing to the Planning and Control of Resources	Element 9.1	Prepare forecasts of income and expenditure
	Element 9.2	Produce draft budget proposals
	Element 9.3	Monitor the performance of responsibility centres against budgets

| Unit 10 Managing Systems and People in the Accounting Environment | Element 10.1 | Manage people within the accounting environment |
| | Element 10.2 | Identify opportunities for improving the effectiveness of an accounting system |

| Unit 22 Contribute to the Maintenance of a Healthy, Safe and Productive Working Environment | Element 22.1 | Contribute to the maintenance of a healthy, safe and productive working environment |
| | Element 22.2 | Monitor and maintain an effective and efficient working environment |

NVQ/SVQ Level 4, continued

Group 2 Optional Units – Choose **one** of the following **four** units.

| Unit 11 Drafting Financial Statements (Accounting Practice, Industry and Commerce) | Element 11.1 Draft limited company financial statements |
| | Element 11.2 Interpret limited company financial statements |

| Unit 12 Drafting Financial Statements (Central Government) | Element 12.1 Draft Central Government financial statements |
| | Element 12.2 Interpret Central Government financial statements |

| Unit 13 Drafting Financial Statements (Local Government) | Element 13.1 Draft Local Authority financial statements |
| | Element 13.2 Interpret Local Authority financial statements |

| Unit 14 Drafting Financial Statements (National Health Service) | Element 14.1 Draft NHS accounting statements and returns |
| | Element 14.2 Interpret NHS accounting statements and returns |

NVQ/SVQ Level 4, continued

Group 3 Optional Units – Choose **two** of the following **four** units.

Unit 15 Operating a Cash Management and Credit Control System	Element 15.1	Monitor and control cash receipts and payments
	Element 15.2	Manage cash balances
	Element 15.3	Grant credit
	Element 15.4	Monitor and control the collection of debts

Unit 17 Implementing Audit Procedures	Element 17.1	Contribute to the planning of an audit assignment
	Element 17.2	Contribute to the conduct of an audit assignment
	Element 17.3	Prepare related draft reports

Unit 18 Preparing Business Taxation Computations	Element 18.1	Prepare capital allowances computations
	Element 18.2	Compute assessable business income
	Element 18.3	Prepare capital gains computations
	Element 18.4	Prepare Corporation Tax computations

Unit 19 Preparing Personal Taxation Computations	Element 19.1	Calculate income from employment
	Element 19.2	Calculate property and investment income
	Element 19.3	Prepare Income Tax computations
	Element 19.4	Prepare Capital Gains Tax computations

Unit 19 Standards of competence

The structure of the Standards for Unit 19

The Unit commences with a statement of the **knowledge and understanding** which underpin competence in the Unit's elements.

The Unit of Competence is then divided into **elements of competence** describing activities which the individual should be able to perform.

Each element includes:

(a)   A set of **performance criteria.** This defines what constitutes competent performance.

(b)   A **range statement.** This defines the situations, contexts, methods etc in which competence should be displayed.

The elements of competence for Unit 19: *Preparing Personal Taxation Computations* are set out below. Knowledge and understanding required for the Unit as a whole are listed first, followed by the performance criteria and range statements for each element.

Unit 19: Preparing Personal Taxation Computations

What is the unit about?

This unit is about preparing tax computations and returns for individuals. It is concerned with the Income Tax and Capital Gains Tax liability of employed individuals, and also of self-employed individuals excluding any calculation of their business income. There are four elements in this unit.

The first element requires you to calculate income from employment, including the amount of taxable benefits.

In the second element you must calculate property and investment income and show that you can apply deductions and reliefs and claim loss set-offs.

The third element is concerned with preparing Income Tax computations, based on your calculations of the client's earned and unearned income.

The final element requires you to prepare Capital Gains Tax computations. As well as calculating chargeable gains and losses, you need to show that you apply reliefs and exemptions correctly.

Throughout the unit you must show that you take account of current tax law and Inland Revenue practice and make submissions within statutory timescales. You also need to show that you consult with the Inland Revenue in an open and constructive manner, give timely and constructive advice to clients and maintain client confidentiality.

BPP
PROFESSIONAL EDUCATION

Knowledge and understanding

To perform this unit effectively you will need to know and understand:

The business environment

1   The duties and responsibilities of the tax practitioner (Elements 19.1, 19.2, 19.3 & 19.4)

2   The issues of taxation liability (Elements 19.1, 19.2, 19.3 & 19.4)

3   Relevant legislation and guidance from the Revenue (Elements 19.1, 19.2, 19.3 & 19.4)

Taxation principles and theory

4   Basic law and practice relating to all issues covered in the range and referred to in the performance criteria (Elements 19.1, 19.2, 19.3 & 19.4)

5   Calculation of assessable employment income including benefits (Element 19.1)

6   Expenses deductible from employment income including pension contributions and payroll giving to charities (Element 19.1)

7   Classification and calculation of income as property income, savings or dividend income (Element 19.2)

8   Identification of the main tax exempt investments (Element 19.2)

9   Calculation and set-off of rental deficits (Element 19.2)

10 Computation of taxable income taking account of gift aid payments and personal allowances for taxpayers aged under 65 (Element 19.3)

11 Calculation of tax on general, savings and dividend income (Element 19.3)

12 Identification of non-business assets disposed of including part disposals and personal shareholdings (Element 19.4)

13 Calculation of gains and losses on disposals of non-business assets including indexation allowance (Element 19.4)

14 Set-off of capital losses, taper relief and annual exemption to arrive at taxable gains (Element 19.4)

15 Calculation of capital gains tax payable on gains on non-business assets disposed of by individuals (Element 19.4)

16 Self assessment including payment of tax and filing of returns by individuals (Elements 19.3 & 19.4)

The client

17 How the taxation liabilities of individuals are affected by their employment status (Elements 19.1, 19.2, 19.3 & 19.4)

18 An understanding of the individual's employment status (Elements 19.1, 19.2, 19.3 & 19.4)

Element 19.1 Calculate income from employment

Performance criteria

In order to perform this element successfully you need to:

A   Prepare accurate computations of **emoluments**, including **benefits**

B   List **allowable expenses** and deductions

C   Record relevant details of income from employment accurately and legibly in the tax return

D   Make computations and submissions in accordance with current tax law and take account of current Revenue practice

E   Consult with Revenue staff in an open and constructive manner

F   Give timely and constructive advice to clients on the recording of information relevant to tax returns

G   Maintain client confidentiality at all times

Range statement

Performance in this element relates to the following contexts:

Emoluments

- Received by UK-resident employees
- Relating to work performed wholly or partly in the UK

Benefits

- Lower paid employees
- Higher paid employees

Allowable expenses

- Contributions to pension schemes
- Contributions to charities under the payroll deduction scheme

Element 19.2 Calculate property and investment income

Performance criteria

In order to perform this element successfully you need to:

A   Prepare schedules of dividends and interest received on shares and securities

B   Prepare schedules of **property income** and determine profits and losses

C   Prepare schedules of investment income from **other sources**

D   Apply deductions and reliefs and claim loss set-offs

E   Record relevant details of property and investment income accurately and legibly in the tax return

F   Make computations and submissions in accordance with current tax law and take account of current Inland Revenue practice

G   Consult with Revenue staff in an open and constructive manner

H   Give timely and constructive advice to clients on the recording of information relevant to tax returns

I   Maintain client confidentiality at all times

Range statement

Performance in this element relates to the following contexts:

Property income taking into account

- Holiday lets
- Wear and tear

Other sources of investment income

- Banks
- Building societies
- Government savings schemes

Element 19.3 Prepare Income Tax computations

Performance criteria

In order to perform this element successfully you need to:

A   List general income, savings income and dividend income and check for completeness

B   Calculate and deduct charges and personal allowances

C   Calculate Income Tax payable

D   Record income and payments legibly and accurately in the tax return

E   Make computations and submissions in accordance with current tax law and take account of current Inland Revenue practice

F   Consult with Revenue staff in an open and constructive manner

G   Give timely and constructive advice to clients on the recording of information relevant to tax returns

H   Maintain client confidentiality at all times

Range statement

Performance in this element relates to the following contexts:

There are no additional contextual requirements in this element.

Element 19.4 Prepare Capital Gains Tax computations

Performance criteria

In order to perform this element successfully you need to:

A   Identify and value **disposed-of chargeable personal assets**

B   Identify shares disposed of by individuals

C   Calculate chargeable gains and allowable losses

D   Apply reliefs and exemptions correctly

E   Calculate Capital Gains Tax payable

F   Record relevant details of gains and the Capital Gains Tax payable legibly and accurately in the tax return

G   Make computations and submissions in accordance with current tax law and take account of current Inland Revenue practice

H   Consult with Revenue staff in an open and constructive manner

I   Give timely and constructive advice to clients on the recording of information relevant to tax returns

J   Maintain client confidentiality at all times

Range statement

Performance in this element relates to the following contexts:

Chargeable personal assets that have been

- Sold
- Gifted
- Lost
- Destroyed

Exam Based Assessment technique

Completing exam based assessments successfully at this level is half about having the knowledge, and half about doing yourself full justice on the day. You must have the right **technique**.

The day of the exam based assessment

1   Set at least one **alarm** (or get an alarm call) for a morning exam.

2   Have **something to eat** but beware of eating too much; you may feel sleepy if your system is digesting a large meal.

3   Allow plenty of **time to get to where you are sitting the exam**; have your route worked out in advance and listen to news bulletins to check for potential travel problems.

4   **Don't forget** pens, pencils, rulers, erasers.

5   Put **new batteries** into your calculator and take a spare set (or a spare calculator).

6   **Avoid discussion** about the exam with other candidates outside the venue.

Technique in the exam based assessment

1   **Read the instructions (the 'rubric') on the front of the exam carefully**

   Check that the format hasn't changed. It is surprising how often assessors' reports remark on the number of students who do not attempt all the tasks.

2   **Read the paper twice**

   Read through the paper twice – don't forget that you are given 15 minutes' reading time. Check carefully that you have got the right end of the stick before putting pen to paper. Use your 15 minutes' reading time wisely.

3   **Check the time allocation for each section of the exam**

   Suggested time allocations are given for each section of the exam. When the time for a section is up, you should go on to the next section.

4   **Read the task carefully and plan your answer**

   Read through the task again very carefully when you come to answer it. Plan your answer to ensure that you **keep to the point**. Two minutes of planning plus eight minutes of writing is virtually certain to produce a better answer than ten minutes of writing. Planning will also help you answer the exam question efficiently, for example by identifying workings that can be used for more than one task.

5   **Produce relevant answers**

   Particularly with written answers, make sure you **answer what has been set**, and not what you would have preferred to have been set. Do not, for example, answer a question on **why** something is done with an explanation of **how** it is done.

6   **Work your way steadily through the exam**

   Don't get bogged down in one task. If you are having problems with something, the chances are that everyone else is too.

7 **Produce an answer in the correct format**

The assessor will state **in the requirements** the format which should be used, for example in a report or memorandum.

8 **Do what the assessor wants**

You should ask yourself what the assessor is expecting in an answer; many tasks will demand a combination of technical knowledge and business commonsense. Be careful if you are required to give a decision or make a recommendation; you cannot just list the criteria you will use, but you will also have to say whether those criteria have been fulfilled.

9 **Lay out your numerical computations and use workings correctly**

Make sure the layout is in a style the assessor likes.

Show all your **workings** clearly and explain what they mean. Cross reference them to your answer. This will help the assessor to follow your method (this is of particular importance where there may be several possible answers).

10 **Present a tidy paper**

You are a professional, and it should show in the **presentation of your work**. You should make sure that you write legibly, label diagrams clearly and lay out your work neatly.

11 **Stay until the end of the exam**

Use any spare time **checking and rechecking** your script. Check that you have answered all the requirements of the task and that you have clearly labelled your work. Consider also whether your answer appears reasonable in the light of the information given in the question.

12 **Don't worry if you feel you have performed badly in the exam**

It is more than likely that the other candidates will have found the exam difficult too. As soon as you get up to leave the venue, **forget** that exam and think about the next – or, if it is the last one, celebrate!

13 **Don't discuss an exam with other candidates**

This is particularly the case if you **still have other exams to sit**. Even if you have finished, you should put it out of your mind until the day of the results. Forget about exams and relax!

Assessment strategy

This Unit is assessed by **exam based assessment** only.

Exam based assessment

An exam based assessment is a means of collecting evidence that you have the **essential knowledge and understanding** which underpins competence. It is also a means of collecting evidence across the **range of contexts** for the standards, and of your ability to **transfer skills**, knowledge and understanding to different situations. Thus, although exams contain practical tests linked to the performance criteria, they also focus on the underpinning knowledge and understanding. You should, in addition, expect each exam to contain tasks taken from across a broad range of the standards.

Format of exam

There will be a three hour exam in two sections.

Section 1:   Element 19.1 (taxation of an individual who is employed)
Section 2:   Element 19.4 (taxation of capital transactions)

Elements 19.2 and 19.3 can appear in either section.

There will be an additional 15 minutes reading time.

Further guidance

The Standard is divided into four elements. Element 19.1 is called 'Calculate income from employment', Element 19.2 is called 'Calculate property and investment income'' Element 19.3 is called 'Prepare Income Tax computations' and Element 19.4 is called ' Prepare Capital Gains Tax Computations. '

The purpose of **Element 19.1** is to calculate the earnings of an individual for inclusion in their income tax computation and/or income tax return. For earnings, the following sources of income need to be considered

(i)   cash received, such as salary, bonuses, commissions

(ii)   benefits, such as car, car fuel, accommodation, living expenses connected with accommodation, assets made available to employees for private usage and cheap taxable loans.

The rules for benefits need to be considered for all levels of income.

Deductibility of allowable expenses will involve: the operation of the 'wholly, exclusively and necessarily incurred' rule, pension contributions and payroll giving to charities.

Students should understand the significance of all the major PAYE forms, such as P11D, P60 and P45. However, detailed knowledge of the mechanics of the PAYE system will not required.

Element 19.2 deals with property and investment income. For property income, students will be required to compute the profit or loss on Schedule A income. This specifically includes rental income, but excludes lease premiums and 'rent-a-room' relief. An understanding of the basis of assessment, allowable expenditure and capital expenditure is required in reference to Schedule A income.

For investment income, students must understand the tax implications of owning a variety of investment assets, such as shares, ISAs and TESSAs. Students should also have an understanding of the tax implications where interest is taxed at source, and where it is not taxed at source. There will be considerable commonality between element 19.2 and element 19.3, as the generation of the income in element 19.2 will be used in the Income Tax computations in element 19.3.

Element 19.3 concerns the preparation of income tax computations. It will not necessarily be a requirement in the examination to complete a full Inland Revenue income tax return, but relevant extracts may be used and the student will need to demonstrate understanding on how it should be properly completed. All sources of income, earned and unearned, will come under this element, though the specifics on how they are individually calculated will come under another element within this unit. Detailed knowledge is required of all personal allowances and reliefs, including personal allowances for taxpayers aged under 65, charges on income and gift aid.

Specifically excluded from this element are eligible interest payments and maintenance payments.

Also, the dates for submission of the income tax return and payment of income tax must be considered, together with the implications of making a late filing of the return.

Element 19.4 deals with the calculation of capital gains for individuals. As disposals of business assets are examined under Unit 18, the type of disposals covered by this unit include: non-business assets, shares and securities, including rights issues and bonus issues, FA 1985 pool and matching rules, chattels, part-disposal of assets, improvement expenditure, principal private residence, including periods of deemed occupation, and exempt assets.

Students should be able to compute the gain, or loss, and then be able to apply tapering relief and the annual exemption. An understanding is also required of the impact of capital gains on the tax liability, assuming gains are the top slice of an individual's income.

Specifically excluded topics are double tax relief, trusts, granting of leases and share take-overs.

Section 1 and Section 2

It is not anticipated that candidates will be required to compute certain topics more than once during the examination. For instance, Schedule A income will only be assessed once in either Section 1 or Section 2. The same principle applies for calculating certain forms of income, although the application of such income in calculating the final income tax due will not be restricted to only one section.

Tax rates and allowances

A Income tax

1 Rates

	2003/04		2004/05	
	£	%	£	%
Starting rate	1 – 1,960	10	1 – 2,020	10
Basic rate	1,961 – 30,500	22	2,021 – 31,400	22
Higher rate	30,501 and above	40	31,401 and above	40

Savings (excl. Dividend) income is taxed at 20% if it falls in the basic rate band. Dividend income in both the starting rate and the basic rate bands is taxed at 10%. Dividend income within the higher rate band is taxed at 32.5%.

2 Allowances

	2003/04	2004/05
	£	£
Personal allowance	4,615	4,745
Blind person's allowance	1,510	1,560

3 Car Benefit

Baseline CO_2 Emissions = 145g/km

4 Car fuel charge – 2004/05

Set figure £14,400

5 Authorised mileage rates (AMR) 2004/05 rates

Car mileage rates

First 10,000 miles	40p per mile
Over 10,000 miles	25p per mile

Bicycles	*Motor cycles*
20p per mile	24p per mile
Passenger payments	5p per mile

6 Personal pension contribution limits

Age	Maximum percentage %
Up to 35	17.5
36 – 45	20.0
46 – 50	25.0
51 – 55	30.0
56 – 60	35.0
61 or more	40.0

Subject to earnings cap of £99,000 for 2003/04 and £102,000 for 2004/05.

Stakeholder pension limit £3,600.

B   Rates of interest

Official rate of interest: 5% (assumed)
Rate of interest on unpaid tax: 6.5% (assumed)
Rate of interest on overpaid tax: 2.5% (assumed)

C   Capital gains tax

1   Annual exemption (individuals)

	£
2003/04	7,900
2004/05	8,200

2   Tapering relief for non-business assets

Number of complete years after 5.4.98 for which asset held	% of gain chargeable
0	100
1	100
2	100
3	95
4	90
5	85
6	80
7	75
8	70
9	65
10 or more	60

P A R T   A

Income tax

An outline
of income tax

Contents

Performance criteria

19.3 A List general income, savings income and dividend income and check for completeness

19.3 B Calculate and deduct charges and personal allowances

19.3 C Calculate Income Tax payable

Range statement

There are no additional contextual requirements in this element relevant to this chapter .

Knowledge and understanding

2   The issues of taxation liability (Elements 19.1, 19.2, 19.3, 19.4)

3   Relevant legislation and guidance from the Revenue (Elements 19.1, 19.2, 19.3, 19.4)

4   Basic law and practice (Elements 19.1, 19.2, 19.3, 19.4)

10   Computation of taxable income taking account of gift aid payments and personal allowances for taxpayers aged under 65 (Element 19.3)

11   Calculation of tax on general, savings and dividend income (Element 19.3)

1 Taxes in the UK

The main taxes suffered by individuals are income tax and capital gains tax. You will study these taxes in this unit.

As a general rule, income tax is charged on receipts which might be expected to recur (such as weekly wages) **whereas capital gains tax is charged on one-off gains** (for example from selling a painting owned for 20 years). Both taxes are charged for tax years.

The **tax year**, or **fiscal year**, or **year of assessment** runs from 6 April to 5 April. For example, the tax year 2004/05 runs from 6 April 2004 to 5 April 2005.

2 Relevant legislation and guidance from the Revenue

The main tax law is incorporated into the following Acts of Parliament.

(i)   The Income and Corporation Taxes Act 1988
(ii)   The Taxation of Chargeable Gains Act 1992

These Acts are amended by the Annual Finance Acts which incorporate proposals set out each year in the Chancellor's Budget Speech. **This text includes the provisions of the Finance Act 2004. The Finance Act 2004 will be examined in June 2005 and December 2005.**

The above statute is interpreted and amplified by **case law**. The Revenue also issue:

(a)   **statements of practice**, setting out how they intend to apply the law

(b)   **extra-statutory concessions**, setting out circumstances in which they will not apply the strict letter of the law

(c)   a wide range of **explanatory leaflets**

(d)   **business economic notes**. These are notes on particular types of business, which are used as background information by the Revenue and are also published

(e)   the **Tax Bulletin**. This is a newsletter giving the Revenue's view on specific points. It is published every two months

(f)   the **Internal Guidance**, a series of manuals used by Revenue staff

However, none of these Revenue publications has the force of law.

A great deal of information and the Revenue publications can now be found on the Revenue's internet site (www.inlandrevenue.gov.uk).

3 Various types of income

3.1 The schedular system

We saw above that individuals must pay income tax on their income and capital gains tax on their capital gains.

Some types of income is taxed under a set of rules known as a schedule. Schedules D is divided into cases. The schedules and cases that you may need to be aware of in Unit 19 are:

Schedule A   Income from land and buildings (rents and so on) in the UK

Schedule D

      Case I   Profits of trades

      Case II   Profits of professions or vocations

      Case III   Interest

      Case VI   Income not falling under any other schedule or case

Schedule F   UK dividends

You will not be expected to compute Schedule D Case I or II income in Unit 19 although you may be expected to include a given amount of such income in the individual's income tax computation.

The schedules and cases are important because each has its own set of rules. Once we have decided that income is taxed under, say, Schedule A, the rules of Schedule A determine the amount of income taxed in any year. Each type of income examinable at Unit 19 is considered in detail later in this text.

The schedular system arose for historical administrative reasons and is likely to become less important in the future as tax law is rewritten. For example, **Schedule E (which taxed employment income and pensions) was abolished in April 2003 and replaced by the provisions of the Income Tax (Earnings and Pensions) Act 2003. The Income Tax (Trading and Other Income) Act 2005 will replace Schedule A, Schedule D and Schedule F for income tax purposes.**

3.2 Interest received net of 20% tax

Individuals receive most interest income **'net of tax'**. This means that the payer of the interest deducts tax from the payment made to the individual and pays that tax to the Revenue on the individual's behalf.

The following interest income is received by individuals net of 20% tax.

    (a)   Interest paid by UK companies on debentures and loan stocks
    (b)   Bank and building society interest (but not National Savings Bank interest)

The amount of interest received must be grossed up by multiplying by 100/80 and it must be included gross in the income tax computation. For example, interest received of £80 must be grossed up to £100 (£80 × 100/80) for inclusion in the income tax computation. The tax suffered on the interest income of £20 can be offset against the individual's income tax payable. If it exceeds the tax payable the excess can be repaid.

In the exam you may be given either the net or the gross amount of such income: read the question carefully. If you are given the net amount (the amount received or credited), you should gross up the figure as shown above. However, if you are given the gross amount include the figure you are given in the income tax computation.

Activity 1.1

Kahlida receives building society interest (net of 20% tax) of £320. What amount of interest must be included in Kahlida's income tax computation?

$$£320 \times \frac{100}{80} = 400$$

Although building society and bank deposit interest are generally paid net of 20% tax a recipient who is not liable to tax can recover the tax suffered For example, net building society interest of £160 is equivalent to gross income of £160 × 100/80 = £200 on which tax of £40 (20% of £200) has been suffered and a non-taxpayer can get the £40 tax suffered repaid to him. Alternatively, he can certify in advance that he is a non-taxpayer and get the interest paid gross.

3.3 Dividends on UK shares

Dividends received on UK shares are received net of a 10% tax credit. This means a dividend received of £90 has a £10 tax credit, giving gross income of £100 to be included in the tax computation. The tax credit attached to dividends **cannot be repaid to non-taxpayers but it is offsettable and can be set against a taxpayer's tax liability.**

Activity 1.2

Harriet receives dividends of £2,250 and building society interest (net of 20% tax) of £2,400 in 2004/05. What are the gross amounts of dividends and interest to be included in her income tax computation for 2004/05?

3.4 Exempt income

Some income is exempt from income tax. This income is not included in the income tax computation.

Several of the exemptions are mentioned at places in this text where the types of income are described in detail, but note the following types of exempt income now.

- (a) Scholarships (exempt as income of the scholar. If paid by a parent's employer, a scholarship may be taxable income of the parent)
- (b) Betting and gaming winnings, including premium bond prizes
- (c) Income on National Savings Certificates
- (d) Gifts
- (e) Income arising on Individual Savings accounts (ISAs)

Learn the different types of exempt income as they are popular items of income in the exam. Always state on your workings sheets that such income is exempt (do not ignore it) to gain an easy mark.

4 The aggregation of income

4.1 Statutory total income

An individual's income from all sources is brought together in a personal tax computation. We split income into non-savings income, savings (excl. dividend) income and dividend income. This means that when preparing an income tax computation you need three columns headed as follows:

Non-savings income £	Savings (excluding dividend income) £	Dividend Income £

Interest and dividends are **'savings income'** All other income is non-savings income.

The total of an individual's income from all sources is known as **statutory total income.**

4.2 Taxable income

Once **statutory total income** has been calculated, **personal allowances are deducted to arrive at taxable income**.

Two allowances, the personal allowance and the blind person's allowance, are deducted from STI. The allowances come off non savings income first, then off savings (excl. dividend) income and lastly off dividend income.

All persons (including children) are entitled to the personal allowance (PA) of £4,745 in 2004/05. There are different allowances for taxpayers aged 65 and over but these are not examinable in Unit 19.

A taxpayer who is registered with a local authority as a blind person gets a blind person's allowance (BPA) of £1,560 in 2004/05. The allowance is also given for the year before registration, if the taxpayer had obtained the proof of blindness needed for registration before the end of that earlier year.

The example below shows the layout of the taxable income computation:

SUE: TAXABLE INCOME FOR 2004/05

	Non-savings income £	Savings (excl dividend) income £	Dividend income £	Total £
Income from employment	36,000			
Building society interest (× 100/80)		1,000		
National savings bank interest		320		
UK dividends (× 100/90)			1,000	
Statutory total income (STI)	36,000	1,320	1,000	38,320
Less personal allowance	(4,745)			
Taxable income	31,255	1,320	1,000	33,575

Remember that National Savings Bank interest is received gross. Building Society interest and UK dividends must, however, be grossed up for inclusion in the income tax computation.

Now follow the above layout to try the next activities for yourself.

Activity 1.3

An individual has the following income in 2004/05.

	£
Earnings from employment	16,000
Building society interest received	4,800
Dividends received	7,875
Premium bond prize	5,000

His personal allowance is £4,745. Show his taxable income split into non-savings, savings (excl dividend) and dividend income.

Activity 1.4

An individual has the following income in 2004/05.

		£
Business profits	21,000	21,000
Building society interest received	6,000	4,800
Dividends received	2,000	1,800
His personal allowance is £4,745. What is his total taxable income?	29,000 – 4,745	

5 Calculation of income tax liability

5.1 Income tax bands

The first step in calculating the income tax liability is to divide the total **taxable income** into three bands:

(i)   the first £2,020 of income; this is called income in the **starting rate band**
(ii)   the next £29,380 of income; this is income in the **basic rate band**
(iii)   the remaining income over the **higher rate threshold** of £31,400

The rate of tax applied to the income in each band depends on whether the income is non-savings income, savings (excluding dividend) income or dividend income.

There is only one set of income tax bands used for all three types of income. These bands **must be allocated to income in the following order:**

(i) **non-savings income**
(ii) **savings** (excluding dividend) **income**
(iii) **dividend income**

Example

Zoë has total taxable income of £32,000. Of this £18,000 is non-savings income, £12,000 is interest and £2,000 is dividend income.

The first £2,020 of non-savings income is in the starting rate band. The remaining £15,980 of non-savings income is in the basic rate band. This leaves £13,400 (£29,380 – £15,980) of the basic rate band.

The next £12,000 of the basic rate band is used by interest income, leaving £1,400 (£13,400 – £12,000) of the basic rate band to be used by dividend income.

The remaining dividend income £600 (£2,000 – £1,400) is income above the higher rate threshold.

18,000   12,000   2,000

5.2 Computing the tax liability

You need to calculate the tax due on taxable income in three steps:

Step 1: Deal with non-savings income first:

Non-savings income in the starting rate band is taxed at 10%. Next any non-savings income in the basic rate band is taxed at 22%, and finally non-savings income above the higher rate threshold is taxed at 40%.

Step 2: Secondly, deal with savings (excl dividend) income:

Savings (excl dividend) income is dealt with after non-savings income. If any of the starting or basic rate bands remain **after taxing non-savings income** they can be used here. Savings (excl dividend) income is taxed at 10% in the starting rate band. If savings (excl dividend) income falls within the basic rate band it is taxed at 20% (not 22%). Once income is above the higher rate threshold, it is taxed at 40%.

Step 3: Thirdly, compute tax on dividend income:

Lastly, tax dividend income. If dividend income falls within the starting or basic rate bands, it is taxed at 10% (never 20% or 22%). If, however, the dividend income exceeds the basic rate threshold of £31,400, it is taxed at 32.5%

32,000

Continuing Zoë's income tax computation from the Example above, the tax liability is:

Income tax	£
Step 1:	
Non savings income	
£2,020 × 10%	202
£15,980 × 22%	3,516
£18,000	
Step 2:	
Savings (excl. dividend) income	
£12,000 × 20%	2,400
Step 3:	
Dividend income	
£1,400 × 10%	140
£600 × 32.5%	195
2,000	
Tax liability	6,453

Activity 1.5

An individual has total taxable income of £50,000 for 2004/05. All of his income is non-savings income. What is the total income tax liability?

5.3 Computing the tax payable

We have seen above how to calculate the income tax liability on non-savings, savings and dividend income. Once this is done there are two final steps to be made in order to compute the tax payable:

Step 4

Deduct the tax credit on dividends from the tax liability. Although deductible, this tax credit cannot be repaid if it exceeds the tax liability calculated so far.

Step 5

Finally deduct the tax deducted at source from savings (excluding dividend) income and any PAYE (PAYE is the tax deducted at source from an individual's earnings. It will be covered later in this text.) These amounts can be repaid to the extent that they exceed the income tax liability.

The resulting figure is the tax payable which is the balance of the liability still to be settled in cash.

Continuing the example of Zoe, above, and assuming all interest was received net of 20% tax:

	£
Income liability	6,453
Less tax suffered	
Tax credit on dividend (£2,000 × 10%)	(200)
Tax on interest (£12,000 × 20%)	(2,400)
Income tax payable	3,853

Activity 1.6

Kate, who is entitled to a personal allowance of £4,745, has a salary of £10,430 (PAYE tax deducted at source £1,000) and building society interest received of £4,000. Calculate Kate's tax payable for 2004/05.

Activity 1.7

Doris received dividend income of £34,200 in 2004/05. She has no other income. Her personal allowance to deduct from dividend income is £4,745. Calculate the tax payable.

We will look at some further examples of the computation of income tax later in this chapter.

6 Charges on income

6.1 Introduction

Charges on income are deducted in computing taxable income.

A **charge on income** is a payment by the taxpayer which income tax law allows as a deduction.

Examples of charges on income are:

(a)   patent royalties
(b)   copyright royalties

Charges on income fall into two categories: those from which basic rate (22%) income tax is first deducted by the payer (charges paid net) and those which are paid without any deduction (charges paid gross).

Patent royalties are an example of a charge on income which is paid net. Copyright royalties are paid gross.

We always deduct the gross figure in the payer's tax computation. If a charge is paid net you must gross it up by multiplying by 100/78. For example if Sue pays a patent royalty of £1,014 you must gross it up to £1,300 (£1,014 × 100/78) and deduct the gross figure in Sue's income tax computation.

Activity 1.8

In 2004/05 Harriet pays a patent royalty of £3,900 and a copyright royalty of £1,000. What is the total amount that Harriet can deduct as charges on income in her income tax computation for 2004/05?

If you are preparing the personal tax computation of someone who *receives* a charge, for example the owner of a patent who gets royalties from someone who exploits the patent, do the following.

(a)   Include the **gross** amount under non-savings income. If the charge is paid gross, the gross amount is the amount received. If it is paid net, the gross amount is the amount received × 100/78.

(b)   If the charge was received net, then under the heading 'less tax suffered' (between tax liability and tax payable) include the tax deducted. This is the gross amount × 22%. This amount can be repaid if it exceeds the gross tax liability.

6.2 Charges in personal tax computations

The gross amount of any charge is deducted from the taxpayer's income to arrive at Statutory Total Income (STI).

Deduct charges from non-savings income then from savings (excl. dividend income) and lastly from dividend income.

If a charge has been paid net, the basic rate income tax deducted (22% of the gross amount) is added into the tax liability. The taxpayer gets tax relief by deducting the gross amount of the payment in computing his STI: he cannot keep the basic rate tax withheld from the payment as well, but he must pay it to the Revenue. This means that the final step in computing the tax liability should be to add on any tax withheld on charges paid net.

Example

Three taxpayers have the following schedule D Case I income and allowances for 2004/05. Taxpayers A and B pay a patent royalty of £176 (net). Taxpayer C pays a patent royalty of £1,248 (net).

	A	B	C
	£	£	£
Schedule D Case I Income	6,000	4,000	37,795
Less: charge on income (× 100/78)	(226)	(226)	(1,600)
	5,774	3,774	36,195
Less: personal allowance	(4,745)	(4,745)	(4,745)
Taxable income	1,029	–	31,450
Income tax			
10% on £1,029/–/£2,020	103	–	202
22% on –/–/£29,380			6,464
40% on –/–/£50			20
	103	–	6,686
Add: 22% tax retained on charge	50	50	352
Tax payable	153	50	7,038

Note that you will not be expected to compute Schedule D Case I Income (income from a trade) in your exam but, as here, you may be expected to include it in an income tax computation.

Activity 1.9

John, who is single and entitled to a personal allowance of £4,745, has Schedule D Case I profits of £8,000 in 2004/05. He also received building society interest of £14,000 and dividends of £450. He paid a patent royalty of £9,360. Show John's income tax liability for 2004/05.

7 Gift aid donations

One-off and regular charitable gifts of money qualify for tax relief under the **gift aid scheme** provided the donor gives the charity a gift aid declaration.

Gift aid declarations can be made in writing, electronically through the internet or orally over the phone. A declaration can cover a one-off gift or any number of gifts for the future or retrospectively.

A gift aid donation is treated as though it was paid net of basic rate tax (22%, 2004/05).

Additional tax relief is given in the personal tax computation by increasing the donor's basic rate band by the gross amount of the gift.

Example

Amarjart has taxable income (all non savings) of £40,000 on 2004/05. He received no other income in the year but he did pay a gift aid donation of £3,900. No claims were made to carry back the gift aid donation (see below).

Compute Amarjat's income tax liability.

Solution

The gift aid donation will have been paid net of 22% tax. This means that the gross amount of the payment was £3,900 × 100/78 = £5,000). Additional rate tax relief is given on this payment by extending Amarjat's basic rate band by £5,000.

Income tax liability:

	£
£2,020 × 10%	202
£29,380 × 22%	6,464
£5,000 (Extended band) × 22%	1,100
£3,600 × 40%	1,440
	9,206

If the basic rate band had not been extended by £5,000, the income tax liability would have been:

	£
£2,020 x 10%	202
£29,380 x 22%	6,464
£8,600 x 40%	3,440
	10,106

∴ Extending the basis rate band reduces the tax liability by £900. Effectively 18% (£5,000 × 18% = £900) relief is given on the gift aid donation.

Activity 1.10

James earns a salary of £58,000 but has no other income. In 2004/05 he paid £7,800 (net) under the gift aid scheme. No claims (see below) were made to carry back the gift aid donation.

Compute James' income tax liability for 2004/05.

Higher rate taxpayers can claim to carry back their additional tax relief (ie relief above the relief at the basic rate) on **gift aid donations for one year**. This means that the basic rate band for the previous year is increased by the gross amount of the gift.

Activity 1.11

Zoë earns £20,000 in 2004/05 and £39,000 in 2003/04. She had no other income. In 2004/05, she paid £7,800 under the gift aid scheme. Zoë made a claim to have additional tax relief on the gift aid donation in 2003/04.

Show Zoë's tax liability in both years. Assume that tax rates and allowances in 2003/04 were the same as in 2004/05.

1.10

58000
4745
53255

10% 2020   202
29380×22   6164
10,000×22   220
4855×40%   4742
            11328

8 Personal tax computations

Now let us work through some complete computations of income tax payable.

Examples: personal tax computations

(a) Kathe has a salary of £10,000 and receives dividends of £4,500.

	Non-savings £	Dividends £	Total £
Earnings	10,000		
Dividends £4,500 × 100/90		5,000	
STI	10,000	5,000	15,000
Less personal allowance	(4,745)		
Taxable income	5,255	5,000	10,255

	£
Income tax	
Non savings income	
£2,020 × 10%	202
£3,235 × 22%	712
Dividend income	
£5,000 × 10%	500
Tax liability	1,414
Less tax credit on dividend	(500)
Tax payable	914

Some of the tax payable has probably already been paid on the salary under PAYE.

The dividend income falls within the basic rate band so it is taxed at 10% (*not* 22%). The tax credit on dividend income is deducted from the tax liability. Remember that the deduction can reduce the tax payable to £NIL but any excess tax credit cannot be repaid.

(b) Jules has a salary of £20,000, business profits of £30,000, net dividends of £6,750 and building society interest of £3,000 net. He pays a copyright royalty of £2,000 and makes a gift aid donation of £780 (net).

	Non-savings £	Savings (excl dividend) £	Dividend £	Total £
Schedule D Case I	30,000			
Earnings	20,000			
Dividends £6,750 × 100/90			7,500	
Building society interest £3,000 × 100/80	–	3,750	–	
	50,000	3,750	7,500	
Less charges	(2,000)			
STI	48,000	3,750	7,500	59,250
Less personal allowance	(4,745)			
Taxable income	43,255	3,750	7,500	54,505

	£
Income tax	
Non savings income	
£2,020 × 10%	202
£29,380 × 22%	6,464
£1,000 (£780 × $\dfrac{100}{78}$) × 22%	220
£10,855 × 40%	4,342
	11,228
Savings (excl. dividend) income	
£3,750 × 40%	1,500
Dividend income	
£7,500 × 32.5%	2,438
	15,166
Less tax credit on dividend income	(750)
Less tax suffered on building society interest	(750)
Tax payable	13,666

Savings (excl. dividend) income and dividend income fall above the basic rate threshold so they are taxed at 40% and 32.5% respectively. The basic rate band is extended by the gross amount of the gift aid donation. Copyright royalties are deducted as charge in income. They are paid gross,

(c)   Jim does not work. He receives net bank interest of £38,000. He pays gross charges of £2,000.

	Savings (excl dividend) £	Total
Bank interest × 100/80	47,500	
Less charges	(2,000)	
STI	45,500	45,500
Less personal allowance	(4,745)	
	40,755	40,755

	£
Savings (excluding dividend) income	
£2,020 × 10%	202
£29,380 × 20%	5,876
£9,355 × 40%	3,742
Tax liability	9,820
Less tax suffered	(9,500)
Tax payable	320

Savings (excl. dividend) income within the basic rate band is taxed at 20% (*not* 22%).

8.1 The complete proforma

Here is a complete proforma computation of taxable income. It is probably too much for you to absorb at this stage, but refer back to it as you come to the chapters dealing with the types of income shown.

	Non-savings £	Savings (excl dividend) £	Dividend £	Total £
Business profits	X			
Wages less occupational pension contributions	X			
Other non-savings (as many lines as necessary)	X			
Building society interest (gross)		X		
Other savings (excl. dividends) (gross) (as many lines as necessary)		X		
Dividends (gross)			X	
	X̄	X̄	X̄	
Less charges (gross)	(X)	(X)	(X)	
STI	X	X	X	X
Less personal allowance	(X)	(X)	(X)	
Taxable income	X̲	X̲	X̲	X

Activity 1.12

Jackie, a single woman aged 45 has the following income and outgoings for 2004/05.

	£
Salary (tax deducted under PAYE £4,750)	24,200
Building society interest received (net)	1,600
Dividends received (net)	14,625
One-off charitable donation qualifying under the gift aid scheme (gross amount)	800

What is Jackie's tax payable for 2004/05?

Activity 1.13

John and Helen Pink who are both in their thirties are a married couple. They have no children. Mr and Mrs Pink received the following income in 2004/05.

	Mr Pink £	Mrs Pink £
Salary (gross)	36,000	30,000
PAYE tax deducted	(6,000)	(4,800)
Dividends (amount received)	1,090	2,538
Bank deposit interest (amount received)	200	76
Building society interest (amount received)	143	420
Premium bond prizes (amount)	–	500

In 2004/05 Mrs Pink paid £200 (gross) under the gift aid scheme.

Task

Compute the net tax payable by Mr Pink and by Mrs Pink for 2004/05.

Key learning points

☑   Individuals suffer **income tax**.

☑   Some income is **received in full** with no tax deducted, some income has **tax deducted** at source.

☑   All sources of income are **aggregated** in a **personal tax computation.**

☑   Some income is **exempt** from income tax and **not included** in the personal tax computation.

☑   All income in the personal tax computation must be included **gross**.

☑   **Dividends** are grossed up by multiplying by 100/90.

☑   **Bank and Building Society interest** is grossed up by multiplying by 100/80.

☑   Income is divided into **non-savings** income, **savings (excluding dividend)** income and **dividend** income.

☑   **Charges** are deducted from the taxpayer's income to arrive at Statutory Total Income.

☑   The **personal allowance** and **blind person's allowance** are deducted from Statutory Total Income to arrive at taxable income.

☑   There is one set of **income tax bands** which applies to all the income.

☑   **Non-savings income is taxed first**, then the **savings (excluding dividends) income** and **finally dividend income**.

☑   **Gift aid donations** are paid net of basic rate (22%) tax. You should extend the basic rate band to give **higher rate tax relief**.

☑   **Tax suffered on interest and PAYE is deducted in computing tax payable and can be repaid.**

☑   The **tax credit on dividends** is **deducted in computing tax payable**. However, **any excess tax credit cannot be repaid**.

Quick quiz

1   At what rates is income tax charged on non-savings income?

2   Under what schedule is UK rental income taxed?

3   List two types of savings income that is received by individuals net of 20% tax.

4   Which charge on income is paid net?

5   How is tax relief given for a gift aid donation?

6   How is dividend income taxed?

Quick quiz answers

1   10%, 22% and 40%

2   Schedule A.

3   Interest paid by UK companies on UK debentures and loan stock and bank and building society interest (but not National Savings Bank interest).

4   Patent royalties

5   Basic rate tax relief is given by treating a gift aid donation as though it were paid of net of basic rate tax. Additional tax relief is given in the personal tax computation by increasing the donor's basic rate band by the gross amount of the gift. Additional tax relief may be given in the year of the gift, or if a claim is made, in the previous tax year.

6   Dividend income in the starting and basic rate band is taxed at 10%. Dividend income in excess of the higher rate threshold is taxed at 32.5%.

Activity checklist

This checklist shows which performance criteria, range statement or knowledge and understanding point is covered by each activity in this chapter. Tick off each activity as you complete it.

Activity

1.1 ☐ This activity deals with Performance Criteria 19.3.A: list general income, savings and dividend income.

1.2 ☐ This activity deals with Performance Criteria 19.3.A: list general income, savings and dividend income.

1.3 ☐ This activity deals with Performance Criteria 19.3.A: list general income, savings and dividend income.

1.4 ☐ This activity deals with Performance Criteria 19.3.A: list general income, savings and dividend income.

1.5 ☐ This activity deals with Performance Criteria 19.3.C: calculate income tax payable.

1.6 ☐ This activity deals with Performance Criteria 19.3.C: calculate income tax payable.

1.7 ☐ This activity deals with Performance Criteria 19.3.C: calculate income tax payable.

1.8 ☐ This activity deals with Performance Criteria 19.3.B: calculate and deduct charges and personal allowances.

1.9 ☐ This activity deals with Performance Criteria 19.3.B: calculate and deduct charges and personal allowances.

1.10 ☐ This activity deals with Knowledge and Understanding point 10: computation of taxable income taking account of gift aid payments and personal allowances for taxpayers aged under 65

1.11 ☐ This activity deals with Knowledge and Understanding point 10: computation of taxable income taking account of gift aid payments and personal allowances for taxpayers aged under 65

1.12 ☐ This activity deals with Performance Criteria 19.3.C: calculate income tax payable.

1.13 ☐ This activity deals with Performance Criteria 19.3.C: calculate income tax payable.

BPP
PROFESSIONAL EDUCATION

Calculation of
employment income

Contents

Performance criteria

19.1 A   Prepare accurate computations of emoluments, including benefits

19.1 B   List allowable expenses and deductions

Range statements

19.1   Emoluments: received by UK-resident employees, relating to work performed wholly or partly in the UK

19.1   Benefits: excluded employees, higher paid employees

19.1   Allowable expenses: contributions to pension schemes, contributions to charities under the payroll deduction scheme

Knowledge and understanding

2   The issues of taxation liability (Elements 19.1, 19.2, 19.3, 19.4)

3   Relevant legislation and guidance from the Revenue (Elements 19.1, 19.2, 19.3, 19.4)

4   Basic law and practice (Elements 19.1, 19.2, 19.3, 19.4)

5   Calculation of assessable employment income including benefits (Element 19.1)

6   Expenses deductible from employment income including pension contributions and payroll giving to charities (Element 19.1)

17   How the tax liabilities of individuals are affected by their employment status (Elements 19.1, 19.2, 19.3 and 19.4)

18   An understanding of an individual's employment status (Elements 19.1, 19.2, 19.3, 19.4)

21

1 Employment income

1.1 Introduction

Employment income includes income of employees and directors of companies. From now on we will use the term 'employee' to mean both these types of people.

There are two types of employment income:

- **General earnings**, and
- **Specific employment income**.

General earnings are an employees' earnings plus the 'cash equivalent' of any taxable non-monetary benefits.

'Earnings' means any salary, wage or fee, any gratuity or other profit or incidental benefit obtained by the employee if it is money or money's worth (something of direct monetary value or convertible into direct monetary value) or anything else which constitutes an emolument of the employment.

'Specific employment income' includes payments on termination of employment. This type of income is covered in the next chapter.

The residence status of an employee determines whether earnings are taxable. If an employee is resident in the UK, **taxable earnings from an employment in a tax year are the general earnings received in that tax year**, whether earned in the UK or outside it.

1.2 When are earnings received?

General earnings consisting of money are treated as received at the earlier of:

- **The time when payment is made**
- **The time when a person becomes entitled to payment of the earnings**.

If the employee is a director of a company, earnings from the company are received on the earliest of:

- The earlier of the two alternatives given in the general rule (above)
- The time when the amount is credited in the company's accounting records
- The end of the company's period of account (if the amount was determined by then)
- The time the amount is determined (if after the end of the company's period of account).

Taxable benefits are generally treated as received when they are provided to the employee.

The receipts basis does not apply to pension income or taxable social security benefits. Both of these sources of income are taxed on the amount accruing in the tax year, whether or not it has actually been received in that year.

Activity 2.1

All directors of a company receive bonuses for the year ended 31 January 2005. On what date are they treated as receiving these bonuses if they are determined on:

(a)   15 January 2005   → *No 31ˢᵗ Janos.*

(b)   30 April 2005

and paid a month after they are determined? (The directors only become entitled to payment of the bonuses when they are paid.) The bonuses are credited to the company's accounts when paid.

1.3 Net taxable earnings

Total taxable earnings less total allowable deductions (see below) **are net taxable earnings of a tax year. Deductions cannot usually create a loss: they can only reduce the net taxable earnings to nil**. If there is more than one employment in the tax year, separate calculations are required for each employment.

1.4 Person liable for tax on employment income

The person liable to tax on employment income is generally the **employee.**

1.5 Employment and self employment

Employment income is the income arising from an employment.

The distinction between employment (taxable as earnings) and self employment (taxed under Schedule D) is a fine one and will depend on the exact facts of a case. **Employment involves a <u>contract of service</u>, whereas self employment involves a <u>contract for services</u>**. Taxpayers tend to prefer self employment, because the rules on deductions for expenses are more generous. Also, self-employed people do not have income tax deducted at source from their earnings. Instead, income tax is paid in three instalments (see later in this text). Employees have tax deducted at source from their earnings under the PAYE system.

Factors which may be of importance include:

- The degree of control exercised over the person doing the work
- Whether he must accept further work
- Whether the other party must provide further work
- Whether he provides his own equipment
- Whether he hires his own helpers
- What degree of financial risk he takes
- What degree of responsibility for investment and management he has
- Whether he can profit from sound management
- Whether he can work when he chooses
- The wording used in any agreement between the parties.

2 Taxable benefits

2.1 Introduction

The Income Tax (Earnings and Pensions) Act 2003 (ITEPA 2003) provides the first comprehensive legislation covering the taxation of benefits. The legislation distinguishes between two groups of employees:

(a)   'excluded' employees

(b)   other employees and directors

An excluded employee is an employee in lower paid employment who is not a director of a company.

2.2 Lower paid employment

Lower paid employment is one where the earnings rate for the tax year is less than £8,500. To decide whether this applies, add together the **total earnings and benefits that would be taxable, if the employee were *not* an excluded employee.**

A number of **specific deductions** must be taken into account to determine lower paid employment. These include **contributions to authorised pension schemes and payroll giving**. (These items are covered in the next chapter) General deductions from employment income (see later in this chapter) are not taken into account.

Activity 2.2

Molly is a part time employee of A plc. She is paid a salary of £6,500 and receives benefits that would have a taxable value of £3,000 under the legislation if she were not an excluded employee. Is Molly an excluded employee?

2.3 General taxation of benefits

The specific rules for taxing certain benefits are dealt with below. If the benefit does not fall within any of the categories below, there is a **general charge for lower paid employees** which taxes the employee on the **"second hand"** value of the benefit. The second hand value is the amount the asset concerned could be sold for second hand. The general charge to other employees and directors is the **cost to their employer of providing any other benefit.**

2.4 General business expenses

If business expenses on such items as travel or hotel stays, are reimbursed by an employer, the reimbursed amount is a taxable benefit for employees other than excluded employees. To avoid being taxed on this amount, **an employee must then make a claim to deduct it as an expense** under the rules set out below. **In practice, however, many such expense payments are not reported to the Revenue and can be ignored because it is agreed in advance that a claim to deduct them would be possible (a P11D dispensation).**

When an individual has to spend one or more nights away from home, his employer may reimburse expenses on items incidental to his absence (for example meals and private telephone calls). **Such incidental expenses are exempt** if:

(a) The expenses of travelling to each place where the individual stays overnight, throughout the trip, are incurred necessarily in the performance of the duties of the employment (or would have been, if there had been any expenses).

(b) The total (for the whole trip) of incidental expenses not deductible under the usual rules is no more than £5 for each night spent wholly in the UK and £10 for each other night. If this limit is exceeded, all of the expenses are taxable, not just the excess.

This incidental expenses exemption applies to expenses reimbursed, and to benefits obtained using credit tokens and non-cash vouchers.

2.5 Vouchers

If any employee (including an excluded employee):

(a) receives cash vouchers (vouchers exchangeable for cash)
(b) uses a credit token (such as a credit card) to obtain money, goods or services, or
(c) receives exchangeable vouchers (such as book tokens), also called non-cash vouchers

he is taxed on the cost of providing the benefit, less any amount made good.

However, the first 15p per working day of meal vouchers (eg luncheon vouchers) is not taxed.

2.6 Accommodation

The taxable value of accommodation provided to an employee (including an excluded employee) is the rent that would have been payable if the premises had been let at their annual value (taken to be their **rateable value**, despite the abolition of domestic rates). **If the premises are rented** rather than owned by the employer, then the **taxable benefit is the higher of the rent actually paid and the annual value.** If property does not have a rateable value the Revenue estimate a value.

If a property cost more than £75,000, an additional amount is chargeable as follows:

(Cost of providing the living accommodation − £75,000) × the official rate of interest at the start of the tax year.

Thus with an official rate of 5%, the total benefit for accommodation costing £90,000 and with an annual value of £2,000 would be £2,000 + £(90,000 − 75,000) × 5% = £2,750.

Any contribution paid by the employee is deducted from the annual value of the property and then from the additional benefit.

The 'cost of providing' the living accommodation is the aggregate of the cost of purchase and the cost of any improvements made before the start of the tax year for which the benefit is being computed. It is therefore not possible to avoid the charge by buying an inexpensive property requiring substantial repairs and improving it.

Where the property was acquired more than six years before first being provided to the employee, the market value when first so provided plus the cost of subsequent improvements is used as the cost of providing the living accommodation. However, unless the actual cost plus improvements up to the start of the tax year in question exceeds £75,000, the additional charge cannot be imposed, however high the market value.

Activity 2.3

A company bought a house in 2003 for £420,000. On 1 January 2004, it was first provided to an employee who has occupied it since then. The rateable value is £1,600. If the official rate of interest was 5% on 6 April 2004, what is the taxable benefit for 2004/05?

There is no taxable benefit in respect of job related accommodation. Accommodation is job related if:

(a)   Residence in the accommodation **is necessary for the proper performance of the employee's duties** (as with a caretaker), or

(b)   The accommodation is provided **for the better performance of the employee's duties** and the employment is of a kind in which it is **customary for accommodation to be provided** (as with a policeman), or

(c)   The **accommodation is provided as part of arrangements in force because of a special threat to the employee's security**.

Directors can only claim exemptions (a) or (b) if:

(i)   They have no **material interest** ('material' means over 5%) in the company, and
(ii)   Either they are **full time working directors** or the company is **non-profit making or is a charity.**

2.7 Expenses connected with living accommodation

In addition to the benefit of living accommodation itself, **employees, other than excluded employees, are taxed on related expenses paid by the employer**, such as:

(a)   **Heating, lighting or cleaning the premises**
(b)   **Repairing, maintaining or decorating the premises**
(c)   **The provision of furniture** (the annual value is 20% of the cost)

Unless the accommodation qualifies as 'job related' (as defined above) the **full cost of ancillary services** (excluding structural repairs) is taxable. **If the accommodation is 'job related', however, taxable ancillary services are restricted to a maximum of 10% of the employee's 'net earnings'.** For this purpose, net earnings are all earnings from the employment (excluding the ancillary benefits (a) – (c) above) less any allowable expenses, statutory mileage allowances and contributions to approved occupational pension schemes (but not personal pension plans) (pensions are dealt with in the following chapter). If there are ancillary benefits other than those falling within (a) – (c) above (such as a telephone) they are taxable in full.

Activity 2.4

Mr Quinton has a gross salary in 2004/05 of £27,400. He normally lives and works in London, but he is required to live in a company house in Scotland which cost £70,000 three years ago, so that he can carry out a two year review of his company's operations in Scotland. The annual value of the house is £650. In 2004/05 the company pays an electricity bill of £550, a gas bill of £400, a gardener's bill of £750 and redecoration costs of £1,800. Mr Quinton makes a monthly contribution of £50 for his accommodation.

Calculate Mr Quinton's taxable employment income for 2004/05.

Council tax and water or sewage charges paid by the employer are taxable in full as a benefit unless the accommodation is 'job-related'.

2.8 Cars

A car provided by reason of the employment to an employee or member of his family or household for private use gives rise to a taxable benefit. This does not apply to excluded employees.

(a)   The starting point for calculating a car benefit is the list price of the car (plus accessories). **The percentage of the list price that is taxable depends on the car's CO_2 emissions.** Accessories include accessories provided when the car was provided to an employee plus accessories fitted later and costing at least £100 each. (Excluding mobile phones and equipment needed by disabled employees.)

(b)   If the list price or market value exceeds £80,000, then £80,000 is used instead of the price or value.

(c)   Capital contributions are payments by the employee in respect of the price of the car or accessories. In any tax year, we take account of capital contributions made in that year and previous years (for the same car). The maximum deductible capital contributions is £5,000: contributions beyond that total are ignored.

(d)   For cars that emit CO_2 of **145g/km (2004/05) or less, the taxable benefit is 15% of the car's list price. This percentage increases by 1% for every 5g/km (rounded down to the nearest multiple of 5) by which CO_2 emissions exceed 145g/km up to a maximum of 35%.**

(e)   Diesel cars have a supplement of 3% of the car's list price added to the taxable benefit. (The benefit is discounted for cars that are particularly environmentally friendly.) The maximum percentage, however, remains 35% of the list price.

(f)   Cars which do not have an approved CO_2 emissions figure are taxed according to engine size.

(g)   **The benefit is reduced on a time basis where a car is first made available or ceases to be made available during the tax year** or is incapable of being used for a continuous period of not less than 30 days (for example because it is being repaired).

(h)   **The benefit is reduced by any payment the user must make for the private use of the car** (as distinct from a capital contribution to the cost of the car). Payments for insuring the car do not count. The benefit cannot become negative to create a deduction from the employee's income.

(i)   Pool cars are exempt. A car is a pool car if **all** the following conditions are satisfied.

- It is used by more than one employee and is not ordinarily used by any one of them to the exclusion of the others.
- Any private use is merely incidental to business use.
- It is not normally kept overnight at or near the residence of an employee.

There are many ancillary benefits associated with the provision of cars, such as insurance, repairs, vehicle licences and a parking space at or near work. No extra taxable benefit arises as a result of these, with the exception of the cost of providing a driver.

Now lets look at an example of the calculation of the taxable benefit.

Example

Shammina is provided with a petrol engined company car by her employer. The list price of the car is £20,000. The car's CO_2 emissions were 157g/km. The company pays insurance of £600 and repair bills of £900 in respect of the car in 2004/05. What taxable benefit arises on Shammina?

Solution

The taxable benefit depends on the car's CO_2 emissions.

Round the CO_2 emissions down to the nearest 5 below, 155g/km.

Amount above baseline figure 155g/km – 145g/km = 10g/km. Divide by 5 = 2

Taxable % = 15% + 2% = 17%

The taxable benefit is 17% x £20,000 = £3,400

No taxable benefit arises as a result of the insurance of the repair bills.

Note that you will be given the baseline CO_2 emissions figure of 145g/km in the tax rates and allowances tables in your exam.

Activity 2.5

On 1 July 2004 Sue was provided with a new petrol driven car by her employer. The list price of the car was £10,000. The car's CO_2 emissions were 228g/km. What is the taxable benefit?

$$225-145 = 80/5 = 16$$

$$15 + 16 = 31\%$$

$$= \frac{31}{100} \times 10,000 \times \frac{9}{12} = £2325$$

2.9 Fuel for cars

Where fuel is provided there is a further be nefit in addition to the car benefit.

No taxable benefit arises where either

(a)   **All the fuel provided was made available only for business travel**, or

(b)   The **employee is required to make good, and has made good, the whole of the cost of any fuel provided for his private use**.

Unlike most benefits, a reimbursement of only part of the cost of the fuel available for private use does not reduce the benefit.

The taxable benefit is a percentage of a base figure. The base figure for 2004/05 is £14,400. The percentage is the same percentage as is used to calculate the car benefit (see above).

The fuel benefit is reduced in the same way as the car benefit **if the car is not available for 30 days or more.**

The fuel benefit is also reduced if private fuel is not available for part of a tax year. However, if private fuel later becomes available in the same tax year, the reduction is not made. If, for example, fuel is provided from 6 April 2004 to 30 June 2004, then the fuel benefit for 2004/05 will be restricted to just three months. This is because the provision of fuel has permanently ceased. However, if fuel is provided from 6 April 2004 to 30 June 2004, and then again from 1 September 2004 to 5 April 2005, then the fuel benefit will not be reduced since the cessation was only temporary.

Activity 2.6

*

An employee was provided with a new car costing £15,000. The car emits 196 g/km of CO_2. During 2004/05 the employer spent £900 on insurance, repairs and a vehicle licence. The firm paid for all petrol, costing £1,500, without reimbursement. The employee paid the firm £270 for the private use of the car. Calculate the taxable benefit arising.

2.10 Vans and heavier commercial vehicles

If a van (of normal maximum laden weight up to 3,500 kg) **is made available for an employee's private use, there is an annual scale charge of £500, or £350 if the van is at least four years old at the end of the tax year.** The scale charge covers ancillary benefits such as insurance and servicing (but not van telephones). Paragraphs 2.7 (g) and (h) above apply to vans as they do to cars.

If a commercial vehicle of normal maximum laden weight over 3,500 kg is made available for an employee's private use, but the employee's use of the vehicle is not wholly or mainly private, no taxable benefit arises except in respect of the provision of a driver.

These rules will be changing from April 2005 but the change is not examinable in Unit 19.

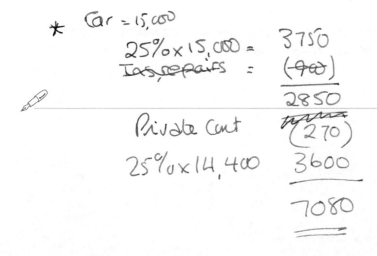

2.11 Statutory mileage allowances

A single authorised mileage allowance for business journeys in an employee's own vehicle applies to all cars and vans. There is no income tax on payments up to this allowance and employers do not have to report mileage allowances up to this amount. The allowance for 2004/05 is 40p per mile on the first 10,000 miles in the tax year with each additional mile over 10,000 miles at 25p per mile. The statutory mileage allowance for employees using their own motor cycle is 24p per mile. For employees using their own pedal cycle it is 20p per mile.

The statutory allowance does not prevent employers from paying higher rates, but any excess will be subject to income tax.

Example

Pratish uses his own car for business travel. In 2004/05 he drove 12,000 business miles. Pratish's employer paid him 40p per business mile.

Pratish receives 40p x 12,000 = £4,800 from his employer.

The tax free mileage allowance is

	£
10,000 x 40p	4,000
2,000 x 25p	500
	4,500

The taxable benefit is the excess or £300 above the tax free amount that Pratish's employer has paid.

Activity 2.7

Sophie uses her own car for business travel. During 2004/05, Sophie drove 15,400 miles in the performance of her duties. Sophie's employer paid her 35p a mile. How is the mileage allowance received by Sophie treated for tax purposes?   15,400 x 35p = 5390

10,000 x 40 = 4,000
5,400 x 25 = 1350

If employers pay less than the statutory allowance, employees can claim tax relief up to that level.

5350 - 5390 = £40.00
Taxable.

Activity 2.8

Megan uses her own car for business travel and her employer reimburses her 25p per mile. In 2004/05 Megan drove 12,000 business miles. What is Megan's tax position in respect of the business mileage?

Employers can make income tax free payments of up to 5p per mile for each fellow employee making the same business trip who is carried as a passenger. If the employer does not pay the employee for carrying business passengers, the employee cannot claim any tax relief.

12,000 x 25p = 3,000

4,500

1,500 claim back

As allowable deduction

2.12 Beneficial loans

2.12.1 Introduction

Employment related loans to employees (other than excluded employees) and their relatives give rise to a benefit equal to:

(a)   **Any amounts written off** (unless the employee has died), and

(b)   **The excess of the interest based on an official rate prescribed by the Treasury, over any interest actually charged ('taxable cheap loan').**

2.12.2 Calculating the interest benefit

There are two alternative methods of calculating the taxable benefit. The simpler **'average' method** automatically applies unless the taxpayer or the Revenue elect for the alternative **'strict' method**. (The Revenue normally only make the election where it appears that the 'average' method is being deliberately exploited.) In both methods, the benefit is the interest at the official rate minus the interest payable.

The 'average' method averages the balances at the beginning and end of the tax year (or the dates on which the loan was made and discharged if it was not in existence throughout the tax year) and applies the official rate of interest to this average. If the loan was not in existence throughout the tax year only the number of complete tax months (from the 6th of the month) for which it existed are taken into account.

The 'strict' method is to compute interest at the official rate on the actual amount outstanding on a daily basis.

Example

Hilary's employer lent her £40,000 in April 2003. Hilary repaid £20,000 of this loan on 5 March 2005. Assume the official rate of interest is 5%.

The benefit in 2004/05 using the average method is

$$\frac{40,000 + 20,000}{2} \times 5\% = £1,500$$

Using the strict method the benefit is

$$\left(£40,000 \times \frac{334}{365} + £20,000 \times \frac{31}{365}\right) \times 5\% = \underline{£1,915}$$

The Revenue may elect to use the strict method.

Activity 2.9

At 6 April 2004 a taxable cheap loan of £30,000 was outstanding to an employee earning £12,000 a year, who repaid £20,000 on 7 December 2004. The remaining balance of £10,000 was outstanding at 5 April 2005. Interest paid during the year was £250. What was the benefit under both methods for 2004/05, assuming that the official rate of interest was 5%?

2.12.3 Exempt benefit

The benefit is not taxable **if the total of all taxable cheap loans to the employee did not exceed £5,000** at any time in the tax year.

When the £5,000 threshold is exceeded, a **benefit** arises on interest **on the whole loan**, not just on the excess of the loan over £5,000.

When a loan is written off and a benefit arises, there is no £5,000 threshold: writing off a loan of £1 gives rise to a £1 benefit.

Activity 2.10

An employer lends an employee £4,000 to buy a car, interest-free for six months. The official rate of interest is 5%. 65% of the loan is then repaid, and the balance is written off. What is the total taxable benefit?

1400.

Activity 2.11

Anna, who is single, has an annual salary of £30,000, and two loans from her employer.

(a)   A season ticket loan of £2,300 at no interest
(b)   A loan to buy a yacht of £54,000 at 3% interest

The official rate of interest is to be taken as 5%.

What is Anna's taxable income for 2004/05?

2.13 Other assets made available for private use

When assets are made available to employees or members of their family or household, the taxable benefit is the higher of 20% of the market value when first provided as a benefit to any employee, or on the rent paid by the employer if higher. The 20% charge is time-apportioned when the asset is provided for only part of the year. The charge after any time apportionment is reduced by any contribution made by the employee.

If an asset made available is subsequently acquired by the employee, **the taxable benefit on the acquisition is the** *greater* **of:**

- The **current market value minus the price paid by the employee.**

- The **market value when first provided minus any amounts already taxed (ignoring contributions by the employee) minus the price paid by the employee.**

This rule prevents tax free benefits arising on rapidly depreciating items through the employee purchasing them at their low secondhand value.

Example: assets made available for private use

A suit costing £400 is purchased by an employer for use by an employee on 6 April 2003. On 6 April 2004 the suit is purchased by the employee for £30, its market value then being £50.

The benefit in 2003/04 is £400 × 20%

£80

The benefit in 2004/05 is £290, being the *greater* of:

		£
(a)	Market value at acquisition by employee	50
	Less price paid	(30)
		20

		£
		400
(b)	Original market value	(80)
	Less taxed in respect of use	320
		(30)
	Less price paid	290

3 Exempt benefits

Various benefits are exempt from tax. These include:

(a) **Entertainment provided to employees by genuine third parties** (eg seats at sporting/cultural events), even if it is provided by giving the employee a voucher.

(b) **Gifts of goods** (or vouchers exchangeable for goods) from third parties (ie not provided by the employer or a person connected to the employer) if the total cost (incl. VAT) of all gifts by the same donor to the same employee in the tax year is £250 or less. If the £250 limit is exceeded, the full amount is taxable, not just the excess.

(c) **Non-cash awards for long service** if the period of service was at least 20 years, no similar award was made to the employee in the past 10 years and the cost is not more than £50 per year of service.

(d)   **Awards under staff suggestion schemes if:**

(i)   There is a formal scheme, open to all employees on equal terms.

(ii)   The suggestion is outside the scope of the employee's normal duties.

(iii)   Either the award is not more than £25, or the award is only made after a decision is taken to implement the suggestion.

(iv)   Awards over £25 reflect the financial importance of the suggestion to the business, and either do not exceed 50% of the expected net financial benefit during the first year of implementation or do not exceed 10% of the expected net financial benefit over a period of up to five years.

(v)   Awards of over £25 are shared on a reasonable basis between two or more employees putting forward the same suggestion.

If an award exceeds £5,000, the excess is always taxable.

(e)   **The first £8,000 of removal expenses if:**

(i)   The employee does not already live within a reasonable daily travelling distance of his new place of employment, but will do so after moving.

(ii)   The expenses are incurred or the benefits provided by the end of the tax year following the tax year of the start of employment at the new location.

(f)   The cost of running a **workplace nursery**. However, cash or vouchers given so that employees can obtain nursery facilities, are taxable.

(g)   **Sporting or recreational facilities available to employees generally and not to the general public**, unless they are provided on domestic premises, or they consist in an interest in or the use of any mechanically propelled vehicle or any overnight accommodation. Vouchers only exchangeable for such facilities are also exempt, but membership fees for sports clubs are taxable.

(h)   **Assets or services used in performing the duties of employment** provided any private use of the item concerned is insignificant. This exempts, for example, the benefit arising on the private use of employer-provided tools.

(i)   **Welfare counselling** and similar minor benefits if the benefit concerned is available to employees generally.

(j)   **Bicycles or cycling safety equipment provided to enable employees to get to and from work or to travel between one workplace and another**. The equipment must be available to the employer's employees generally. Also, it must be used mainly for the aforementioned journeys.

(k)   **Workplace parking**

(l)   **Up to £7,000 a year paid to an employee who is on a full-time course lasting at least a year**, with average full-time attendance of at least 20 weeks a year. If the £7,000 limit is exceeded, the whole amount is taxable.

(m)   **Work related training and related costs. This includes the costs of** training material and assets either made during training or incorporated into something so made.

(n)   **Air miles or car fuel coupons** obtained as a result of business expenditure but used for private purposes.

(o) **The cost of work buses and minibuses or subsidies to public bus services**.

A works bus must have a seating capacity of 12 or more and a works minibus a seating capacity of 9 or more but not more than 12 and be available generally to employees of the employer concerned. The bus or minibus must mainly be used by employees for journeys to and from work and for journeys between workplaces.

(p) Transport/overnight costs where public transport is disrupted by industrial action, late night taxis and travel costs incurred where car sharing arrangements unavoidably breakdown.

(q) The private use of a **mobile phone** and the **first £500 of any benefit arising in respect of the private use of computer equipment**.

(r) **Employer provided uniforms** which employees must wear as part of their duties.

(s) The cost of **staff parties** which are open to staff generally provided that the **cost per staff member per year (including VAT) is £150 or less**. The £150 limit may be split between several parties. If exceeded, the full amount is taxable, not just the excess over £150.

(t) **Private medical insurance premiums paid to cover treatment when the employee is outside the UK in the performance of his duties**. Other medical insurance premiums are taxable as is the cost of medical diagnosis and treatment except for routine check ups.

(u) **The first 15p per day of meal vouchers (eg luncheon vouchers).**

(v) Cheap loans **that do not exceed £5,000** at any time in the tax year (see earlier).

(w) **Job related accommodation.** (see earlier)

(x) **Employer contributions towards additional household costs incurred by an employee who works wholly or partly at home.** Payments up to £2 pw (£104 pa) may be made without supporting evidence. Payments in excess of that amount require supporting evidence that the payment is wholly in respect of additional household expenses.

(y) Meals or refreshments for cyclists provided as part of official 'cycle to work' days.

Activity 2.12

On 6 March 2004, Tim's employer lent him computer equipment costing £3,800. This equipment, which was situated at Tim's home, was used by Tim for both personal and work purposes. What taxable benefit arises in 2004/05 in respect of Tim's use of the computer?

3800
×20% = 760 −500
= 260

4 Allowable deductions

4.1 Introduction

Certain expenditure is specifically deductible in computing net taxable earnings:

(a) **Contributions** (within certain limits) **to approved occupational pension schemes** (see the next chapter).

(b) **Subscriptions to professional bodies** on the list of bodies issued by the Revenue (which includes most UK professional bodies), if relevant to the duties of the employment

(c) Payments for liabilities relating to the employment and for insurance against them (see below)

(d) Payments to charity made under the payroll deduction scheme operated by an employer (see next chapter)

(e) Mileage allowance relief (see above)

Otherwise, allowable deductions are notoriously hard to obtain. They are limited to:

- **Qualifying travel expenses** (see below)

- **Other expenses the employee is obliged to incur and pay as holder of the employment which are incurred wholly, exclusively and necessarily in the performance of the duties of the employment**

- **Capital allowances on plant and machinery (other than cars or other vehicles) necessarily provided for use in the performance of those duties. You will not be expected to compute the amount of any capital allowances in Unit 19. However, you may be expected to deduct a given capital allowance figure in computing net taxable earnings.**

4.2 Liabilities and insurance

If a director or employee incurs a liability related to his employment or pays for insurance against such a liability, the cost is, in general, a deductible expense. If the employer pays such amounts, there is no taxable benefit.

4.3 Travel expenses

4.3.1 Introduction

Tax relief is not available for an employee's normal commuting costs. This means relief is not available for any costs an employee incurs in getting from home to his normal place of work. However **employees are entitled to relief for travel expenses which basically are the full costs that they are obliged to incur and pay as holder of the employment in travelling in the performance of their duties or travelling to or from a place which they have to attend in the performance of their duties (other than a permanent workplace).**

To prevent manipulation of the basic rule normal commuting will not become a business journey just because the employee stops en-route to perform a business task (eg make a 'phone call'). Nor will relief be available if the journey is essentially the same as the employee's normal journey to work.

Example: travel in the performance of duties

Judi is an accountant. She often travels to meetings at the firm's offices in the North of England returning to her office in Leeds after the meetings. Relief is available for the full cost of these journeys as the travel is undertaken in the performance of her duties.

Activity 2.13

Zoe lives in Wycombe and normally works in Chiswick. Occasionally she visits a client in Wimbledon and travels direct from home. Distances are shown in the diagram below:

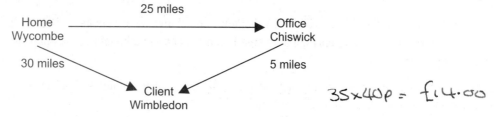

35 x 40p = £14.00

What tax relief is available for Zoe's travel costs?

Example: Normal commuting

Judi is based at her office in Leeds City Centre. One day she is required to attend a 9.00 am meeting with a client whose premises are around the corner from her Leeds office. Judi travels from home directly to the meeting. As the journey is substantially the same as her ordinary journey to work relief is not available.

4.3.2 Site based skills

Site based employees (eg construction workers, management consultants etc) who do not have a permanent workplace, are entitled to relief for the costs of all journeys made from home to wherever they are working. This is because these employees do not have an ordinary commuting journey or any normal commuting costs. However there is a caveat that the employee does not spend more than 24 months of continuous work at any one site.

4.3.3 Temporary workplace

Tax relief is available for travel, accommodation and subsistence expenses incurred by an employee who is working at a temporary workplace on a secondment expected to last up to 24 months. If a secondment is initially expected not to exceed 24 months, but it is extended, relief ceases to be due from the date the employee becomes aware of the change. When looking at how long a secondment is expected to last, the Revenue will consider not only the terms of the written contract but also any verbal agreement by the employer and other factors such as whether the employee buys a house etc.

Activity 2.14

Philip works for Vastbank at its Newcastle City Centre branch. Philip is sent to work full-time at another branch in Morpeth for 20 months at the end of which he will return to the Newcastle branch. Morpeth is about 20 miles north of Newcastle.

What travel costs is Philip entitled to claim as a deduction?

4.4 Other expenses

The word 'exclusively' strictly implies that the expenditure must give no private benefit at all. If it does, none of it is deductible. In practice inspectors may ignore a small element of private benefit or make an apportionment between business and private use.

Whether an expense is 'necessary' is not determined by what the employer requires. The test is whether the duties of the employment could not be performed without the outlay.

The cost of clothes for work is not deductible, except that for certain trades requiring protective clothing there are annual deductions on a set scale.

An employee required to work at home may be able to claim a deduction for an appropriate proportion of his or her expenditure on lighting, heating and (if a room is used exclusively for work purposes) the council tax. Employers can pay up to £2 per week without the need for supporting evidence of the costs incurred by the employee. Payments above the £2 limit require evidence of the employee's actual costs.

Activity 2.15

Taker is employed at an annual salary of £36,000. He receives the following benefits in 2004/05.

(a)   He has the use of a petrol engined motor car, which cost £20,000. Its CO_2 emissions are 182g/km. Fuel is provided for both business and private motoring, and Taker contributes £500 a year (half the cost of fuel for private motoring) for fuel.

(b)   He makes occasional private calls on the mobile phone provided by his employer. *non benefit*

(c)   He usually borrows his employer's video camera (which cost £600) at weekends, when he uses it to record *20%* weddings and parties for friends. He receives no payment for this, and he supplies blank tapes himself.

(d)   He has an interest free loan of £3,000 from his employer. Take the official rate of interest to be 5%. *non benefit*

(e)   His employer pays £4,000 a year to a registered childminder with whom the employer has a contract. The childminder looks after Taker's three year old son. *non benefit*

In 2004/05, Taker pays expenses out of his earnings as follows.

(a)   He pays subscriptions to professional bodies (relevant to his employment) of £180.   *Allowable deduction*

(b)   He makes business telephone calls from home. The cost of business calls is £45. The cost of renting the line for the year is £100, and 40% of all Taker's calls are business calls.   *Allowable deduction*

(c)   He pays a golf club subscription of £150. He does not play golf at all, but goes to the club to discuss business with potential clients. These discussions frequently lead to valuable contracts.   *non allowable*

Task

Compute Taker's taxable earnings for 2004/05.

Salary		36,000
Car benefit		
22% of 20,000	4,400	
22% of 14,400	3,168	7,568
Use of company Assets		120
600 × 20%		
Childminding		4,000
		47,688
Allowable deductions - subs		(180)
Telephone		(45)
		47,463

Key learning points

☑   An employee is taxed on **employment income**: **general earnings** and **specific employment income**.

☑   Net taxable earnings are **total taxable earnings** less **allowable deductions**.

☑   Earnings includes **salary, wages, gratuities and other benefits in money or money's worth**.

☑   Employees are also taxable on **benefits**: **excluded employees** (non-directors earning **less than £8,500**) are **only taxable on certain benefits**.

☑   **Accommodation** is a taxable benefit on **all employees** unless the accommodation is **job related**. There is a 'basic' benefit equal to the annual value of the accommodation. There is an 'additional' benefit if the property originally cost £75,000.

☑   **Employees other than excluded employees** are also taxable on **expenses connected with living accommodation.**

☑   **Cars and fuel** provided for **private use** are taxable in relation to a **% of CO_2 emissions.**

☑   **Beneficial loans** are taxable if **any amount of the loan is written off** or the loan is at a **cheap rate of interest.**

☑   Other assets made available for **private use** are generally taxable at **20% of the market value** of the asset per year.

☑   There are various **exempt benefits.**

☑   There are a few **allowable deductions**, including contributions to **pension schemes** and contributions under the **payroll deduction scheme**.

☑   Travel expenses incurred in **travelling in the performance of duties** or in **travelling to a temporary workplace** are deductible. Tax relief is not available for an employee's ordinary commuting costs.

Quick quiz

1   Earnings are taxed on a .... basis. Fill in the blank.

2   What accommodation does not give rise to a taxable benefit?   *Job related*

3   Sue is a director of Stowe Ltd. On 6 July 2003 Stowe Ltd lent Sue video equipment which it had just bought for £1,000. On 6 April 2004 the equipment was sold to Sue for £600, when its open market value was £700.

        What benefit arises on Sue in 2004/05 in respect of the video equipment?

        A   £100
        B   £150
        C   £200
        D   £250

4   Julia's employer provided her with a petrol engine company car on 1 January 2004. The car's market value on this date was £10,000. The list price of the car when new on 1 June 2003 was £18,000. The car's CO_2 emissions figure is 170g/km.

        What taxable benefit arises in respect of the car in 2004/05?

        A   £2,000
        B   £3,420
        C   £3,600
        D   £1,900

5   Edmund's employer granted him an interest free loan of £5,200 on 6 April 2004. The loan was intended to help Edmund to purchase his annual season ticket for travel to work.

        Assuming the official rate of interest is 5% what assessable benefit arises in respect of the loan made to Edmund?

        A   £NIL
        B   £10
        C   £250
        D   £260

6   What are the conditions for expenses other than travel expenses to be deductible?

Answers to quick quiz

1   Earnings are taxed on a **receipts** basis.

2   Job related accommodation.

3   D

		£
Market value on 6.7.03		1,000
Assessed in 2003/04 ($20\% \times 1,000 \times {}^{9}/_{12}$)		(150)
		850
Less: price paid		(600)
		250

	£
Market value 6.4.04	700
Price paid	(600)
	100

The assessable benefit is the higher amount of £250.

4   C   £18,000 × 20% = £3,600

The taxable % is (170 – 145) = 25 ÷ 5 = 5 + 15 = 20%.

The list price of the car is used to calculate the assessable benefit.

Tutorial note. The car was available throughout 2004/05 so there is no need to time apportion the benefit.

5   D   As the loan exceeds £5,000, a taxable benefit arises in respect of the full amount of the loan.

£5,200 x 5% = £260

6   They must be incurred wholly, exclusively and necessarily in the performance of the employment.

Activity checklist

This checklist shows which performance criteria, range statement or knowledge and understanding point is covered by each activity in this chapter. Tick off each activity as you complete it.

Activity

2.1 [ ] This activity deals with Performance Criteria 19.1.A: prepare accurate computations of emoluments, including benefits.

2.2 [ ] This activity deals with Performance Criteria 19.1.A: prepare accurate computations of emoluments, including benefits.

2.3 [ ] This activity deals with Performance Criteria 19.1.A: prepare accurate computations of emoluments, including benefits.

2.4 [ ] This activity deals with Performance Criteria 19.1.A: prepare accurate computations of emoluments, including benefits.

2.5 [ ] This activity deals with Performance Criteria 19.1.A: prepare accurate computations of emoluments, including benefits.

2.6 [ ] This activity deals with Performance Criteria 19.1.A: prepare accurate computations of emoluments, including benefits.

2.7 [ ] This activity deals with Performance Criteria 19. A: prepare accurate computations of emoluments including benefits.

2.8 [ ] This activity deals with Performance Criteria 19.1.B: list allowable expenses and deductions.

2.9 [ ] This activity deals with Performance Criteria 19.1.A: prepare accurate computations of emoluments, including benefits.

2.10 [ ] This activity deals with Performance Criteria 19.1.A: prepare accurate computations of emoluments, including benefits.

2.11 [ ] This activity deals with Performance Criteria 19.1.A: prepare accurate computations of emoluments, including benefits.

2.12 [ ] This activity deals with Performance Criteria 19.1.A: prepare accurate computations of emoluments, including benefits.

2.13 [ ] This activity deals with Performance Criteria 19.1.B: list allowable expenses and deductions.

2.14 [ ] This activity deals with Performance Criteria 19.1.B: list allowable expenses and deductions.

2.15 [ ] This activity deals with Performance Criteria 19.1.A and B: prepare accurate computations of emoluments, including benefits; list allowable expenses and deductions.

chapter 3

Employment income – additional aspects

Contents

Performance criteria

19.1.B List allowable expenses and deductions

19.1.C Record relevant details of income from employment accurately and legibly in the tax return

19.1.D Make computations and submissions in accordance with current tax law and taking account of current Revenue practice.

Range statement

19.1 Allowable expenses: contributions to pension schemes, contributions to charity under the payroll deduction scheme

Knowledge and understanding

2   The issues of taxation liability (Elements 19.1, 19.2, 19.3, 19.4)

3   Relevant legislation and guidance from the Revenue (Elements 19.1, 19.2, 19.3, 19.4)

4   Basic law and practice (Elements 19.1, 19.2, 19.3, 19.4)

6   Expenses deductible from employment income including pension contributions and payroll giving to charities (Element 19.1)

1 The PAYE system

1.1 Introduction

The objective of the PAYE system is to deduct the correct amount of tax over the year. Its scope is very wide. It applies to most cash payments, other than reimbursed business expenses, and to certain non cash payments.

In addition to wages and salaries, PAYE applies to taxable lump sum payments on leaving, most lump sum payments on joining, round sum expense allowances and payments instead of benefits. It also applies to any readily convertible asset.

It is the employer's duty to deduct income tax from the pay of his employees, whether or not he has been directed to do so by the Revenue. **If he fails to do this he** (or sometimes the employee) **must pay over the tax which he should have deducted and the employer may be subject to penalties**. Interest will also run from 14 days after the end of the tax year concerned on any underpaid PAYE. Officers of the Revenue can inspect employer's records in order to satisfy themselves that the correct amounts of tax are being deducted and paid.

1.2 Payment under the PAYE system

Under PAYE income tax and national insurance is normally paid over to the Revenue monthly, 14 days after the end of each tax month.

The PAYE system is also used to collect student loan repayments.

1.3 Employer's responsibilities: year end returns and employees leaving or joining

At the end of each tax year, the employer must provide each employee with a form P60. This shows total taxable emoluments for the year, tax deducted, code number, national insurance (NI) number and the employer's name and address. **The P60 must be provided by 31 May following the year of assessment.**   In your exam you may be given a P60 as a source document provided by the client. You would then be expected to obtain information for salary and tax deducted at source from the form. A sample P60 is included within Practice Exam 1 later in this text. Familiarise yourself with it now.

Following the end of each tax year, the employer must send the Revenue:

    (a)   **by 19 May:**

        (i)   **End of year Returns P14** (showing the same details as the P60);
        (ii)   **Form P35** (summary of tax and NI deducted).

    (b)   **by 6 July:**

        (i)   **Forms P11D** (benefits etc for directors and employees paid £8,500+ pa);
        (ii)   **Forms P9D** (benefits etc for excluded employees).

A copy of the form P11D (or P9D) must also be provided to the employee by 6 July. The details shown on the P11D include the full cash equivalent of all benefits, so that the employee may enter the details on his self-assessment tax return. Specific reference numbers for the entries on the P11D are also used on the employee's self assessment tax return.

The full value of any assessable benefits must usually be entered on Form P11D. Employees must then make a separate claim in respect of any expenses incurred wholly, exclusively and necessarily for the purposes of the employment. Alternatively, employers sometimes reach an agreement with the Revenue that certain expenses reimbursed to employees are tax deductible and do not need to be entered on form P11D. The company is then said to have a **'P11D Dispensation'** covering these items.

A copy of Form P11D is produced in Practice Exam 1 later in this text. Have a look at it now. Again you may be provided with the form in your exam. You will not be required to fill in a P11D in the exam.

When an employee leaves, a certificate on form P45 (particulars of Employee Leaving) must be prepared. This form shows the employee's code and details of his income and tax paid to date and is a four part form. One part is sent to the Revenue, and three parts handed to the employee. One of the parts (part 1A) is the employee's personal copy. If the employee takes up a new employment, he must hand the other two parts of the form P45 to the new employer. The new employer will fill in details of the new employment and send one part to the Revenue, retaining the other. The details on the form are used by the new employer to calculate the PAYE due on the next payday.

1.4 Charitable donations under the payroll deduction scheme

Employees can make tax deductible donations under the payroll deduction scheme to an approved charity of their choice by asking their employer to deduct the donation from their gross earnings prior to calculating the PAYE due.

This scheme is sometimes known as a **'payroll giving'** scheme.

2 Pensions

The main ways in which individuals can provide for a pension are:

- the state pension scheme
- occupational pension schemes
- personal pension schemes

The state scheme has no impact on income tax during an individual's working career, but the other two systems are discussed below.

2.1 Occupational pension schemes

2.1.1 Introduction

An employer may set up an **occupational pension scheme** for employees. Such a scheme may either require contributions from employees or be non-contributory.

Schemes can be of two kinds: Revenue approved and unapproved. **Approved schemes have significant tax advantages** that have made them very popular.

The advantages for an employee are:

- **contributions made by the employee are deductible from his earnings** (up to a limit of 15% of gross earnings, with gross earnings limited to the earnings cap (see below));

- **the employer's contributions are not regarded as benefits for the employee**;

- **the fund of contributions, and the income and gains arising from their investment, are not, in general, liable to tax**. It is this long-term tax-free accumulation of funds that makes approved schemes so beneficial;

- provision can be made for a **lump sum** to be **paid on the employee's death in service**. Provided that it does not exceed four times his final remuneration, it is **tax-free**;

- **a tax-free lump sum may be paid to the employee on retirement.**

The following limits apply to an approved occupational pension scheme.

- The maximum pension is normally two thirds of the individual's final remuneration, being calculated as one sixtieth for each year of service, with a maximum of 40 years.

- A scheme may provide for part of the pension to be taken as a lump sum. The maximum lump sum is 1.5 times final remuneration, being calculated as 3/80 for each year of service, with a maximum of 40 years.

The Revenue have discretion to approve schemes which do not comply with these limits. In particular, many schemes provide for a pension of two thirds of final salary after less than 40 years service.

2.1.2 The earnings cap

An earnings cap applies to tax-approved occupational pension schemes. The cap is £102,000 for 2004/05.

The earnings cap has two consequences.

    (a)   The maximum pension payable from an approved scheme is the cap × 2/3.
    (b)   The maximum tax-free lump sum is the cap × 1.5.

2.1.3 Additional voluntary contributions

An employee who feels that his employer's scheme is inadequate may make additional voluntary contributions (AVCs), either to the employer's scheme or to a separate scheme (freestanding AVCs). **AVCs are deductible from the employee's taxable pay**, but only to the extent that they, plus any contributions by the employee to the employer's scheme, do not exceed 15% of gross earnings (limited to the earnings cap). The limits on pensions and lump sums which may be taken must be applied to the total sums derived from the employer's scheme and the AVCs.

2.1.4 Unapproved schemes

Employers can set up unapproved schemes, to operate alongside approved schemes. Employer's contributions to unapproved schemes are taxed as earnings of the employee. Employee's contributions are not tax-deductible.

Activity 3.1

An employee earns £105,000 in 2004/05 and pays £3,500 a year in contributions to his employer's pension scheme. What is the maximum tax-deductible amount he may pay in AVCs? ~~£102,000 earning cap × 2/3~~ – 3,500

102,000 × 15% – 3,500 = 64,500
                                       ↘ 11,800

2.2 Personal pension schemes

An alternative way of providing a pension is to take out a personal pension known as a **'Stakeholder' pension**.

2.2.1 Eligibility

An individual who is below the age of 75 may, in general, contribute to a personal pension scheme.

It is possible for a personal pension scheme to accept payments from a person other than the scheme member. Thus a parent may make contributions for his child (even under the age of 18) or a working spouse could contribute on behalf of a housewife/husband. **If a scheme member is employed his employer may make contributions to the personal pension scheme.**

2.2.2 Limits

2.2.2.1 Time of retirement

Normal Retirement Age can, in general, be at any time between 50 and 75.

2.2.2.2 Benefits

There are **no limits** on the amount of the pension allowable. At retirement the fund can be used to buy the highest annuity available.

It is also possible to take out a **tax-free cash lump sum** on retirement. There is **no restriction** on the **amount** of tax-free cash but it is limited to 25% of the size of the fund at the time. The individual effectively takes a reduced pension in order to obtain the tax free cash simply because only the balance (75%) of the fund remains for an annuity purchase (ie buying an annual pension).

2.2.2.3 Contributions

Although benefits are not limited, there is a restriction placed on **contributions**.

In certain circumstances, contributions can be made into a stakeholder scheme for an individual with no earnings. In this case, **annual contributions (by the scheme member and anyone else, eg employer, parent) to the personal pension scheme cannot in total exceed the contributions threshold**.

The contributions threshold is fixed at £3,600 for 2004/05. This figure includes tax relief at the basic rate. Therefore, net payments of £2,808 can be made into the scheme. This would be increased by tax relief of £792 (at 22%) given by the Revenue to the pension provider to make up the total of £3,600 (see further below for more details on tax relief).

For individuals with net relevant earnings, **annual contributions (by the scheme member and anyone else, eg employer) to the personal pension scheme cannot in total exceed the greater of**:

   (a)   the contributions threshold, and
   (b)   the relevant percentage of net relevant earnings of the basis year (see further below).

Again, the amount determined under this test includes tax relief at basic rate. For example, if the permitted contributions were £5,000, a net payment of £3,900 could be made on which tax relief of £1,100 would be given by the Revenue to the pension provider, resulting in a total payment of £5,000 into the personal pension fund.

Net relevant earnings in a tax year cannot exceed the earnings cap (£102,000 for 2004/05).

Broadly, net relevant earnings (NRE) are calculated as follows:

	£
Earnings under Schedule D Cases I and II	X
Employment earnings not providing occupational pension scheme rights	X
Schedule A income from furnished holiday lettings	X
	X
Less: Deductions from earnings	(X)
Net relevant earnings	X

2.2.3 Basis year

In any tax year in which he has actual net relevant earnings, an individual may choose a basis year for his deemed net relevant earnings on which contributions are based. This can be the **current tax year or one of the previous five tax years**. Therefore, for 2004/05 the basis year may be any year from 1999/00 to 2004/05.

The basis year need not be a tax year in which the individual was a member of the personal pension scheme.

Once a basis year has been chosen, the level of net relevant earnings will be presumed to be the same in the basis year and the next five tax years. Therefore, if 2004/05 is chosen as the basis year, the level of NRE will be deemed to be the same for the years 2004/05 to 2009/10 inclusive and no further evidence of earnings needs to given. However, it is also possible to choose a new basis year with higher earnings within this time if the individual wishes to make increased contributions.

Having determined the basis year, the next stage is to determine the relevant percentage for the tax year of the contribution. The maximum contributions are:

Age at start of tax year of contribution	% of NRE of the basis year
Up to 35	17.5
36 – 45	20
46 – 50	25
51 – 55	30
56 – 60	35
61 – 74	40

Activity 3.2

An individual (born 13 January 1959) first has net relevant earnings for 2004/05 and wishes to make maximum personal pension contributions in that year and all following years. He expects to have the following net relevant earnings: *Age* ~~46~~ 45

2004/05	£30,000
2005/06	£25,000
2006/07	£20,000
2007/08	£28,000
2008/09	£27,500
2009/10	£24,000
2010/11	£20,000
2011/12	£34,000

Show the maximum amount of pension contributions he can pay for 2004/05 up to 2011/12, assuming the rules in 2004/05 stay the same in later years.

Tax yr	Age	%	Basis Yr	Max Cont	
04/05	45	20	4/5	(30,000 × 20%) =	6,000
05/06	46	25	4/5	(30,000 × 25%) =	7,500
06/07	47	25	4/5	(30k × 25%) =	7,500
07/08	48	25	4/5	" =	7,500
08/09	49	25	4/5	" =	7,500
09/10	50	25	4/5	(30k × 25%) =	7,500
10/11	51	30	7/8	(28k × 30%) =	8,400
11/12	52	30	11/12	(34k × 30%) =	10,200

2.2.4 Carrying back premiums

It is possible in certain circumstances to treat a contribution as if it had been paid in the previous tax year. This is especially useful to self employed people who wish to maximise their contributions, but cannot determine their net relevant earnings until after the end of the tax year.

An irrevocable election must be made at or before the time the contribution is made for the carry back to take effect. The contribution must be made by 31 January following the end of the tax year in which the contribution is to be treated has having been paid. So, if a contribution is to be treated as paid in 2003/04 it must be paid by 31 January 2005.

2.3 Tax treatment of contributions

All contributions to a personal pension scheme are treated as amounts paid net of basic rate tax. The Revenue then pays the basic rate tax to the pension provider.

Further tax relief is given if the scheme member is a higher rate taxpayer. **The relief is given by increasing the basic rate band for the year by the gross amount of contributions for which he is entitled to relief.**

Activity 3.3

Joe has earnings of £46,000 in 2004/05. He pays a personal pension contribution of £7,020 (net). He has no other taxable income.

Show Joe's tax liability for 2004/05.

3 Payments on the termination of employment

3.1 Charge on termination payments

Termination payments may be entirely exempt, partly exempt or entirely chargeable.

The following payments on the termination of employment are exempt.

- Payments on account of injury, disability or accidental death

- Lump sum payments from approved pension schemes

- Legal costs recovered by the employee from the employer following legal action to recover compensation for loss of employment, where the costs are ordered by the court or (for out-of-court settlements) are paid directly to the employee's solicitor as part of the settlement.

Payments to which the employee is contractually entitled are, in general, taxable in full as general earnings. Payments for work done (terminal bonuses), for doing extra work during a period of notice, payments in lieu of notice where stated in the original contract, or for extending a period of notice are therefore taxable in full. A payment by one employer to induce an employee to take up employment with another employer is also taxable in full.

BPP PROFESSIONAL EDUCATION

Other payments on termination (such as compensation for loss of office and including statutory redundancy pay), which are not taxable under the general earnings rules because they are not in return for services, are nevertheless brought in as amounts which count as employment income. Such payments **are partly exempt: the first £30,000 is exempt; any excess is taxable as specific employment income.**

Payments and other benefits provided in connection with termination of employment (or a change in terms of employment) **are taxable in the year in which they are received.** 'Received' in this case means when it is paid or the recipient becomes entitled to it (for cash payments) or when it is used or enjoyed (non-cash benefits).

Employers have an obligation to report termination settlements which include benefits to the Revenue by 6 July following the tax year end. No report is required if the package consists wholly of cash. Employers must also notify the Revenue by this date of settlements which (over their lifetime) may exceed £30,000.

The provision of counselling for unemployment or to help an employee leaving to find new employment or self-employment is not a taxable benefit, nor is the reimbursement of the cost of such counselling taxable. There are a number of other excluded benefits such as continued use of a mobile telephone, work related training and continued provision of computer equipment (if within the £500 limit).

If the termination package is a partially exempt one and exceeds £30,000 then the £30,000 exempt limit is allocated to earlier benefits and payments. In any particular year the exemption is allocated to cash payments before non-cash benefits.

Example: redundancy package

Jonah is made redundant on 31 December 2004. He receives (not under a contractual obligation) the following redundancy package:

- cash in total of £40,000 payable as £20,000 in January 2005 and £20,000 in January 2006
- use of company car for period to 5 April 2006 (benefit value per annum £5,000)
- use of computer for period to 5 April 2006 (benefit value per annum £400)

In 2004/05 Jonah receives as redundancy:

	£
Cash	20,000
Car ($£5,000 \times {}^3/_{12}$)	1,250
	21,250

Wholly exempt (allocate £21,250 of £30,000 exemption to cash first then benefit).

In 2005/06 Jonah receives:

	£
Cash	20,000
Car	5,000
	25,000
Exemption (remaining)	(8,750)
Taxable	16,250

Thus of the cash payment £11,250 (£20,000 less £8,750) is taxable and PAYE at the basic rate should have been applied to this by Jonah's former employer. There is no tax on the provision of the computer as it is an excluded benefit.

 first 30k exempt from Tax

4 Forms

Sample copies of the following forms are included in Practice Exam 1 in this text.

- A P11D
- A P60
- The supplementary pages to the income tax return form that must be completed by employed taxpayers

You may have to take information from Forms P60 and P11D in your exam so you should ensure that you have a look at the forms and note where the information is provided. You will not be required to complete these forms in your exam.

In your exam you may, however, have to complete the employment pages that accompany the income tax return. You can practice completing these pages in several of the activities and practice exams later in this text.

See page (vi) of this text for a note regarding the forms.

Activity 3.4

The Pay as You Earn (PAYE) regulations requires certain forms to be completed and deadlines to be met.

In relation to these regulations you are required to state:

(a)   Which form is given to an employee when leaving employment. *P45*

(b)   Which form is used to inform the Revenue of each employee's total tax and National Insurance Contributions for the year.   *P60*

(c)   Which form summaries ALL the forms in (ii) above.

(d)   By what date the forms in (ii) and (iii) above are to be submitted to the Revenue.

(e)   Which form details an employee's benefits where the employee earns less than £8,500 per year (ie where the employee is an excluded employee)

(f)   By what date the form in (v) above is to be submitted to the Revenue.

Key learning points

☑ The **PAYE system** collects **tax on employment income**.

☑ The employer is responsible for providing employee **year end forms** (**P60**, **P11D**, **P9D**)

☑ The employer must also provide a **P45** form when an employee leaves.

☑ An employer may set up an **occupational pension scheme** for employees. **Employee contributions** are deducted in arriving at taxable earnings.

☑ **Maximum employee contributions** are **15% of earnings,** subject to the **earnings cap.**

☑ An employee may make **additional voluntary contributions** (AVCs). (subject to the maximum level of contribution).

☑ Alternatively, a pension may be provided under a **personal pension scheme** (including a **stakeholder pension**).

☑ **Anyone can contribute** to a personal pension scheme, but **higher contributions** can be made by individuals with **net relevant earnings**, (subject to the earnings cap).

☑ Contributions can be **carried back** one tax year**.**

☑ **Basic rate tax relief** is given on personal pension contributions by treating contributions as being made **net of 22% tax. Higher rate tax relief** is given by **extending the basic rate band**.

☑ **Ex gratia payments of up to £30,000**, made in the termination employment are **tax free**. Contractual payments and payments in excess of £30,000 are tax free.

Capital allowance is a deductable benefit.

Quick quiz

1   Which form will be given by an employer to an employee who leaves employment?

    A   P11D
    B   P35
    C   P45
    D   P60

2   The limit on employee contributions to an occupational pension scheme is 17½% of earnings. TRUE/FALSE.

3   Ursula is aged 37. In 2004/05 she has net relevant earnings of £50,000. This was the highest amount of NRE she has had. What is her maximum personal pension contribution for the year?

4   How is higher rate tax relief given for personal pension contributions?

5   Which payments made on termination of employment are tax free?

Answers to quick quiz

1   C

2   FALSE. The limit on employee contributions to an occupational pension scheme is **15** % of earnings.

3   20% x £50,000 = £10,000 maximum gross contribution.

4   By extending the basic rate band by the gross amount of the contribution.

5   Ex gratia payments of up to £30,000.

Activity checklist

This checklist shows which performance criteria, range statement or knowledge and understanding point is covered by each activity in this chapter. Tick off each activity as you complete it.

Activity

3.1 ☐ This activity deals with Performance Criteria 19.1.B: list allowable expenses and deductions.

3.2 ☐ This activity deals with Performance Criteria 19.1.B: list allowable expenses and deductions.

3.3 ☐ This activity deals with Performance Criteria 19.1.B: list allowable expenses and deductions.

3.4 ☐ This activity deals with Performance Criteria 19.1.D: make computations and submissions in accordance with current tax law and taking account of Revenue practice.

Investments and land

Contents

Performance criteria

19.2 A Prepare schedules of dividends and interest received on shares and securities

19.2 B Prepare schedules of property income and determine profits and losses

19.2 C Prepare schedules of investment income from other sources

19.2 D Apply deductions and reliefs and claim loss set-offs

19.2.E Record relevant details of property and investment income accurately and legibly in the tax return

Range statements

19.2 Property income taking into account: holiday lets, wear and tear

19.2 Other sources of investment income: banks, building societies, government saving schemes

Knowledge and understanding

2 The issues of taxation liability (Elements 19.1, 19.2, 19.3, 19.4)

3 Relevant legislation and guidance from the Revenue (Elements 19.1, 19.2, 19.3, 19.4)

4 Basic law and practice (Elements 19.1, 19.2, 19.3, 19.4)

7 Classification and calculation of income as property income, savings or dividend income (Element 19.2)

8 Identification of the main tax exempt investments (Element 19.2)

9 Calculation and set-off of rental deficits (Element 19.2)

1 Schedule D Case III

Schedule D Case III taxes interest. The taxable income is the full amount arising without any deductions. Some interest is received gross. Examples of interest received gross are:

- loans between individuals;
- 3½% War Loan;
- most government stocks (gilt edged securities);
- National Savings Bank accounts;
- certificates of tax deposit.

The amount of income taxable for a tax year is the amount arising in that year. Income arises when it is paid or credited: accrued income not yet paid or credited is ignored.

2 Schedule D Case VI

This case deals with any income not falling under any other schedule or case.

Examples are income or profits from:

- the sale of patent rights
- casual commission

The income arising in a tax year is taxed in that year.

3 Other financial investments

3.1 Tax-free investments

The proceeds of National Savings Certificates (including index-linked issues), **children's bonus bonds** and **Premium Bond winnings are tax-free**. All income arising on **individual savings accounts (ISAs)** (see below) are also tax-free.

Income arising on **Tax Exempt Special Savings Accounts** (TESSAs) is tax free. Also there is no tax on income or gains arising in a **Personal Equity Plan** (PEP). It has not been possible to open new TESSAs or PEPs since 6 April 1999 but TESSAs and PEPs that existed at that date retain their tax free status.

3.2 Taxable National Savings products

The return on some National Savings products is taxable. These include:

- Capital bonds. A lump sum is invested, and interest is added gross once a year. The rates are fixed in advance for five years.

- Fixed rate savings bonds. 20% tax is deducted at source. Bonds are available for various fixed terms.

- Income bonds. Interest is paid gross each month. The rate of interest may vary.

- Pensioners' guaranteed income bonds. These are like income bonds except that the interest rate is fixed for a period of up to five years. The investor must be aged 60 or over.

3.3 Bank and building society interest

Bank deposit interest and building society interest paid to individuals is paid net of 20% tax. The tax is refundable to individuals who are not liable to pay the tax.

Banks and building societies may pay interest gross to investors who certify themselves as non-taxpayers. If tax turns out to be due after all, the interest is taxed under Schedule D Case III.

Banks and building societies may also pay interest gross on fixed deposits and certificates of deposit of at least £50,000 which must be repaid at the end of a specified period of five years or less.

National Savings Bank interest is paid gross and taxed under Schedule D Case III.

3.4 Interest on company securities

Interest paid by UK companies on debentures and loan stock is paid net of 20% tax to individuals. This is refundable to individuals who are not liable to pay tax.

Activity 4.1

Denis receives the following in 2004/05 (cash amounts)

National Savings Bank easy access a/c interest	£80
Interest on National Savings Certificates *Exempt*	£100
Interest on ISA *Exempt*	£250
Interest from NatWest Bank deposit a/c	£80
Interest on $3^{1}/_{2}$% War Loan	£50

Show the total taxable interest assessable on Denis for 2004/05. State clearly any amounts that are exempt.

3.5 Interest in the personal tax computation

Interest is included gross in the savings (excl dividend) column of the personal tax computation. It is taxed at 10% if it falls in the starting rate band, at 20% if it falls in the basic rate band and at 40% if it exceeds the higher rate threshold. **Any tax suffered on the interest is deducted in computing tax payable and may be repaid.**

Activity 4.2

A single taxpayer's only income in 2004/05 is bank deposit interest of £9,600 net. No arrangement to receive interest gross is made. What tax repayment is due?

3.6 Dividends

Dividends on UK shares are deemed to be paid net of a 10% tax credit. This means a dividend received must be grossed up for inclusion in the tax computation by multiplying by 100/90.

The 10% tax credit cannot be repaid.

Dividend income is taxed as the top slice of income. If it is above the basic rate threshold of £31,400 (2004/05), it is taxed at 32.5%. Otherwise it is taxed at 10%.

Activity 4.3

Emma's only income in 2004/05 was dividend income of £12,600 (net). Emma, who is aged 40, is single. What tax is payable / repayable?

Activity 4.4

Maureen held 10,000 shares in ABC plc and £20,000 of loan stock in the company.

In 2004/05, ABC plc paid a net dividend of 18p per share and paid 5% interest on its loan stock.

Calculate the taxable amounts of dividend and interest income received by Maureen from ABC plc for 2004/05.

4 Individual savings accounts (ISAs)

4.1 Tax Treatment

Individual savings accounts are tax efficient savings accounts..

Investments within an ISA are exempt from both income and capital gains tax.

There is no statutory minimum period for which an ISA must be held. A full or partial withdrawal may be made at any time without loss of the tax exemption.

5 Schedule A

5.1 Calculation of profit/loss

Income from land and buildings in the UK, including caravans and houseboats which are not moved, is taxed under Schedule A.

A taxpayer with rental income is treated as running a business, his 'Schedule A' business. All the rents and expenses for all properties are pooled, to give a single profit or loss. Profits and losses are computed on an accruals basis.

Expenses are deductible in computing taxable net rental income if those expenses are incurred wholly and exclusively for the letting business. Expenses will often include rent payable, where a landlord is himself renting the land which he in turn lets to others. Interest on loans to buy or improve properties is treated as an expense (on an accruals basis).

Capital allowances are a form of tax depreciation given on plant and machinery used in the Schedule A business and on industrial and agricultural buildings. If you study Unit 18 Preparing Business Tax Computations you will learn how to compute capital allowances. In this Unit you would be given the relevant figure for capital allowances and just expected to deduct it as an expense from accrued rental income.

Capital allowances are not available on plant or machinery used in a dwelling, so someone who lets property furnished cannot normally claim capital allowances on the furniture (but see below). Instead, he can choose between the renewals basis and the 10% wear and tear allowance.

(a)   Under the *renewals* basis, there is no deduction for the cost of the first furniture provided, but the cost of replacement furniture is treated as a revenue expense. However, the part of the cost attributable to improvement, as opposed to simple replacement, is not deductible.

(b)   Under the *10% wear and tear* basis, the actual cost of furniture is ignored. Instead, an annual deduction is given of 10% of rents. The rents are first reduced by amounts which are paid by the landlord but are normally a tenant's burden. These amounts include any water rates and council tax paid by the landlord.

Schedule A profits are computed for tax years. Each tax year's profit is taxed in that year.

Rent for furniture supplied with premises is taxed as part of the rent for the premises, unless there is a separate trade of renting furniture.

Activity 4.5

Michael let out his house from 1 July 2004. The rent charged was £500 per month. Michael paid 15% per month of the gross rents to a managing agent. He also paid buildings insurance of £360 on 1 September 2004 for 12 months cover. The house was let furnished and Michael chose to deduct the wear and tear allowance.

Show the Schedule A profit for Michael for 2004/05.

9 months × 500 = 4,500

15% managing agent   (675)

Insurance $\frac{7}{12}$ × 360 = (210)

10% wear & tear   (450)

3165

5.2 Loss relief

If there is a loss in a Schedule A business, it is carried forward to set against the first future Schedule A profits. It may be carried forward until the Schedule A business ends, but it must be used as soon as possible.

Activity 4.6

Joanne bought a flat on 1 October 2004. She let it out to a tenant at a rent of £300 per month. She incurred the following expenses:

3600

Cleaning   £50 per month
Water rates   £20 per month
Interest on loan £210 per month

On 1 May 2005, Joanne increased the rent to £350 per month. The flat was let furnished and Joanne chose to deduct the wear and tear allowance.

Show the Schedule A profit or loss for 2004/05 and 2005/06.

5.3 Furnished holiday lettings

There are special rules for furnished holiday lettings. The income from such lettings is taxed under Schedule A but the following rules apply.

(a)   Relief for losses is available as if they were trading losses. This means losses can be set against other income. The usual Schedule A loss relief does not apply.

(b)   Capital allowances are available on furniture: the renewals basis and the 10% wear and tear basis do not apply if capital allowances are claimed. You will not be expected to compute capital allowances in Unit 19 but you may be given the figure which you should deduct in computing profits and losses.

(c)   The income qualifies as net relevant earnings for personal pension relief (see earlier in this text).

The letting must be of furnished accommodation made on a **commercial basis with a view to the realisation of profit**. The property must satisfy the following conditions.

(a)   It is **available** for commercial letting to the public **for not less than 140 days in a tax year, and is so let for at least 70 days in that 140 day period.** If two or more properties each pass the 140 day test separately, then they need only pass the 70 day test on average. That is, the test becomes: [(sum of numbers of days let)/(number of properties)] must be at least 70. A landlord may choose to leave particular properties out of the averaging computation if they would pull the average down to below 70 days.

(b)   For at least seven months (including the 70 days) it is not normally in the same occupation for more than 31 days.

If someone has furnished holiday lettings and other lettings, **draw up two profit and loss accounts as if they had two separate Schedule A businesses**. The profit/losses from furnished holiday lets must always be kept separately.

6 Forms

A sample of the supplementary pages to the income tax return form that need to be completed by taxpayers with property income is included in Practice Exam 1 in this text. You may need to complete details on the second page of this form in your exam. Familiarise yourself with the form now. Please see page (vi) for a note regarding forms.

Activity 4.7

(a) On 1 May 2004, Hamburg started to invest in rented properties. He bought three houses in the first three months, as follows.

House 1

Hamburg bought house 1 for £62,000 on 1 May 2004. It needed a new roof, and Hamburg paid £5,000 for the work to be done in May. He also spent £1,200 on loft insulation. He then let it unfurnished for £600 a month from 1 June to 30 November 2004. The first tenant then left, and the house was empty throughout December 2004. On 1 January 2005, a new tenant moved in. The house was again let unfurnished. The rent was £6,000 a year, payable annually in advance.

Hamburg paid water rates of £320 for the period from 1 May 2004 to 5 April 2005 and a buildings insurance premium of £480 for the period from 1 June 2004 to 31 May 2005.

House 2

Hamburg bought house 2 for £84,000 on 1 June 2004. He immediately bought furniture for £4,300, and let the house fully furnished for £5,000 a year from 1 August 2004. The rent was payable quarterly in arrears. Hamburg paid water rates of £240 for the period from 1 June 2004 to 5 April 2005. He claimed the 10% wear and tear allowance for furniture.

House 3

Hamburg bought house 3 for £45,000 on 1 July 2004. He spent £1,200 on routine redecoration and £2,300 on furniture in July, and let the house fully furnished from 1 August 2004 for £7,800 a year, payable annually in advance. Hamburg paid water rates of £360 for the period from 1 July 2004 to 5 April 2005, a buildings insurance premium of £440 for the period from 1 July 2004 to 30 June 2005 and a contents insurance premium of £180 for the period from 1 August 2004 to 31 July 2005. He claimed the 10% wear and tear allowance for furniture.

Task

Compute Hamburg's Schedule A income for 2004/05.

(b) Hamburg is thinking about investing in two holiday cottages in Cornwall.

Task

Outline the requirements for the cottages to be furnished holiday lettings and the income tax treatment of such lettings.

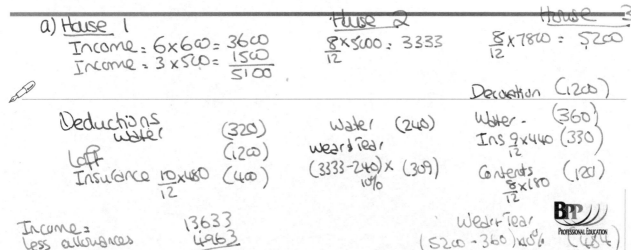

Key learning points

☑   **Schedule D Case III** income and **Schedule D Case VI** income are taxed in the **year of receipt**.

☑   Income arising in an ISA or on National Savings Certificates is tax free.

☑   **Premium bond prizes** are tax free.

☑   **Interest** on a **National Savings Bank account** is received **gross**.

☑   **Bank and building society interest** is generally received **net of 20% tax** which is **repayable**.

☑   **Dividends** are received with a **10% tax credit** which is **not repayable.**

☑   Income from **land** is taxed under **Schedule A.**

☑   All rents and expenses for all properties are **pooled** to give an **overall profit or loss**. The overall profit or loss is computed on an accruals basis.

☑   If there is a **Schedule A loss**, it is **carried forward** to set against **first available Schedule A profit**.

☑   If property is let furnished either a **10% wear and tear allowance** may be claimed or a tax relief for the cost of furniture may be taken on a **renewals basis**.

☑   There are special rules for **furnished holiday lettings**.

Quick quiz

1   Kevin receives £80 interest on his National Savings Bank easy access account in 2004/05.

     What is the taxable amount of interest?

     A   nil – the interest is exempt
     B   £10
     C   £80 ✓
     D   £100

2   How many of the following investments give rise to tax free income?

     (i)   Shares in an ISA
     (ii)   3 ½ War Loan
     (iii) National Savings income bonds

     A   All three of them
     B   Two of them
     C   One of them
     D   None of them

3   Lorna rented out her furnished flat in 2004/05. She received rents of £5,000 and paid council tax of £1,000. Her Schedule A assessment for the year is:

     A   £3,500
     B   £3,600
     C   £4,000
     D   £5,000

4   What are the conditions for a letting to be a furnished holiday letting?

Answers to quick quiz

1   C   Interest on the National Savings Easy Access Account is received gross.

2   C   Income arising in an ISA is tax free. Interest from both the other investments is taxable under Schedule D Case III.

3   B

	£
Rents	5,000
Less: council tax	(1,000)
wear and tear 10% x £(5,000 – 1,000)	(400)
Schedule A	3,600

4   FHL is – available for letting at least 140 days per tax year
         – actually let for at least 70 days per tax year
         – for at least 7 months not normally in the same occupation for more than 31 days

Activity checklist

This checklist shows which performance criteria, range statement or knowledge and understanding point is covered by each activity in this chapter. Tick off each activity as you complete it.

Activity

4.1	☐	This activity deals with Performance Criteria 19.2.C: prepare schedules of investment income from other sources.
4.2	☐	This activity deals Performance Criteria 19.2.C: prepare schedules of investment income from other sources.
4.3	☐	This activity deals Performance Criteria 19.2.C: prepare schedules of investment income from other sources.
4.4	☐	This activity deals with Performance Criteria 19.2.A: prepare schedules of dividends and interest received on shares and securities.
4.5	☐	This activity deals with Performance Criteria 19.2.B: prepare schedules of property income and determine profits and losses.
4.6	☐	This activity deals with Knowledge and Understanding point 9: calculation and set-off of rental deficits and Performance Criteria 19.2.D: apply deductions and reliefs and claim loss set offs.
4.7	☐	This activity deals with Performance Criteria 19.2.B: prepare schedules of property income and determine profits and losses.

P A R T B

Capital gains tax

chapter 5

An outline of
capital gains tax

Contents

Performance criteria

19.4 A   Identify and value disposed-of chargeable personal assets

19.4 D   Apply reliefs and exemptions correctly

19.4 E   Calculate capital gains tax payable

19.4.F   Record relevant details of gains and captal gains tax payable legibly and accurately in the tax return

Range statement

19.4   Chargeable personal assets that have been: sold, gifted, lost, destroyed

Knowledge and understanding

2   The issues of taxation liability (Elements 19.1, 19.2, 19.3, 19.4)

3   Relevant legislation and guidance from the Revenue (Elements 19.1, 19.2, 19.3, 19.4)

4   Basic law and practice (Elements 19.1, 19.2, 19.3, 19.4)

14   Set-off capital losses, taper relief and annual exemption to arrive at taxable gains (Element 19.4)

15   Calculation of capital gains tax payable on gains on non-business assets disposed of by individuals (Element 19.4)

1 The charge to CGT

1.1 Introduction

Broadly, an individual's **taxable gains** for a tax year **are current year chargeable gains less current year allowable losses less the annual exemption**.

There is an annual exemption for each tax year. For 2004/05 it is £8,200. It is the last deduction to be made in the calculation of taxable gains.

Activity 5.1

In 2004/05, Carol, a single woman, has the following gains and losses. What are Carol's taxable gains for 2004/05?

	£
Chargeable gains	26,100
Allowable capital losses	8,000

1.2 Rates of CGT

Taxable gains are chargeable to capital gains tax as if the gains were an extra slice of savings (excl dividend) income for the year of assessment concerned. This means that CGT may be due at 10%, 20% or 40%.

The rate bands are used first to cover income and then gains. If a gift aid payment is made, the basic rate can be extended, as for income tax calculations (see Chapter 1). Similarly, the payment of a personal pension contribution can extend the basic rate band.

Example

Sase has taxable income of £18,000 in 2004/05. Her taxable gains in the year were £4,000.

Calculate the CGT payable.

Solution

The taxable income uses the £2,020 starting rate band and £15,980 of the basic rate band. £13,400 of the basic rate band remains to use against gains. All the gains are taxed at 20%.

£4,000 × 20% = £800

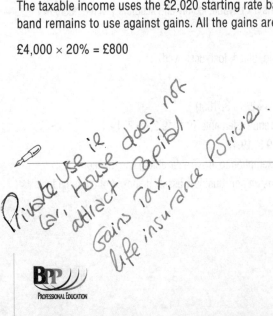

Private use ie does not (ar, House) attract Capital Gains Tax, life insurance policies.

BPP PROFESSIONAL EDUCATION

Activity 5.2.

Nissan has taxable income of £28,215 and taxable gains of £5,285 in 2004/05.

Task

Calculate Nissan's CGT payable.

[handwritten:] 28215   5285
10% 2020   202
22% 26195   5763
20% 3185   637
40% 2100   840   = 1477

Activity 5.3

David had gross bank interest of £24,500 and gains of £35,000 in 2004/05.

Task

Calculate David's capital gains tax liability for 2004/05.

[handwritten:] 8 800   26800
24,500
4 745
S.T.I 19755

2 Allowable losses

2.1 Introduction

[handwritten:] Annual Exemption "£8,200"

(31400 − 19755) = 11645 × 20%   2329
15155 × 40% = 6062 = £8391.

Deduct allowable capital losses from chargeable gains in the tax year in which they arise. Any loss which cannot be set off is carried forward to set against future chargeable gains. Losses must be used as soon as possible (subject to the following paragraph). Losses may not normally be set against income.

Allowable losses brought forward are only set off to reduce current year chargeable gains less current year allowable losses to the annual exempt amount. No set-off is made if net chargeable gains for the current year do not exceed the annual exempt amount.

Example: the use of losses

(a) George has chargeable gains for 2004/05 of £10,000 and allowable losses of £6,000. As the losses are *current year losses* they must be fully relieved against the £10,000 of gains to produce net gains of £4,000, despite the fact that net gains are below the annual exemption.

(b) Bob has gains of £12,400 for 2004/05 and allowable losses brought forward of £6,000. Bob restricts his loss relief to £4,200 so as to leave net gains of £(12,400 − 4,200) = £8,200, which will be exactly covered by his annual exemption for 2004/05. The remaining £1,800 of losses will be carried forward to 2005/06.

(c) Tom has chargeable gains of £5,000 for 2004/05 and losses brought forward from 2003/04 of £4,000. He will leapfrog 2004/05 and carry forward all of his losses to 2005/06. His gains of £5,000 are covered by his annual exemption for 2004/05.

Activity 5.4

Amarjat realised capital gains of £15,000 and allowable losses of £3,000 in 2004/05. He also had allowable losses of £9,000 brought forward from 2003/04.

Task

What amount of capital losses are carried forward to 2005/06?

[Handwritten annotations:
Gains 15,000
losses 3,000
12,000
8,200 All
3800
5200 carried forward.*]*

2.2 Losses in the year of death

The only facility to carry back capital losses arises on the death of an individual. **Losses arising in the tax year in which an individual dies can be carried back to the previous three tax years, later years first, and used so as to reduce gains for each of the years to an amount covered by the appropriate annual exemption.** Only losses in excess of gains in the year of death can be carried back.

Activity 5.5

Joe dies on 1 January 2005. His chargeable gains (no taper relief available – see later) and allowable loss have been as follows.

	Gain/(loss) £	Annual exemption £
2004/05	2,000	8,200
	(12,000)	
2003/04	8,100	7,900
2002/03	4,000	7,700
2001/02	28,000	7,500

[Handwritten annotations:
{10,000 loss
used 200 →0
(9800) loss used*]*

How will the loss be set off?

3 Taper relief

3.1 Relief for non-business assets

Taper relief may be available to reduce gains realised after 5 April 1998.

Taper relief reduces the percentage of the gain chargeable according to how many complete years the asset had been held since acquisition or 6 April 1998, if earlier. Taper relief is more generous for business assets than for non-business assets. In unit 19 you will only be expected to deal with non-business assets. If you study unit 18 you will learn how to calculate gains on the disposal of business assets.

The percentages of gains which remain chargeable after taper relief are set out below.

Non business assets No of complete years after 5.4.98 for which asset held	% of gain chargeable
0	100
1	100
2	100
3	95
4	90
5	85
6	80
7	75
8	70
9	65
10 or more	60

You should be given the above rates in the tax rates and allowances section of your exam paper. Non-business assets acquired before 17 March 1998 qualify for an addition of 1 year (a 'bonus year') to the period for which they are actually held after 5 April 1998.

Example: complete years held for taper relief

Peter buys a non business asset on 1 January 1998 and sells it on 1 July 2004. For the purposes of the taper Peter is treated as if he had held the asset for 7 complete years (six complete years after 5 April 1998 plus one additional year).

3.2 Taper relief and losses

Taper relief is applied to net chargeable gains after the deduction of current year and brought forward losses. The annual exemption is then deducted from the tapered gains.

Losses brought forward are only deducted from net current gains to the extent that the gains exceed the CGT annual exemption.

Activity 5.6

William sold a non-business asset in December 2004 realising a chargeable gain of £14,000 before taper relief. He had purchased the asset in May 1997. In January 2005 William sold another asset realising a loss of £1,300 but he made no other disposals in 2004/05. What are William's taxable gains for 2004/05?

12700 x 75% = 9525
Less Exemp   8200
              1325

Activity 5.7

Ruby sold a non-business asset in July 2004 which she had purchased in January 1992. She realised a chargeable gain (before taper relief) of £17,500. She also sold a non-business asset in 2004/05 realising a capital loss of £6,000. She

17500
6000

11500
loss (10000) 300
8200 8,200   6150
Taper relief   Annual (8200)
(6 year + Bonus) 6150   Exemp
£ 6,700 loss carried forward.   = NIL   we can only bring to zero

has a capital loss brought forward from 2003/04 of £10,000. Calculate Ruby's taxable gain and any losses carried forward at 5.4.05.

3.3 Allocation of losses to gains

Allocate losses to gains in the way that produces the lowest tax charge. Losses should therefore be deducted from the gains attracting the lowest rate of taper (ie where the highest percentage of the gain remains chargeable).

Example: allocation of losses to gains

Alastair made the following capital losses and gains in 2004/2005:

	£
Loss	10,000
Gains (before taper relief)	
Asset A (non-business asset)	25,000
Asset B (non-business asset)	18,000

Asset A was purchased in December 2000 and sold in January 2005. Taper relief reduces the gain to 90% of the original gain (4 years; non-business asset). Asset B was purchased on 5 November 2001 and sold on 17 December 2004. Taper relief reduces the gain to 95% of the original gain (3 years; non-business asset).

The best use of the loss is to offset it against the gain on the asset B:

	£	£
Gain – Asset A	25,000	
Gain after taper relief (£25,000 × 90%)		22,500
Gain – Asset B	18,000	
Less loss	(10,000)	
Net gain before taper relief	8,000	
Gain after taper relief £8,000 × 95%		7,600
Gains after taper relief		30,100
Less annual exemption		(8,200)
Taxable gains		21,900

Activity 5.8

In 2004/05 Ross sold a non business asset that had been owned for 2 complete years realising a chargeable gain of £20,000. He also realised a gain of £50,000 on a non business asset he had owned since 1993. At the start of 2004/05 he had bought forward losses of £10,000. Compute Ross' taxable gains for 2004/05.

3.4 Shares and securities

Special rules apply to shares and securities. We cover these later in this text. However, note that quoted shares in a trading company are a non-business asset for taper relief purposes, provided:

(a)   The shareholder is not an officer or employee of the company, and

(b)   The shareholder does not own 5% or more of the voting rights in the company.

In addition shares in a non-trading company are a non-business asset provided the shareholder is not an officer or employee of the company or broadly, that the shareholder does not have a more than a 10% interest in the company.

4 Chargeable persons, disposals and assets

4.1 Chargeable persons

Individuals are the only type of chargeable person that you will meet at Unit 19.

4.2 Chargeable disposals

The following are chargeable disposals.

- Sales of assets or parts of assets
- Gifts of assets or parts of assets
- Receipts of capital sums following the surrender of rights to assets
- The loss or destruction of assets

A **chargeable disposal occurs on the date of the contract** (where there is one, whether written or oral), or the date of a conditional contract becoming unconditional. This may differ from the date of transfer of the asset. However, when a capital sum is received on a surrender of rights, the disposal takes place on the day the sum is received.

Where a disposal involves an acquisition by someone else, the date of acquisition is the same as the date of disposal.

The following are exempt disposals.

- Transfers of assets on death (the heirs inherit assets as if they bought them at death for their then market values, but there is no capital gain or allowable loss on death)

- Transfers of assets as security for a loan or mortgage

- Gifts to charities and national heritage bodies

Betting winnings are not subject to CGT.

4.3 Chargeable assets

All forms of property, wherever in the world they are situated, are chargeable assets for CGT purposes unless they are specifically designated as exempt.

The following are exempt assets (thus gains are not taxable and losses on their disposal are not in general allowable losses)

- Motor vehicles suitable for private use
- National savings certificates and premium bonds
- Foreign currency for private use
- Decorations for valour unless acquired by purchase
- Damages for personal or professional injury
- Life assurance policies (only exempt in the hands of the original beneficial owner)
- Works of art, scientific collections and so on given for national purposes
- Gilt-edged securities
- Qualifying corporate bonds (QCBs)
- Certain chattels
- Debts (except debts on a security)
- Pension rights and annuity rights
- Investments held in individual savings accounts (ISAs) or personal equity plans (PEPs)

Activity 5.9

In 1990, Jane bought a vintage motor car as an investment. She never drove it. She sold it in 2004, making a gain of £75,000. Is the gain chargeable to CGT?   *Cars of exempt*

5 Married couples

A husband and wife are taxed as two separate people. Each has an annual exemption, and losses of one spouse cannot be set against gains of the other.

Disposals between spouses who are living together give rise to no gain and no loss, whatever actual price (if any) **was charged by the person transferring the asset** to their spouse. A couple are treated as living together unless they are separated under a court order or separation deed, or are in fact separated in circumstances which make permanent separation likely.

Where an asset is jointly owned, the beneficial interests of the spouses will determine the treatment of any gain on disposal. If, for example, there is evidence that the wife's share in an asset was 60%, then 60% of any gain or loss on disposal would be attributed to her. If there is no evidence of the relative interests, the Revenue will normally accept that the asset is held in equal shares. Where a declaration of how income from the asset is to be shared for income tax purposes has been made, there is a presumption that the same shares will apply for CGT purposes.

If a spouse who would be liable to pay tax at 40% wishes to dispose of an asset on which a gain would arise, and the other spouse would be taxed on the gain at a lower rate, the asset should first be transferred to the spouse with the lower tax rate. Similarly, assets or parts of assets should be transferred between spouses to use both CGT annual exemptions.

Where there has been a transfer of assets between spouses taper relief on a subsequent disposal is based on the combined period of holding by the spouses.

Activity 5.10

Edwina disposed of assets as follows.

(a) On 1 January 2004 she sold her car at a loss of £10,700.
(b) On 28 February 2004 she sold some shares at a loss of £6,300.
(c) On 1 May 2004 she sold some quoted shares (acquired August 2002) and realised a gain of £7,800.
(d) On 1 October 2004 she sold some shares at a loss of £2,000.
(e) On 1 December 2004 she sold a picture (acquired July 2003) to a collector for £50,000, making a gain of £3,000.
(f) On 1 April 2005 she sold some gilt-edged securities (acquired May 2003), making a gain of £10,000.

Task

What loss, if any, is available to be carried forward at the end of 2004/05?

Key learning points

☑ An individual pays **CGT** on his **net taxable gains** in a tax year.

☑ There is an **annual exemption** for each tax year.

☑ Taxable gains are taxed as an **extra slice of savings (excluding dividend) income.**

☑ **Capital losses** are deducted against gains in the **same tax year.**

☑ Excess losses are **carried forward**, except in the **year of death** when they can be **carried back 3 years**.

☑ **Brought forward losses cannot reduce taxable gains below the annual exempt amount.**

☑ **Taper relief** reduces gains. Taper relief is applied to net gains after the deduction of current year and brought forward losses.

☑ The percentage of gains taxable after deducting taper relief depends on the **number of complete years after 5 April 1998 that the asset was held for**. If the asset was held on **17 March 1998 an additional year is added** to the number of years that it is treated as held for taper relief purposes.

☑ There needs to be three things for a capital gain to arise: **chargeable person, chargeable disposal, chargeable asset.**

☑ Disposals between spouses are on a **no gain/ no loss** basis.

Quick quiz

1   CGT is payable at ..... %, ... % and ......%. Fill in the blanks

2   Niall made a chargeable gain (no taper relief) of £10,000 and an allowable loss of £(4,000) in 2004/05.

    His loss carried forward to 2005/06 is:

    A   Nil
    B   £(1,900)
    C   £(2,200)
    D   £(4,000)

3   Mark acquired a non-business asset on 1 July 1997. He sold the asset on 1 September 2004.

    His qualifying period for taper relief is:

    A   4 years
    B   5 years
    C   6 years
    D   7 years

4   Give some examples of chargeable disposals.

Answers to quick quiz

1   CGT is payable at **10**%, **20**% and **40**%.

2   A   As the loss is a current year loss, it is set against the gain, even though this brings the gain below the annual exemption.

3   D   The ownership period runs from 6 April 1998 to 5 April 2004 = 6 years, plus a bonus year as the asset was held on 17 March 1998.

4   (a)   Sales of assets or parts of assets
    (b)   Gifts of assets or parts of assets
    (c)   Receipts of capital sums following the surrender of rights to assets
    (d)   The loss or destruction of an asset.

Activity checklist

This checklist shows which performance criteria, range statement or knowledge and understanding point is covered by each activity in this chapter. Tick off each activity as you complete it.

Activity

5.1		This activity deals with Knowledge and Understanding point 14: set-off capital losses, taper relief and annual exemption to arrive at a taxable gain.
5.2		This activity deals with Performance Criteria 19.4E: calculate Capital Gains Tax payable.
5.3		This activity deals with Performance Criteria 19.4E: calculate Capital Gains Tax payable.
5.4		This activity deals with Performance Criteria 19.4D: apply reliefs and exemptions correctly.
5.5		This activity deals with Performance Criteria 19.4D: apply reliefs and exemptions correctly.
5.6		This activity deals with Knowledge and Understanding point 14: set-off capital losses, taper relief and annual exemption to arrive at a taxable gain.
5.7		This activity deals with Performance Criteria 19.4D: apply reliefs and exemptions correctly.
5.8		This activity deals with Knowledge and Understanding point 14: set-off capital losses, taper relief and the annual exemption to arrive at a taxable gain.
5.9		This activity deals with Performance Criteria 19.4A: identify and value disposed-of or chargeable personal assets.
5.10		This activity deals with Knowledge and Understanding point 14: set-off capital losses, taper relief and the annual exemption to arrive at a taxable gain.

chapter 6

The computation of gains and losses

Contents

Performance criteria

19.4 A   Identify and value disposed-of chargeable personal assets

19.4 C   Calculate chargeable gains and allowable losses

Range statement

19.4   Chargeable personal assets that have been: sold, gifted, lost, destroyed

Knowledge and understanding

2   The issues of taxation liability (Elements 19.1, 19.2, 19.3, 19.4)

3   Relevant legislation and guidance from the Revenue (Elements 19.1, 19.2, 19.3, 19.4)

4   Basic law and practice (Elements 19.1, 19.2, 19.3, 19.4)

12   Identification of non-business assets disposed of including part disposals and personal shareholdings (Element 19.4)

13   Calculation of gains and losses on disposals of non-business assets including indexation allowance (Element 19.4)

1 The basic computation

1.1 Introduction

A chargeable gain (or an allowable loss) is generally calculated as follows.

	£
Disposal consideration (or market value)	45,000
Less incidental costs of disposal	(400)
Net proceeds	44,600
Less allowable costs	(21,000)
Unindexed gain	23,600
Less indexation allowance (if available)	(8,500)
Indexed gain	15,100

Taper relief may then apply. Taper relief was discussed in the previous chapter.

1.2 Incidental costs of disposal

Incidental costs of disposal may include:

- valuation fees (but not the cost of an appeal against the Revenue's valuation);
- estate agency fees;
- advertising costs;
- legal costs.

These costs should be deducted separately from any other allowable costs (because they do not qualify for any indexation allowance if it was available on that disposal).

1.3 Allowable costs

Allowable costs include:

- the original cost of acquisition
- incidental costs of acquisition
- capital expenditure incurred in enhancing the asset

Incidental costs of acquisition may include the types of cost listed above as incidental costs of disposal, but acquisition costs do qualify for indexation allowance (from the month of acquisition) if it is available on the disposal.

1.4 Enhancement expenditure

Enhancement expenditure is capital expenditure which enhances the value of the asset and is reflected in the state or nature of the asset at the time of disposal, or expenditure incurred in establishing, preserving or defending title to, or a right over, the asset. Excluded from this category are:

- costs of repairs and maintenance

- costs of insurance
- any expenditure deductible for income tax purposes
- any expenditure met by public funds (for example council grants)

Enhancement expenditure may qualify for indexation allowance from the month in which it becomes due and payable.

Activity 6.1

Daniella buys a plot of land for £100,000, and spends £6,000 on clearing it. However, by the time she sells the land (at a large profit) it has become overgrown, and is in the same state as it would have been if the work had not been done. Is the £6,000 deductible as enhancement expenditure?

1.5 Disposal considerations

Usually the disposal consideration is the proceeds of sale of the asset, but a disposal is deemed to take place at market value:

    (a)   where the disposal is **not a bargain at arm's length**

    (b)   where the disposal is made for a **consideration which cannot be valued**

    (c)   where the disposal is by way of a **gift**

2 The indexation allowance

2.1 Introduction

Indexation was introduced from March 1982. The purpose of having an indexation allowance was to remove the inflationary element of a gain from taxation.

Individuals are entitled to an indexation allowance until April 1998, but not thereafter.

You will not have to deal with assets acquired before 31 March 1982 in the exam.

Example: indexation allowance

John bought a painting on 2 January 1987 and sold it on 19 November 2004.

Indexation allowance will be available for the period January 1987 to April 1998 only.

2.2 Calculation of indexation allowance

Indexation is calculated from the month of acquisition of an asset.

The indexation factor for individuals is:

$$\frac{\text{RPI for April 1998} - \text{RPI for month of acquisition}}{\text{RPI for month of acquisition}}$$

The calculation is expressed as a decimal and is normally rounded to three decimal places.

The indexation factor is then multiplied by the cost of the asset to calculate the indexation allowance. If the RPI has fallen, the indexation allowance is zero: it is not negative.

You will be given the indexation factor in the exam. You will not be expected to calculate it.

Activity 6.2

An asset is acquired by an individual on 15 February 1983 at a cost of £5,000. Enhancement expenditure of £2,000 is incurred on 10 April 1984. The asset is sold for £20,500 on 20 December 2004. Calculate the indexation allowance.

Assume indexation factors:

February 1983 to April 1998 = 0.960
April 1984 to April 1998 = 0.834

2.3 Indexation and losses

The indexation allowance cannot create or increase an allowable loss. If there is a gain before the indexation allowance, the allowance can reduce that gain to zero, but no further. If there is a loss before the indexation allowance, there is no indexation allowance.

Activity 6.3

Simon bought a picture for £97,000 in August 1990 and sold it for £24,000 in April 2004. What is the allowable loss?

Assume indexation factor: August 1990 to April 1998 = 0.269

BPP
PROFESSIONAL EDUCATION

3 Connected persons

A disposal to a connected person is deemed to take place for a consideration equal to the market value of the asset, rather than the actual price paid.

If a loss results on a disposal to a connected person, **it can be set only against gains arising in the same or future years on disposals to the same connected person and the loss can only be set off if he or she is still connected with the person sustaining the loss.**

An individual is connected with:

- his spouse;
- his relatives (brothers, sisters, ancestors and lineal descendants);
- the relatives of his spouse;
- the spouses of his and his spouse's relatives.

Activity 6.4

On 1 August 2004 Holly sold a painting to her sister, Emily for £40,000. The market value of the painting on the date of sale was £50,000. Holly bought the painting on 1 September 2002 for £60,000.

What allowable loss arises on disposal of the painting and how may this be relieved?

4 Intraspouse transfers of assets

Disposals between spouses living together do not give rise to chargeable gains or allowable losses. (See the previous chapter.)

A special rule applies to indexation on no gain/no loss disposals. To illustrate the rule, we assume a husband (H) buys an asset and later transfers it to his wife (W) who then sells it to an outsider. The rules are exactly the same if the roles of H and W are reversed.

If H buys the asset, W is deemed to have bought the asset when H transferred it to her. Her cost is H's cost plus indexation allowance up to the date of transfer (or 6 April 1998). When W sells the asset, she computes indexation allowance from the time of the transfer. If the transfer was made after 5 April 1998 there is no further indexation allowance.

Activity 6.5

Sylvia bought an antique vase for £18,000 on 1 January 1991. On 1 January 1994 she gave it to her husband Nicholas. On 12 April 2004 he sold it for £50,000. What is his chargeable gain before taper relief?

Assume indexation factors:

January 1991 to January 1994 = 0.085
January 1994 to April 1998 = 0.151

5 Part disposals

The disposal of part of a chargeable asset is a chargeable event for the purpose of capital gains tax. The chargeable gain (or allowable loss) is computed by deducting from the disposal value a fraction of the original cost of the whole asset.

The fraction is:

$$\frac{A}{A + B} = \frac{\text{value of the part disposed of}}{\text{value of the part disposed of} + \text{market value of the remainder}}$$

A is the proceeds (for arm's length disposals) *before* deducting incidental costs of disposal.

The part disposal fraction should not be applied indiscriminately. Any expenditure incurred wholly in respect of a particular part of an asset should be treated as an allowable deduction in full for that part and not apportioned. An example of this is incidental selling expenses, which are wholly attributable to the part disposed of.

Activity 6.6

Mr Heal owns a painting which originally cost him £27,000 in March 1984. He sold a quarter interest in the painting in July 2004 for £18,000. The market value of the three-quarter share remaining is estimated to be £36,000. What is the chargeable gain after taper relief?

Assume indexation factor: March 1984 to April 1998 = 0.859

Activity 6.7

Androulla bought a plot of land for £150,000 in January 2000. In August 2004, she sold part of the land for £187,000, which was net of legal fees on the sale of £3,000. At that time, the value of the remaining land was £327,000. What expenditure could she deduct in computing her chargeable gain?

Activity 6.8

Hardup made the following disposals in 2004/05. All disposals were to unconnected persons except where otherwise stated.

(a)   On 12 May 2004 he sold an antique vase for £100,000. He had bought it for £65,000 on 1 July 1988.

(b)   On 18 June 2004 he sold a plot of land for £47,000. He had bought it for £20,000 on 14 January 1990, and had spent £5,000 on permanent improvements in July 1992 and £4,000 on defending his title to the land in July 1999.

(c)   On 25 March 2005 he exchanged contracts for the sale of a house (which he had always rented to tenants) for £173,000. Completion took place on 24 April 2004. He had bought the house for £65,000 on 16 October 1988.

(d)   On 16 October 2004 he sold an antique table to his wife (with whom he was living) for £130,000, its market value. He had bought it a year earlier for £120,000.

(e)   On 1 December 2004 he sold a bungalow (which he had never lived in) to his brother for £32,000, its market value. He had bought the bungalow for £35,000 on 15 December 1999.

Hardup will pay income tax at the marginal rate of 40% in 2004/05.

Tasks

(a)   Compute the chargeable gain/allowable loss before taper relief on disposal of the vase.
(b)   Compute the chargeable gain/allowable loss before taper relief on disposal of the land.
(c)   Compute the chargeable gain/allowable loss before taper relief on the disposal of the house.
(d)   Compute the chargeable gain/allowable loss before taper relief arising on disposal of the table.
(e)   Compute the chargeable gain/allowable loss before taper relief arising on disposal of the bungalow.
(f)   Compute Hardup's net taxable gains after taper relief and the annual exemption.
(g)   Compute the CGT payable by Hardup for 2004/05.

Assume indexation factors:

July 1988 to April 1998 = 0.524
January 1990 to April 1998 = 0.361
July 1992 to April 1998 = 0.171
October 1988 to April 1998 = 0.485

Key learning points

☑   A chargeable gain is the **proceeds** less **cost** and **indexation allowance** (if any).

☑   **Enhancement expenditure** can only be deducted if it is reflected in the **state and nature** of the asset **at the time of disposal**.

☑   **Indexation allowance** runs from the **date of acquisition** to **April 1998**.

☑   Indexation allowance **cannot create or increase a loss.**

☑   In some cases, **market value** is used in a CGT computation.

☑   Disposals between **connected persons** are at **market value.**

☑   A **loss** arising on a disposal between **connected persons can only be set against gains arising in the same** or **future years on disposals to the same connected person.**

☑   There are **special rules on indexation** for **intraspouse transfers**.

☑   On a **part disposal**, the **cost must be apportioned** between the **part disposed of** and the **part retained**.

Quick quiz

1   Josie buys a house. She repairs the roof and builds an extension. The extension blows down in a storm and is not replaced. She pays legal fees on defending a legal action by a neighbour about the boundary.

Which of the additional expenditure will be allowable on a sale of the house?

A   legal fees only
B   legal fees and extension only
C   extension and roof only
D   all of it

2   Lenny is married to Sharon. He sells an asset worth £10,000 to Sharon's mother for £8,000. The asset cost £5,000 2 years ago. What is Lenny's gain on the sale?

3   10 acres of land are sold for £15,000 out of 25 acres. The original cost was £9,000. The costs of sale were £2,000. The rest of the land is valued at £30,000. What is the allowable expenditure?

Answers to quick quiz

1   A   Repairs to roof – not allowable because not capital in nature
          Extension – not allowable as not reflected in the state of the asset at disposal
          Legal fees – allowable as incurred in defending title to asset

2
	£
Market value	10,000
Less: cost	(5,000)
Gain	5,000

Sharon's mother is a connected person so the disposal is at market value.

3    $\dfrac{15,000}{15,000 + 30,000} \times £9,000 = £3,000 + £2,000$ (costs of disposal) $= £5,000$

Activity checklist

This checklist shows which performance criteria, range statement or knowledge and understanding point is covered by each activity in this chapter. Tick off each activity as you complete it.

Activity

6.1 ⬜ This activity deals with Performance Criteria 19.4C: calculate chargeable gains and allowable losses.

6.2 ⬜ This activity deals with Performance Criteria 19.4C: calculate chargeable gains and allowable losses.

6.3 ⬜ This activity deals with Performance Criteria 19.4C: calculate chargeable gains and allowable losses.

6.4 ⬜ This activity deals with Performance Criteria 19.4A: identify and value disposed of chargeable personal assets.

6.5 ⬜ This activity deals with Performance Criteria 19.4C: calculate chargeable gains and allowable losses.

6.6 ⬜ This activity deals with Knowledge and Understanding point 12: identification of non-business assets disposed of including part disposals and personal shareholdings.

6.7 ⬜ This activity deals with Knowledge and Understanding point 12: identification of non-business assets disposed of including part disposals and personal shareholdings.

6.8 ⬜ This activity deals with Performance Criteria 19.4C: calculate chargeable gains and allowable losses and Performance Criteria 19.4E: calculate capital gains tax payable.

PROFESSIONAL EDUCATION

chapter 7

Shares and securities

Contents

Performance criteria

19.4 B Identify shares disposed of by individuals

Range statement

19.4   Chargeable personal assets that have been: sold, gifted, lost, destroyed

Knowledge and understanding

2   The issues of taxation liability (Elements 19.1, 19.2, 19.3, 19.4)

3   Relevant legislation and guidance from the Revenue (Elements 19.1, 19.2, 19.3, 19.4)

4   Basic law and practice (Elements 19.1, 19.2, 19.3, 19.4)

12   Identification of non-business assets disposed of including part disposals and personal shareholdings (Element 19.4)

1 The matching rules for individuals

1.1 The problem

Shares and securities present special problems when attempting to compute gains or losses on disposal. For instance, suppose that an individual buys some quoted shares in X plc as follows.

Date	Number of shares	Cost £
5 May 1988	100	150
17 January 2000	100	375

On 15 June 2004, he sells 120 of its shares for £1,450. To determine the chargeable gain, we need to be able to work out which shares out of the two original holdings were actually sold.

1.2 The solution

We therefore need **matching rules**. These **allow us to decide which shares have been sold and so work out what the allowable cost on disposal should be.**

In what follows, we will use 'shares' to refer to both shares and securities.

Share disposals are matched with acquisitions in the following order.

(a)   Same day acquisitions.
(b)   Acquisitions within the following 30 days.
(c)   Previous acquisitions after 5 April 1998 identifying the most recent acquisition first (a LIFO basis).
(d)   Any shares in the **FA 1985 pool** (shares acquired between 6.4.82 and 5.4.98).

The FA 1985 pool is looked at in detail below. You will not have to deal with shares acquired before 6.4.82 so they are not considered here.

Example

Catherine acquired the following shares in X plc.

	No of shares
1.4.90	10,000
1.9.98	5,000
10.11.01	7,000
30.12.04	2,000

On 11.12.04 Catherine sold 12,000 shares. With which acquisitions is Catherine's share disposal matched?

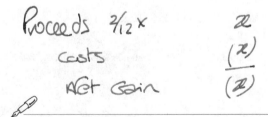

Solution

Catherine will initially match the disposal with the 2,000 shares bought on 30.12.04 (next 30 days). She will then match with the other post April 1998 acquisitions on a LIFO basis, so the 7,000 shares bought on 10.11.01 and 3,000 of the shares bought on 1.9.98 are deemed to be sold. 2,000 of the shares acquired on 1.9.98 and the FA 1985 pool shares remain.

Activity 7.1

[handwritten annotations:]

Proceeds $\frac{1000}{1600} \times 14,000 = 8750$

1st → Cost $\qquad$ (1260)

Gain $\qquad$ 7490

2nd Proceeds $\frac{600}{1600} \times 14000 = 5250$

Cost $\frac{600 \times 1900}{1800} = $ (633)

$\qquad$ 4617

June made the following purchases of ordinary shares in Read plc, a quoted company.

Date	Number	Cost £
15 May 2002	1,800 *2nd*	1,900
1 March 2003	1,000 *1st*	1,260

On 30 September 2004 she sold 1,600 of the shares for £14,000. The shares were not a business asset for taper relief purposes.

Compute the capital gain after taper relief or allowable loss on the sale of June's shares.

[handwritten:] no taper relief — Gain £12107

100% for 3 years — less all — 8200

3907

2 The FA 1985 pool

2.1 Introduction

Until taper relief was introduced we used to treat shares as a 'pool' which grew as new shares were acquired and shrank as they were sold. **The FA 1985 pool** (so called because it was introduced by rules in the Finance Act 1985) **comprises the following shares of the same class in the same company.**

[handwritten:] 6.4.82 – 5.4.85
6.4.85 – 5.4.98

- **Shares held on 6 April 1985 and acquired on or after 6 April 1982.**
- **Shares acquired on or after 6 April 1985.**

The FA 1985 pool closes on 6 April 1998. This is the date from which taper relief starts.

In making computations which use the FA 1985 pool, we must keep track of:

(a)   the **number** of shares;
(b)   the **cost** of the shares ignoring indexation;
(b)   the **indexed cost** of the shares.

Each FA 1985 **pool is started by aggregating the cost and number of shares acquired between 6 April 1982 and 6 April 1985** inclusive. In order to calculate the indexed cost of these shares, an indexation allowance, computed from the relevant date of acquisition of the shares to April 1985, is added to the cost.

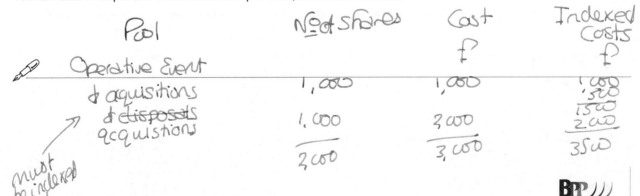

[handwritten table:]

Pool	No of shares	Cost £	Indexed Costs £
Operative Event			
+ acquisitions	1,000	1,000	1,000
			500
+ disposals acquisition	1,000	3,000	1500 2,000
	2,000	3,000	3500

must be indexed first

Example: the FA 1985 pool

Oliver bought 1,000 shares in Judith plc for £2,750 in August 1984 and another 1,000 for £3,250 in December 1984. The FA 1985 pool at 6 April 1985 is as follows.

Assume indexation factors:

August 1984 to April 1985 = 0.054
December 1984 to April 1985 = 0.043

Solution

	No of shares	Cost £	Indexed cost £
August 1984 (a)	1,000	2,750	2,750
December 1984 (b)	1,000	3,250	3,250
	2,000	6,000	6,000
Indexation allowance			
0.054 × £2,750			149
0.043 × £3,250			140
Indexed cost of the pool at 6 April 1985			6,289

2.2 Operative events

Disposals and acquisitions of shares which affect the indexed value of the FA 1985 pool are termed **'operative events'**. **Prior to reflecting each such operative event within the FA 1985 share pool, a further indexation allowance (described as an indexed rise) must be computed up to the date of the operative event concerned from the date of the last such operative event** (or from April 1985 if the operative event in question is the first one).

Indexation calculations within the FA 1985 pool (after its April 1985 value has been calculated) **are not rounded to three decimal places**. This is because rounding errors would accumulate and have a serious effect after several operative events.

If there are several operative events before 6 April 1998 the indexation procedure described above will have to be performed several times over.

Activity 7.2   Always index Before new acquisition

Following on from the above example, assume that Oliver acquired 2,000 more shares on 10 July 1986 at a cost of £4,000. Recalculate the value of the FA 1985 pool on 10 July 1986 following the acquisition.

Assume indexation factor: April 1985 to July 1986 = 0.029

	No of shares	Cost	Indexed costs
April 85	2000	6,000	6289
Index	6289 × 0.029		182
10/7/86	2,000	6,000	6471
	2,000	4,000	4000
10/7/86	4,000	10,000	10,471

2.3 Disposals and the FA 1985 pool

In the case of a disposal, following the calculation of the indexed rise to the date of disposal, the cost and the indexed cost attributable to the shares disposed of are deducted from the amounts within the FA 1985 pool. The proportions of the cost and indexed cost to take out of the pool should be computed using the same A/(A + B) fraction that is used for any other part disposal. However, we are not usually given the value of the remaining shares (B in the fraction). We then just use numbers of shares.

2.4 Shares held at 5.4.98

For all FA 1985 pools held on 5 April 1998 **indexation allowance to April 1998 is calculated and then effectively the pool is closed.**

Activity 7.3

In activity 7.2 you should have calculated the value of the pool on 10 July 1986 as:

	No of shares	Cost £	Indexed cost £
10 July 1986	4,000	10,000	10,471

Handwritten annotations:
To work out gain –
Proceeds x 5,000
Costs
Indexation (8728 Jaw) 3728
8728

Continue this example and show the value of the FA 1985 pool when it closes on 6.4.98.

Handwritten: 10471 x 0.667 = 6984

Assume indexation factor: July 1986 to April 1998 = 0.667

Handwritten: 17455

When FA 1985 pool shares are sold after 6.4.98, the gain is calculated using the cost and indexed cost on 6 April 1998. Taper relief may then apply if appropriate. Now let us work through a complete example with a disposal of shares after 6.4.98.

Example: Post April 1998 disposals for individuals

Ron acquired the following shares in First plc:

Date of acquisition	No of shares	Cost
9.11.90	12,000	25,000
4.8.03	3,000	11,400
1.6.04	5,000	19,000

He disposed of all the shares on 30 July 2004 for £80,000. The shares are not business assets for the purposes of taper relief. Calculate the chargeable gain arising.

Assume indexation factor: November 1990 to April 1998 = 0.251

Solution

Matching of shares

    (a)   Post 5.4.98 acquisitions: 1.6.04

	£
Proceeds $\dfrac{5,000}{20,000} \times £80,000$	20,000
Less cost	(19,000)
Gain	1,000

Note: No taper relief against this gain as the period of ownership was one month only.

    (b)   Post 5.4.98 acquisitions: 4.8.03

	£
Proceeds $\dfrac{3,000}{20,000} \times £80,000$	12,000
Less cost	(11,400)
Gain	600

Note. No taper relief is due against this gain since the period of ownership was only 11 months.

    (c)   FA 1985 pool

	Number of shares	Cost £	Indexed cost £
11.90 Acquisition	12,000	25,000	25,000
Index to 4.98 $0.251 \times £25,000$			6,275
Pool closes at 5.4.98	12,000	25,000	31,275
7.04 sales	12,000	25,000	31,275

Gain

	£
Proceeds $\dfrac{12,000}{20,000} \times £80,000$	48,000
Less cost	(25,000)
	23,000
Less indexation from FA 1985 pool £(31,275 − 25,000)	(6,275)
Gain before taper relief	16,725

The period of ownership of this non-business asset is 7 years (6 years post 5.4.98 plus the additional year). The gain after taper relief is therefore £12,544 (£16,725 × 75%).

Total gains £(1,000 + 600 + 12,544)   £14,144

3 Bonus and rights issues

3.1 Bonus issues (scrip issues)

When a company issues bonus shares all that happens is that the size of the original holding is increased. Since bonus shares are issued at no cost there is no need to adjust the original cost. Instead the numbers purchased at particular times are increased by the bonus. The normal matching rules will then be applied.

Example: bonus issues

The following transactions in the ordinary shares of X plc would be matched as shown below

6.4.86	Purchase of 600 shares
6.4.90	Purchase of 600 shares
6.4.02	Purchase of 1,000 shares
6.10.04	Bonus issue of one for four
6.12.04	Sale of 1,500 shares

(a) **Post 6.4.98 acquisition**

		No of shares
6.4.02	Purchase	1,000
6.10.04	Bonus	250
		1,250
6.12.04	Sold	(1,250)

(b) **FA 1985 pool**

		No of shares
6.4.86	Purchase	600
6.4.90	Purchase	600
		1,200
6.10.04	Bonus	300
		1,500
6.12.04	Sold	(250)
Number of shares remaining in FA 1985 pool		1,250

Activity 7.4

On 1 May 2002 Bruce bought 10,000 shares for £42,000. On 1 December 2003 there was a bonus issue of one for five. On 1 August 2004 Bruce sold 4,000 shares for £15,000. Calculate any chargeable gain arising after taper relief. The shares are not a business asset for taper relief purposes.

3.2 Rights issues

The difference between a bonus issue and a rights issue is that in a rights issue the new shares are paid for and this results in an adjustment to the original cost. As with bonus issues, rights shares derived from shares in the 1985 pool go into that holding and those derived from post 5.4.98 holdings attach to those holdings. You should add the number and cost of each of right issue to each holding as appropriate.

The length of the period of ownership for taper relief purposes depends on the date of acquisition of the original holding **not** the date of acquisition of the rights shares.

For the purposes of calculating the indexation allowance, expenditure on a rights issue is taken as being incurred on the date of the issue and not on the date of acquisition of the original holding.

Activity 7.5

Simon had the following transactions in S plc.

1.10.95	Bought 10,000 shares for £15,000
11.9.01	Bought 2,000 shares for £5,000
1.2.02	Took up rights issue 1 for 2 at £2.75 per share ~~= 3000 @ 5,500~~
14.10.04	Sold 5,000 shares for £15,000

Compute the gain arising in October 2004, after taper relief (if applicable). The shares are not a business asset for taper relief purposes.

Assume indexation factor: October 1995 to April 1998 = 0.085

4 Gilts and qualifying corporate bonds

For CGT purposes, **gilts are British Government and Government guaranteed securities** as shown on Treasury list. Gilt strips (capital or interest entitlements sold separately) are also gilts. You may assume that the list of gilts includes all issues of Treasury Loan, Treasury Stock, Exchequer Loan, Exchequer Stock and War Loan.

Disposals of gilt edged securities (gilts) and qualifying corporate bonds by individuals are exempt from CGT.

Handwritten annotations:

Total Gain = 1498
1188
2686

Post '98 first

Sept '01 / Rights issue 1:2 @ 2.75

	No of Shares	Costs
	2000	5000
	1000	2750
	3000	7750

Proceeds = 3/5 x 15000 = 9,050
less cost 7750
1250
Taper relief 95% 1188
5 Sep 01 → 14.10.04

Proceeds = 3/5 x 15 = 6,000
Costs = 3833
Index = 170
Gain 1997
Taper Relief 75% = 1498

FA85 pool (Indexed)

	No of Shares	Costs	
1.10.95	10,000	15000	15000
Index 0.085 x 15k			1275
	10,000	15000	16275
Right Issue 1:2 @ 2.75	5000	13750	13750
	15000	28750	30025
Disposal	(2,000)	(3833)	(4003)
	13000	24917	26022

BPP PROFESSIONAL EDUCATION

Activity 7.6

Frances sold her ordinary shares in The Hastings Hardening Company plc on 17 May 2004 for £24,000. She had bought ordinary shares in the company on the following dates.

	No of shares	Cost £
19 September 1985	2,000	1,700
12 December 2001	2,000	5,500
17 January 2002	2,000	6,000

Task

Calculate, before the annual exemption, the capital gain for 2004/05. The shares are a non-business asset for taper relief purposes.

Assume indexation factor: September 1985 to April 1998 = 0.704

(handwritten working)

	No of shares	Cost	Indexed Cost
disposal	2,000	~~6,000~~ 1,700	~~1700~~ ~~2896~~
19th Sep 1985 1700×0.704			1197
			2897
April 1998	2,000	1,700	2897

Jan02
Proceeds 3/6 × 24000 = 8,000
Cost   (6,000)
Gain   2,000

Dec 01
Proceeds 2/6 × 24000 = 8,000
Cost   5,500
                         2,500

19th Jan / Sep 85
Proceeds 2/6 × 24000 = ~~8000~~ 8000
Cost   (1700)
Indexation (2897−1700) (1197)
                         5103
Taper Relief (6yrs+1) 75% 3827

Total Gain   2,000
              2,500
              3827
              8327

Key learning points

☑   We need **special rules for matching** shares sold with shares purchased.

☑   Shares acquired **after 5 April 1998** are matched on a **last in first out** (LIFO) basis

☑   The **FA 1985 pool** contains shares acquired between **6.4.82** and **5.4.98.** The FA 1985 pool will need to be indexed to 6.4.98.

☑   **Bonus and rights issues** are attached to the **holding to which they relate**. The length of the period of ownership for taper relief purposes depends on the date of acquisition of the original holding.

☑   **Gilts** and **QCBs** held by individuals are **exempt** from CGT.

Quick quiz

1   Disposals of shares by individuals are identified with acquisitions in the following order:

.... acquisitions

Next .... days acquisitions

Acquisitions after .... on a .... basis

Shares in the .... pool

2   Julie bought 1,000 shares on 1 July 2004, 1,000 shares on 1 July 2003, 1,000 shares on 1 July 2002 and 1,000 shares on 1 July 1997. She sold 2,500 shares on 15 June 2004.

What shares does Julie hold after the sale

A   1,000 shares bought 1.7.04, 500 shares bought 1.7.97
B   500 shares bought 1.7.03, 1,000 shares bought 1.7.97
C   500 shares bought 1.7.02, 1,000 shares bought 1.7.97
D   1,000 shares bought 1.7.04, 500 shares bought 1.7.03

3   How is taper relief calculated in relation to a rights issue?

4   Chargeable gains arising on disposals of gilt edged securities are exempt from CGT. TRUE/FALSE?

Answers to quick quiz

1   **Same day** acquisitions
Next 30 days acquisitions
Acquisitions after **5.4.98** on a **LIFO** basis
Shares in the **FA 1985** pool

2   C   The shares are matched in the following order:

Next 30 days (1.7.04) 1,000 shares
Post 5.4.98 (LIFO) (1.7.03) 1,000 shares
Post 5.4.98 (LIFO) (1.7.02) 500 shares

Therefore she is left with:

Post 5.4.88 (LIFO) (1.7.02) 500 shares
FA 1985 pool (1.7.97) 1,000 shares

3   Taper relief applies by reference to the original holding, not from the rights issue.

4   TRUE

Activity checklist

This checklist shows which performance criteria, range statement or knowledge and understanding point is covered by each activity in this chapter. Tick off each activity as you complete it.

Activity

7.1		This activity deals with Performance Criteria 19.4B: identify shares disposed of by individuals.
7.2		This activity deals with Knowledge and Understanding point 12: identification of non-business assets disposed of including part disposals and personal shareholdings.
7.3		This activity deals with Knowledge and Understanding point 12: identification of non-business assets disposed of including part disposals and personal shareholdings.
7.4		This activity deals with Performance Criteria 19.4B: identify shares disposed of by individuals.
7.5		This activity deals with Performance Criteria 19.4B: identify shares disposed of by individuals.
7.6		This activity deals with Performance Criteria 19.4B: identify shares disposed of by individuals.

chapter 8

CGT – additional aspects

Contents

Performance criteria

19.4 C   Calculate chargeable gains and allowable losses

19.4 D   Apply reliefs and exemptions correctly

Range statement

19.4   Chargeable personal assets that have been: sold, gifted, lost, destroyed

Knowledge and understanding

2   The issues of taxation liability (Elements 19.1, 19.2, 19.3, 19.4)

3   Relevant legislation and guidance from the Revenue (Elements 19.1, 19.2, 19.3, 19.4)

4   Basic law and practice (Elements 19.1, 19.2, 19.3, 19.4)

13   Calculation of gains and losses on disposals of non-business assets including indexation allowance (Element 19.4)

1 Chattels

1.1 Gains on chattels

A **chattel** is tangible movable property.

Any gain arising on the disposal of a chattel will be exempt from CGT if the asset is sold for gross proceeds of £6,000 or less.

If sale proceeds exceed £6,000, any gain is limited to a maximum of 5/3 × (gross proceeds − £6,000).

Example

Jo sold an antique desk in 2004 for £8,000. The desk had been acquired in 2001 for £4,500. Calculate the chargeable gain arising.

Solution

Your first step should be to calculate the gain in the normal way:

	£
Disposal proceeds	8,000
Less: cost	(4,500)
Gain	3,500

Secondly calculate the gain using the formula.

5/3 (8,000 − 6,000) = £3,333

The **gain before taper relief** is therefore limited to **£3,333**

Activity 8.1

Adam purchased a Chippendale chair on 1 June 2001 for £1,458. On 10 October 2004 he sold the chair at auction for £6,300 (which was net of the auctioneer's 10% commission). What was the chargeable gain?

1.2 Losses

Where a chattel is sold for less than £6,000 and a loss arises, the allowable loss is restricted by assuming that the chattel was sold for £6,000. However, this rule cannot turn a loss into a gain, only reduce the loss, perhaps to zero.

Activity 8.2

Eve purchased a rare first edition on 1 July 1999 for £8,000 which she sold in October 2004 at auction for £2,700 (which was net of 10% commission). Compute the allowable loss.

Activity 8.3

In 2004/05, Mr California sold the following chattels.

Chattel	Date of purchase	Cost £	Date of sale	Proceeds £
Vase	1.4.03	800	2.11.04	7,000
Sideboard	1.5.00	7,000	1.12.04	5,000

All proceeds are shown before selling expenses of 5% of the gross proceeds.

Task

Compute the chargeable gain or allowable loss on each chattel before taper relief.

2 Private residences

2.1 Exemption for private residences

A gain arising on the sale of an individual's only or main private residence (his principal private residence or PPR) is exempt from CGT.

The exemption also normally covers grounds of up to half a hectare. The grounds can exceed half a hectare if the house is large enough to warrant it, but if not, only the gain on the excess grounds is taxable. If the grounds do not adjoin the house (for example when a road separates the two), they *may* still qualify but they may not: each case must be argued on its merits. However, if the grounds are to qualify they must not be sold later than the house.

Buildings within the grounds of a main dwelling house may form part of the taxpayer's principal private residence and therefore be exempt. Each case must be argued on its merits.

The gain is wholly exempt where the owner has occupied the whole of the residence throughout his period of ownership. Conversely, any loss arising will not be an allowable loss.

Activity 8.4

Zoë purchased a house on 1 April 2000 for £100,000. She lived in the house until she sold it in December 2004 for £250,000. What gain arises? What if she sold the house for £80,000?

2.2 Periods of non occupation

Where occupation has been for only part of the period, the proportion of the gain exempted is

$$\text{Total gain} \times \frac{\text{Period of occupation}}{\text{Total period of ownership}}$$

A further proportionate restriction is made where only part of the property has been occupied as the owner's residence.

The **last 36 months of ownership are always** treated as **a period of occupation**, if at some time the residence has been the taxpayer's main residence, even if within those last 36 months the taxpayer also has another house which is his principal private residence.

Where a loss arises but all or a proportion of any gain would have been exempt, all or the same proportion of the loss is not allowable.

Activity 8.5

Nitin bought a house on 1 June 1998 for £150,000 and lived in it until 31 May 2000. On 1 June 2000 Nitin moved into another house he had purchased. He never moved back to the first house which he sold on 31 May 2004 for £450,000. What chargeable gain, if any, arises on the disposal of the first house?

2.3 Periods of deemed occupation

The period of occupation is also deemed to include certain periods of absence, provided the individual had no other exempt residence at the time and the period of absence was at some time both preceded by and followed by a period of actual occupation. Deemed but non-actual occupation during the last 36 months of ownership does not count for this purpose.

These periods of deemed occupation are:

(a)   Any period (or periods taken together) of absence, for any reason, up to three years, and

(b)   Any periods during which the owner was required by his employment (ie employed taxpayer) to live abroad, and

(c)   Any period (or periods taken together) up to four years during which the owner was required to live elsewhere due to his work (ie both employed and self employed taxpayer) so that he could not occupy his private residence.

It does not matter if the residence is let during the absence.

Exempt periods of absence must normally be preceded and followed by periods of actual occupation. An extra-statutory concession relaxes this where an individual who has been required to work abroad or elsewhere (ie the latter two categories mentioned above) is unable to resume residence in his home because the terms of his employment require him to work elsewhere.

Activity 8.6

Mr A purchased a house on 31 March 1982 for £50,000. He lived in the house until 30 June 1982. He then worked abroad for two years before returning to the UK to live in the house again on 1 July 1984. He stayed in the house until 31 December 1997 before retiring and moving out to live with friends in Spain until the house was sold on 28 December 2004 for £150,000.

Assume indexation factor: March 1982 to April 1998 = 1.047

Tasks

(a)   Prepare a schedule showing the chargeable periods and the exempt periods in respect of Mr A's ownership fo the house.

(b)   Calculate any chargeable gain arising.

1.3 More than one residence

1.3.1 The election for a residence to be treated as the main residence

Where a person has more than one residence (owned or rented), he may elect for one to be regarded as his main residence within two years of commencing occupation of the second residence. An election can have effect for any period beginning not more than two years prior to the date of election until it is varied by giving further notice. (The further notice may itself be backdated by up to two years.)

In order for the election to be made, the individual must actually reside in both residences.

Any period of ownership of a residence not nominated as the main residence will be a chargeable period for that residence.

Where there are two residences and the second one is being treated as a residence under the 'delay in moving in' rule (see above), the election is not needed and both may count as principal private residences simultaneously.

1.3.2 Job-related accommodation

The rule limiting people to only one main residence is relaxed for individuals living in job-related accommodation.

Such individuals will be treated as occupying any second dwelling house which they own if they intend in due course to occupy the dwelling house as their only or main residence. Thus it is not necessary to establish any actual residence in such cases. This rule extends to self-employed persons required to live in job-related accommodation (for example tenants of public houses).

A person lives in **job-related accommodation** where:

- it is necessary for the proper performance of his duties; or

- it is provided for the better performance of his duties and his is one of the kinds of employment in which it is customary for employers to provide accommodation; or

- there is a special threat to the employee's security and use of the accommodation is part of security arrangements.

1.4 Lettings

The principal private residence exemption is extended to any gain accruing while the property is let, up to a certain limit. The two main circumstances in which the letting exemption applies are:

- when the owner is absent and lets the property;
- when the owner lets part of the property while still occupying the rest of it.

In both cases the letting must be for residential use. **The extra exemption is restricted to the lowest of:**

(a)   the gain accruing during the letting period (the **letting part of the gain**);

(b)   **£40,000**;

(c)   the amount of the total **gain** which is already **exempt under the PPR provisions.**

The letting exemption cannot convert a gain into an allowable loss.

Where a lodger lives as a member of the owner's family, sharing their living accommodation and eating with them, the whole property is regarded as remaining the owner's main residence.

Activity 8.7

On 30 September 2004 Dr Prance sold his house. He had bought it on 31 March 2000 for £120,000. The proceeds were £300,000 before estate agent's fees of £5,000 and legal fees of £1,200. Dr Prance lived in the property until 1 October 2000, when he moved into a flat he had purchased nearby. Whilst he was living in it the flat became Dr Prance's principal private residence. He sold the flat and moved back into the house on 1 October 2001 and lived there until it was sold. He let the house from 1 October 2000 to 30 September 2001.

Tasks

(a)   Prepare a schedule which shows the number of chargeable and the number of exempt months arising during Mr Prance's ownership of the house.

(b)   Calculate any chargeable gain before taper relief arising on the disposal of the house.

Activity 8.8

Miss Coe purchased a house on 31 March 1992 for £90,000. She sold it on 31 August 2004 for £340,000. In 1994 the house was redecorated and Miss Coe began to live on the top floor renting out the balance of the house (constituting 60% of the total house) to tenants between 1 January 1995 and 31 December 2002. On 2 January 2003 Miss Coe put the whole house on the market but continued to live only on the top floor until the house was sold. What was the chargeable gain?

Assume indexation factor: March 1992 to April 1998 = 0.189

Key learning points

☑   If a **chattel** is sold for **up to £6,000**, there is **no chargeable gain.**

☑   If a **chattel** is **sold for up to £6,000,** any **loss is restricted** by assuming that the **chattel was sold for £6,000**.

☑   If a **chattel is sold for more than £6,000,** any **gain** (before taper relief) **is limited** to a **maximum of 5/3 (gross proceeds – £6,000).**

☑   There is an **exemption** for **private residences**. The exemption is **reduced** by periods of **non-occupation.**

☑   Certain periods of non-occupation are treated as periods of **deemed occupation** for the private residence exemption purposes. The **last 36 months** are always treated as a period of occupation.

☑   A **letting exemption** may be available for **up to £40,000 of gain.**

Quick quiz

1   Karen buys an antique vase for £3,000 in July 2003. She sold it for £8,000 in August 2004.

What is her gain on sale?

A   nil
B   £3,000
C   £3,333
D   £5,000

2   Matthew buys a painting for £7,000 in April 2003. He sold it for £4,000 in October 2004.

What is his allowable loss on sale?

A   nil
B   £(1,000)
C   £(1,667)
D   £(3,000)

3   The last .... months of ownership of a principal private residence are always deemed to be a period of occupation. Fill in the blank.

4   Iris sells her house after owning it for exactly 8 years. Her gain on sale is £160,000. She lived in the house for the first 4 years of ownership, and then let it for 1 year. It was then empty for three years until sale. What is her letting exemption?

Answers to quick quiz

1   C
	£
Proceeds	8,000
Less: cost	(3,000)
Gain	5,000

Gain restricted to 5/3 x £(8,000 – 6,000) = £3,333.

2   B
	£
Proceeds (deemed)	6,000
Less: cost	(7,000)
Loss	(1,000)

3   The last **36** months of ownership of a principal private residence are always deemed to be a period of occupation.

4   The PPR exemption is 7/8 x £160,000 = £140,000
(**Note.** The last 36 months count is a period of deemed occupation)
The remaining gain is 1/8 x £160,000 = £20,000.
The maximum letting exemption is £40,000.
The letting exemption is the lowest of these ie £20,000.

Activity checklist

This checklist shows which performance criteria, range statement or knowledge and understanding point is covered by each activity in this chapter. Tick off each activity as you complete it.

Activity

8.1 ☐ This activity deals with Performance Criteria 19.4D: apply reliefs and exemptions correctly.

8.2 ☐ This activity deals with Performance Criteria 19.4C: calculate chargeable gains and allowable losses.

8.3 ☐ This activity deals with Performance Criteria 19.4C and 19.4D: calculate chargeable gains and allowable losses; apply reliefs and exemptions correctly.

8.4 ☐ This activity deals with Performance Criteria 19.4D: apply reliefs and exemptions correctly.

8.5 ☐ This activity deals with Performance Criteria 19.4C: calculate chargeable gains and allowable losses.

8.6 ☐ This activity deals with Performance Criteria 19.4C: calculate chargeable gains and allowable losses.

8.7 ☐ This activity deals with Performance Criteria 19.4D: apply reliefs and exemptions correctly.

8.8 ☐ This activity deals with Performance Criteria 19.4D: apply reliefs and exemptions correctly.

P A R T   C

Administration

chapter 9

Administration

Contents

Performance criteria

19.1 C   Record relevant details of income from employment accurately and legibly in the tax return

19.2 E   Record relevant details of property and investment income accurately and legibly in the tax return

19.3 D   Record income and payments accurately and legibly in the tax return

19.4 F   Record relevant details of gains and the Capital Gains Tax payable legibly and accurately in the tax return

19.1D, 19.2F, 19.3E, 19.4G

Make computations and submissions in accordance with current tax law and take account of Revenue practice.

19.1E, 19.2G, 19.3F, 19.4H

Consult with Revenue staff in an open and constructive manner.

19.1F, 19.2H, 19.3G, 19.4I

Give timely and constructive advice on the recording of information relevant to tax returns

19.1G, 19.2I. 19.3H, 19.4J

Maintain client confidentiality at all times

Range statement

There are no additional contextual requirements in this element, relevant to this chapter.

Knowledge and understanding

1   The duties and responsibilities of the tax practitioner (Elements 19.1, 19.2, 19.3, 19.4)
2   The issues of taxation liability (Elements 19.1, 19.2, 19.3, 19.4)
3   Relevant legislation and guidance from the Revenue (Elements 19.1, 19.2, 19.3, 19.4)
4   Basic law and practice (Elements 19.1, 19.2, 19.3, 19.4)
16   Self assessment including payment of tax and filing of returns by individuals (Elements 19.1, 19.2, 19.3, 19.4)

1 The administration of taxation

The **Treasury** formally imposes and collects taxation. The management of the Treasury is the responsibility of the Chancellor of the Exchequer. The Treasury appoint the **Board of Inland Revenue** (sometimes referred to as the **Commissioners of Inland Revenue (CIR))**, a body of civil servants. The Board administers income tax and capital gains tax.

For income tax purposes, the UK has historically been divided into **tax districts**. These are being merged into larger areas, with separate offices in each **area** being responsible for different aspects of the Revenue's work. Each area is headed by an **area director**.

The Revenue staff were historically described as '**Inspectors**' and '**Collectors**', although these terms are now less commonly used. The legislation now commonly refers to an '**officer of the board**' rather than an 'inspector' when setting out the Revenue's powers. They are responsible for supervising the self-assessment system and agreeing tax liabilities. Collectors may be referred to a **receivables management officers**, and are local officers who are responsible for following up amounts of unpaid tax referred to then by the **Revenue Accounts Office**.

The structure of Revenue offices is also being changed. **Taxpayer service offices** are being set up to do routine checking, computation *and* collection work, while **Taxpayer district offices** investigate selected accounts and enforce the payment of tax. **Taxpayer assistance offices** handle enquiries and arrange specialist help for taxpayers.

The **General Commissioners** (not to be confused with the CIR) are appointed by the Lord Chancellor to hear **appeals** against Revenue decisions. They are part-time and unpaid. They are appointed for a local area (a **division**). They appoint a clerk who is often a lawyer or accountant and who is paid for his services by the Board of Revenue.

The **Special Commissioners** are also appointed by the Lord Chancellor. They are full-time paid professionals. They generally hear the more complex appeals.

Many taxpayers arrange for their accountants to prepare and submit their tax returns. The taxpayer is still the person responsible for submitting the return and for paying whatever tax becomes due: the accountant is only acting as the taxpayer's agent.

2 Notification of chargeability

Individuals who are chargeable to tax for any tax year and who have not received a notice to file a return are, in general, required to give notice of chargeability to an officer of the Board within six months from the end of the year ie by 5 October 2005 for 2004/05.

The maximum mitigable penalty where notice of chargeability is not given is 100% of the tax assessed which is not paid on or before 31 January following the tax year.

3 Tax returns and keeping records

3.1 Tax returns

An individual's tax return comprises a Tax Form, together with supplementary pages for particular sources of income.

3.2 Time limit for submission of tax returns

The **filing due date for filing a tax return is the later of:**

- 31 January following the end of the tax year which the return covers.
- three months after the notice to file the return was issued.

If an individual wishes the Revenue to prepare the self-assessment on their behalf, earlier deadlines apply. The filing date is then the later of:

- 30 September following the tax year; eg for 2004/05, by 30 September 2005.
- two months after notice to file the return was issued.

3.3 Penalties for late filing

3.3.1 Individual returns

The maximum penalties for delivering a tax return after the filing due date are:

(a)	**Return up to 6 months late:**	**£100**
(b)	**Return more than 6 months but not more than 12 months late:**	**£200**
(c)	**Return more than 12 months late:**	**£200 + 100% of the tax liability**

In addition, the General or Special Commissioners can direct that a maximum penalty of £60 per day be imposed where failure to deliver a tax return continues after notice of the direction has been given to the taxpayer. In this case the additional £100 penalty, imposed under (b) if the return is more than six months late, is not charged.

The fixed penalties of £100/£200 can be set aside by the Commissioners if they are satisfied that the taxpayer had a reasonable excuse for not delivering the return. If the tax liability shown on the return is less than the fixed penalties, the fixed penalty is reduced to the amount of the tax liability. The tax geared penalty is mitigable by the Revenue or the Commissioners.

Activity 9.1

Adrian was sent his 2003/04 tax return on 6 April 2004. He filed it on 1 March 2006. His tax liability was £4,000. What is the maximum penalty that can be imposed?

200 +
4000

4200

3.3.2 Reasonable excuse

A taxpayer only has a reasonable excuse for a late filing if a default occurred because of a factor outside his control. This might be non-receipt of the return by the taxpayer, serious illness of the taxpayer or a close relative, or destruction of records through fire and flood. Illness is only accepted as a reasonable excuse if the taxpayer was taking timeous steps to complete the return, and if the return is filed as soon as possible after the illness etc.

3.3.3 Returns rejected as incomplete

If a return, filed before the filing date, is rejected by the Revenue as incomplete later than 14 days before the filing deadline of 31 January, a late filing penalty will not be charged if the return is completed and returned within 14 days of the rejection. This only applies if the omission from the return was a genuine error. It does not apply if a return was deliberately filed as incomplete in the hope of extending the time limit.

3.4 Standard accounting information

'Three line' accounts (ie income less expenses equals profit) only need be included on the tax return of businesses with a turnover (or gross rents from property) of less than £15,000 pa. This is not as helpful as it might appear, as underlying records must still be kept for tax purposes (disallowable items etc) when producing three line accounts.

Large businesses with a turnover of at least £5 million which have used figures rounded to the nearest £1,000 in producing their published accounts can compute their profits to the nearest £1,000 for tax purposes.

The tax return requires trading results to be presented in a standard format. Although there is no requirement to submit accounts with the return, accounts may be filed. If accounts accompany the return, the Revenue's power to raise a discovery assessment (see below) is restricted.

3.5 Keeping of records

All taxpayers must keep and retain all records required to enable them to make and deliver a correct tax return.

Records must be retained until the later of:

   (a)   (i)   **5 years after the 31 January following the tax year where the taxpayer is in business** (as a sole trader or partner or letting property)

         (ii)   **1 year after the 31 January following the tax year otherwise**

(b)   provided notice to deliver a return is given before the date in (a):

    (i)   **the time after which enquiries by the Revenue into the return can no longer be commenced**

    (ii)   **the date any such enquiries have been completed**

Where a person receives a notice to deliver a tax return after the normal record keeping period has expired, he must keep all records in his possession at that time until no enquiries can be raised in respect of the return or until such enquiries have been completed.

The maximum (mitigable) penalty for each failure to keep and retain records is £3,000 per tax year/accounting period.

Record keeping failures are taken into account in considering the mitigation of other penalties. Where the record keeping failure is taken into account in this way, a penalty will normally only be sought in serious and exceptional cases where, for example, records have been destroyed deliberately to obstruct an enquiry or there has been a history of serious record keeping failures.

4 Self-assessment and claims

4.1 Self-assessment

Every personal tax return must be accompanied by a self-assessment.

A self assessment is a calculation of the amount of taxable income and gains after deducting reliefs and allowances, and a calculation of the income tax and CGT payable after taking into account tax deducted at source and tax credits.

The self-assessment calculation may either be made by the taxpayer or the Revenue. If a return is filed within certain time limits (normally, 30 September following the tax year to which it relates, see above) an officer of the board must make a self-assessment on the taxpayer's behalf on the basis of the information contained in the return. He must send a copy of the assessment to the taxpayer. These assessments, even though raised by the Revenue, are treated as self-assessments.

If the taxpayer files a return after the above deadline but without completing the self-assessment, the Revenue will not normally reject the return as incomplete. However the Revenue are not then bound to complete the self-assessment in time to notify the taxpayer of the tax falling due on the normal due date (generally the following 31 January), and it is the taxpayer's responsibility to estimate and pay his tax on time.

Within nine months of receiving a tax return, the Revenue can amend a taxpayer's self-assessment to correct any obvious errors or mistakes; whether errors of principle, arithmetical mistakes or otherwise. The taxpayer does have the right to reject any corrections of obvious errors made by the Revenue.

Within 12 months of the due filing date (*not* the actual filing date), the taxpayer can give notice to an officer to amend his tax return and self-assessment. Such amendments by taxpayers are not confined to the correction of obvious errors. They may not be made whilst the Revenue are making enquiries into the return.

The same rules apply to corrections and amendments of partnership statements and stand alone claims (see below).

4.2 Claims

4.2.1 General rules

All claims and elections which can be made in a tax return must be made in this manner if a return has been issued. A claim for any relief, allowance or repayment of tax must normally be quantified at the time it is made.

Certain claims have a time limit that is longer than the time limit for filing or amending a tax return. A claim may therefore be made after the time limit for amending the tax return has expired. Claims not made on the tax return are referred to as **'stand alone' claims**.

4.2.2 Claims involving more than one year

Self-assessment is intended to avoid the need to reopen earlier years, so relief should be given for the year of the claim. This rule can best be explained by considering a claim to carry back a trading loss to an earlier year of assessment:

    (a)   the claim for relief is treated as made in relation to the year in which the loss was actually incurred;

    (b)   the amount of any tax repayment due is calculated in terms of tax of the earlier year to which the loss is being carried back; and

    (c)   any tax repayment etc is treated as relating to the later year in which the loss was actually incurred.

4.2.3 Error or mistake claims

An error or mistake claim may be made for errors in a return or partnership statement where tax would otherwise be overcharged. The claim may not be made where the tax liability was computed in accordance with practice prevailing at the time the return or statement was made.

An error or mistake claim may not be made in respect of a claim. If a taxpayer makes an error or mistake in a claim, he may make a supplementary claim within the time limits allowed for the original claim.

The taxpayer may appeal to the Special Commissioners against any refusal of an error or mistake claim.

5 Payment of tax, interest and penalties

5.1 Payments of tax

The self-assessment system may result in the taxpayer making three payments of income tax:

Date	Payment
31 January in the tax year	**1st payment on account**
31 July after the tax year	**2nd payment on account**
31 January after the tax year	**Final payment to settle the remaining liability**

Payments on account are usually required where the income tax due in the previous year exceeded the amount of income tax deducted at source; this excess is known as **'the relevant amount'**. Income tax deducted at source includes tax suffered, PAYE deductions and tax credits on dividends.

The payments on account are each equal to 50% of the relevant amount for the previous year.

[handwritten margin note:]
9200 –
(1700)
(1500)
8000/2
= 3000
each installment

Activity 9.2

Gordon paid tax for 2004/05 as follows:

	£
Total amount of income tax assessed	9,200
This included: Tax deducted under PAYE	1,700
Tax deducted on savings income	1,500
He also paid: Capital gains tax	4,800

How much are the payments on account for 2005/06?

Payments on account are not required if the relevant amount falls below a de minimis limit of £500. Also, payments on account are not required from taxpayers who paid 80% or more of their tax liability for the previous year through PAYE or other deduction at source arrangements.

If the previous year's liability increases following an amendment to a self-assessment, or the raising of a discovery assessment, an adjustment is made to the payments on account due.

Payments on account are normally fixed by reference to the previous year's tax liability but if a taxpayer expects his liability to be lower than this **he may claim to reduce his payments on account to:**

    (a)   a **stated amount**, or

    (b)   **nil**.

The claim must state the reason why he believes his tax liability will be lower, or nil.

If the taxpayer's eventual liability is higher than he estimated he will have reduced the payments on account too far. Although the payments on account will not be adjusted, the taxpayer will suffer an interest charge on late payment.

A penalty of the difference between the reduced payment on account and the correct payment on account may be levied if the reduction was claimed fraudulently or negligently.

The balance of any income tax together with all CGT due for a year, is normally payable on or before the 31 January following the year.

Activity 9.3

Giles made payments on account for 2004/05 of £6,500 each on 31 January 2005 and 31 July 2005, based on his 2003/04 liability. He then calculates his total income tax for 2004/05 at £18,000 of which £2,750 was deducted at source. In addition he calculated that his CGT liability for disposals in 2004/05 is £5,120.

What is the final payment due for 2004/05?

In one case the due date for the final payment is later than 31 January following the end of the year. **If a taxpayer has notified chargeability by 5 October but the notice to file a tax return is not issued before 31 October, then the due date for the payment is three months after the issue of the notice.**

Tax charged in an amended self-assessment is usually payable on the later of:

(a)   the normal due date, generally 31 January following the end of the tax year; and

(b)   the day following 30 days after the making of the revised self-assessment.

Tax charged on a discovery assessment is due thirty days after the issue of the assessment.

5.2 Surcharges

Surcharges are normally imposed in respect of amounts paid late:

Paid		*Surcharge*
(a)	within 28 days of due date:	none
(b)	more than 28 days but not more than six months after the due date:	5%
(c)	more than six months after the due date:	10%

Surcharges apply to:

(a)   balancing payments of income tax and any CGT under self-assessment or a determination

(b)   tax due on the amendment of a self-assessment

(c)   tax due on a discovery assessment

The surcharge rules do not apply to late payments on account.

No surcharge will be applied where the late paid tax liability has attracted a tax-geared penalty on the failure to notify chargeability to tax, or the failure to submit a return, or on the making of an incorrect return (including a partnership return).

5.3 Interest

Interest is chargeable on late payment of both payments on account and balancing payments. In both cases interest runs from the due date until the day before the actual date of payment.

Interest is charged from 31 January following the tax year (or the normal due date for the balancing payment, in the rare event that this is later), even if this is before the due date for payment on:

(a)   tax payable following an amendment to a self-assessment;

(b)   tax payable in a discovery assessment; and

(c)   tax postponed under an appeal which becomes payable.

Since a determination (see below) is treated as if it were a self-assessment, interest runs from 31 January following the tax year.

If a taxpayer claims to reduce his payments on account and there is still a final payment to be made, interest is normally charged on the payments on account as if each of those payments had been the lower of:

(a)   the reduced amount, plus 50% of the final income tax liability; and

(b)   the amount which would have been payable had no claim for reduction been made.

Activity 9.4

Herbert's payments on account for 2004/05 based on his income tax liability for 2003/04 were £4,500 each. However, when he submitted his 2003/04 income tax return in January 2005, he made a claim to reduce the payments on account for 2004/05 to £3,500 each. The first payment on account was made on 29 January 2005, and the second on 12 August 2005.

Herbert filed his 2004/05 tax return in December 2005. The return showed that his tax liabilities for 2004/05 (before deducting payments on account) were income tax: £10,000, capital gains tax: £2,500. Herbert paid the balance of tax due of £5,500 on 19 February 2006.

For what periods and in respect of what amounts will Herbert be charged interest?

Where interest has been charged on late payments on account but the final balancing settlement for the year produces a repayment, all or part of the original interest is remitted.

5.4 Repayment of tax and repayment supplement

Tax is repaid when claimed unless a greater payment of tax is due in the following 30 days, in which case it is set-off against that payment.

Interest is paid on overpayments of:

(a)   payments on account

(b)   final payments of income tax and CGT, including tax deducted at source or tax credits on dividends

(c)   penalties and surcharges

Repayment supplement runs from the original date of payment (even if this was prior to the due date), until the day before the date the repayment is made. Income tax deducted at source and tax credits are treated as if they were paid on the 31 January following the tax year concerned.

6 Enquiries, determinations and discovery assessments

6.1 Enquiries into returns

An officer of the Board has a limited period within which to commence enquiries into a return or amendment. The officer must give written notice of his intention by:

(a) the **first anniversary of the due filing date (not the actual filing date)**; or

(b) **if the return is filed after the due filing date, the quarter day following the first anniversary of the actual filing date. The quarter days are 31 January, 30 April, 31 July and 31 October**.

If the taxpayer amended the return after the due filing date, the enquiry 'window' extends to the quarter day following the first anniversary of the date the amendment was filed. Where the enquiry was not raised within the limit which would have applied had no amendment been filed, the enquiry is restricted to matters contained in the amendment.

Enquiries may be made into partnership returns (or amendments) upon which a partnership statement is based within the same time limits. A notice to enquire into a partnership return is deemed to incorporate a notice, to enquire into each individual partner's return.

Enquiries may also be made into stand alone claims, provided notice is given by the officer of the Board by the later of:

(a) The quarter day following the first anniversary of the making or amending of the claim

(b) 31 January next but one following the tax year, if the claim relates to a tax year

(c) the first anniversary of the end of the period to which a claim relates if it relates to a period other than a tax year

The procedures for enquiries into claims mirror those for enquiries into returns.

The officer does not have to have, or give, any reason for raising an enquiry. In particular the taxpayer will not be advised whether he has been selected at random for an audit. Enquiries may be full enquiries, or may be limited to 'aspect' enquiries.

In the course of his enquiries **the officer may require the taxpayer to produce documents, accounts or any other information required. The taxpayer can appeal to the Commissioners.**

During the course of his enquiries an officer may amend a self-assessment if it appears that insufficient tax has been charged and an immediate amendment is necessary to prevent a loss to the Crown. This might apply if, for example, there is a possibility that the taxpayer will emigrate.

If a return is under enquiry the Revenue may postpone any repayment due as shown in the return until the enquiry is complete. The Revenue have discretion to make a provisional repayment but there is no facility to appeal if the repayment is withheld.

At any time during the course of an enquiry, the taxpayer may apply to the Commissioners to require the officer to notify the taxpayer within a specified period that the enquiries are complete, unless the officer can demonstrate that he has reasonable grounds for continuing the enquiry.

If both sides agree, disputes concerning a point of law can be resolved through litigation without having to wait until the whole enquiry is complete.

An officer must issue a notice that the enquiries are complete, and a statement of the amount of tax that he considers should be included in the tax return, or the amounts which should be contained in the partnership statement, or the amount of the claim. The taxpayer then has thirty days to amend his self-assessment, partnership statement or claim to give effect to the officer's conclusions. He may also make any other amendments that he could have made had the enquiry not been commenced (amendments may not be made whilst enquiries are in progress).

If the officer is not satisfied with the taxpayer's amendment he has thirty days in which to amend the self-assessment, partnership statement or claim. Also if a claim has been disallowed, but does not affect the self-assessment, he must advise the taxpayer of the extent to which it has been disallowed.

If the taxpayer is not satisfied with the officer's amendment he may, within 30 days, appeal to the Commissioners.

Once an enquiry is complete the officer cannot make further enquiries. The Revenue may, in limited circumstances, raise a discovery assessment if they believe that there has been a loss of tax (see below).

The majority of investigation cases are handled by local inspectors, but serious cases are dealt with by the Special Compliance Office.

Where an irregularity is detected, unless it appears to be of a very serious nature, the first overture will often be made by the local inspector writing to the taxpayer or his agent suggesting that he has reason to doubt that full and correct returns have been made and inviting the taxpayer's comments. Correspondence will be followed by interviews at which the inspector will try to collect further evidence, and the taxpayer's accountant may be asked to prepare a detailed report showing the estimated tax unpaid.

The Revenue use various methods to attempt to calculate undisclosed income. Gross profit margins either for previous periods or for similar businesses are standardly used. As a last resort, some indication can be derived from the taxpayer's personal assets. A growth in these, taken together with an assumed level of personal expenditure, can point to an unexplained source, presumably undisclosed income. A sensible taxpayer will co-operate with the Revenue as any resistance on his part at this stage will count heavily against him in the final assessment or penalties.

6.2 The Revenue's powers

The Revenue's powers include the following.

(a) **The power to call for documents of taxpayers and others**. The Revenue may require any person to produce any documents which may contain information relevant to any taxpayer's tax liability. The Revenue may also require the taxpayer to provide written answers about questions of fact. The Inspector must give the person holding the documents reasons for applying for the right to demand documents, unless the commissioner is satisfied that giving reasons would prejudice the assessment or collection of tax.

(b) **The power to call for papers of tax accountants**. The Revenue is not normally empowered to demand documents from the taxpayer's accountant. but if he has either:

(i) been convicted of an offence in relation to tax
(ii) been penalised for assisting in making an incorrect return

the Revenue can, in certain circumstances, demand documents relating to the taxpayer's affairs. A tax accountant is anyone (including a barrister or solicitor) who helps a taxpayer to prepare or deliver documents for tax purposes.

(c)   **The power of entry with a warrant to obtain documents**. Where there are reasonable grounds for suspecting that an offence involving fraud in connection with tax has been, is being or is about to be committed and that evidence is to be found on certain premises, a warrant can be obtained authorising an officer of the Board to search the premises and remove anything which he has reasonable cause to suppose may be required as evidence.

(d)   **The power to obtain information about interest and dividends**. The Revenue can require details from banks and building societies.

6.3 Determinations

The Revenue may only raise enquiries if a return has been submitted.

If notice has been served on a taxpayer to submit a return but the return is not submitted by the due filing date, an officer of the Board may make a determination of the tax due. Such a determination must be made to the best of the officer's information and belief, and is then treated as if it were a self-assessment. This enables the officer to seek payment of tax, including payments on account for the following year and to charge interest.

6.4 Discovery assessments

If an officer of the Board discovers that profits have been omitted from assessment, that any assessment has become insufficient, or that any relief given is, or has become excessive, an assessment may be raised to recover the tax lost.

If the tax lost results from an error in the taxpayer's return but the return was made in accordance with prevailing practice at the time, no discovery assessment may be made.

A discovery assessment may only be raised where a return has been made if:

(a)   there has been fraudulent or negligent conduct by the taxpayer or his agent

(b)   at the time that enquiries into the return were completed, or could no longer be made, the officer did not have information to make him aware of the loss of tax

These rules do not prevent the Revenue from raising assessments in cases of genuine discoveries, but prevent assessments from being raised due to the Revenue's failure to make timely use of information or to a change of opinion on information made available.

6.5 Appeals and postponement of payment of tax

A taxpayer may appeal against an amendment to a self-assessment or partnership statement, or an amendment to or disallowance of a claim, following an enquiry, or against an assessment which is not a self-assessment, such as a discovery assessment.

The appeal must normally be made within 30 days of the amendment or self-assessment.

The notice of appeal must state the **grounds** of appeal. These may be stated in general terms. At the hearing the Commissioners may allow the appellant to put forward grounds not stated in his notice if they are satisfied that his omission was not wilful or unreasonable.

In some cases it may be possible to agree the point at issue by negotiation with the Revenue, in which case the appeal may be settled by agreement. If the appeal cannot be agreed, it will be heard by the General or Special Commissioners.

An appeal does not relieve the taxpayer of liability to pay tax on the normal due date unless he obtains a 'determination' of the Commissioners or agreement of the Inspector that payment of all or some of the tax may be postponed pending determination of the appeal. The amount not postponed is due 30 days after the determination or agreement is issued, if that is later than the normal due date.

If any part of the postponed tax becomes due a notice of the amount payable is issued and the amount is payable 30 days after the issue of the notice. Interest, however, is still payable from the normal due date.

7 Client confidentiality

Whenever you prepare accounts or returns on behalf of a client you should remember that you are bound by the ethical guideline of client confidentiality. This means that you should not discuss a client's affairs with third parties without the client's permission. You should also take care not to leave documents relating to a client's affairs in public places such as on trains or in restaurants.

Activity 9.5

Tim is a medical consultant. His total tax liability for 2003/04 was £16,800. Of this £7,200 was paid under the PAYE system, £800 was withheld at source from bank interest and £200 was suffered on dividends received during the year.

Tim's total tax liability for 2004/05 was £22,000. £7,100 of this was paid under PAYE system, £900 was withheld at source from bank interest and there was a £250 tax credit on dividends.

Tim did not make any claim in respect of his payments on account for 2004/05. The Revenue issued a 2004/05 tax return to Tim on 5 May 2005.

Task

State what payments Tim was required to make in respect of his 2004/05 tax liability and the due dates for the payment of these amounts.

03/04   16,800
ded at source 7,200 + 800 + 200 = 8200

04/05   = 22,000
ded at source = 7100 + 900 + 250 = 8250

31st Jan 05 = 4300
31st Jul 05 = 4300
31st Jan 06 = 5150   (22,000 - 8250 - 8600)

Key learning points

☑   The **tax return** is due for filing by **31 January following the end of the tax year**.

☑   However, if the taxpayer wants the **Revenue to calculate tax**, he must file it by **30 September following the end of the tax year.**

☑   **Two payments on account** of income tax are due on **31 January in the tax year** and **31 July following the end of the tax year.**

☑   Payments on account are based on the **previous year's tax bill**.

☑   On **31 January following the end of the tax year**, the **balance** of any income tax is due.

☑   **CGT** is due to be paid on **31 January following the end of the tax year.**

☑   There is an extensive regime of **penalties**, **surcharges** and **interest**.

☑   The Revenue have extensive, but not unlimited, **powers to enquire into returns**.

Quick quiz

1 Julia is sent her 2004/05 tax return on 6 August 2005.

 By what date must she file the tax return if she does not want to calculate her tax liability?

 A 30 September 2005
 B 5 October 2005
 C 5 November 2005
 D 31 January 2006

2 What penalty is due if a tax return is delivered 4 months late?

3 Christopher had a tax liability of £6,000 for 2003/04. In 2004/05, his tax liability was £10,000.

 How is Christopher's tax liability for 2004/05 paid?

4 Oliver should have made a balancing payment of £10,000 on 31 January 2005. He actually paid it on 31 May 2005.

 What surcharge is due?

Answers to quick quiz

1 B later of 30 September 2005 and 2 months after the issue of the tax return.

2 £100

3 Two payments of £3,000 each on 31 January 2005 and 31 July 2005, balance of £4,000 on 31 January 2006.

4 5% x £10,000 = £500

Activity checklist

This checklist shows which performance criteria, range statement or knowledge and understanding point is covered by each activity in this chapter. Tick off each activity as you complete it.

Activity

9.1 ☐ This activity deals with Knowledge and Understanding point 16: self assessment including payment of tax and filing of returns by individuals.

9.2 ☐ This activity deals with Knowledge and Understanding point 16: self assessment including payment of tax and filing of returns by individuals.

9.3 ☐ This activity deals with Knowledge and Understanding point 16: self assessment including payment of tax and filing of returns by individuals.

9.4 ☐ This activity deals with Knowledge and Understanding point 16: self assessment including payment of tax and filing of returns by individuals.

9.5 ☐ This activity deals with Knowledge and Understanding point 16: self assessment including payment of tax and filing of returns by individuals.

P A R T   D

Answers to activities

Answers to activities

Chapter 1: An outline of income tax

Activity 1.1

The interest must be grossed up to £320 × 100/80 = £400

Activity 1.2

The gross amounts are:
Dividends (£2,250 × 100/90) £2,500
Building society interest (£2,400 × 100/80) £3,000

Activity 1.3

	Non-savings Income £	Savings (excl. dividend) income £	Dividend income £	Total £
Earnings	16,000	0	0	
Building society interest £4,800 × 100/80	0	6,000	0	
Dividends £7,875 × 100/90	0	0	8,750	
Premium bond prize: exempt	0	0	0	
STI	16,000	6,000	8,750	30,750
Less personal allowance	(4,745)			
Taxable income	11,255	6,000	8,750	26,005

Did you remember to gross up dividends by 100/90 and building society interest by 100/80?

Did you remember that premium bond prizes are exempt?

Activity 1.4

	Non-savings Income £	Savings (excl. dividend) income £	Dividend income £	Total £
Business profits				
Building society interest (× 100/80)	21,000	6,000	2,000	
Dividends (×100/90)		6,000	2,000	29,000
Personal allowance	(4,745)			
Taxable income	16,255	6,000	2,000	24,255

Activity 1.5

	£
£2,020 × 10%	202
£29,380 × 22%	6,464
£18,600 × 40%	7,440
£50,000	14,106

Did you remember that taxable income is income **after** deducting the personal allowance?

Activity 1.6

	Non-savings income £	Savings (excl dividend) income) £	Total £
Earnings	10,430		
Building society interest (× 100/80)		5,000	
	10,430	5,000	15,430
Less personal allowance	(4,745)		
	5,685	5,000	10,685

	£
Tax on non-savings income	
£2,020 × 10%	202
£3,665 × 22%	806
Tax on savings (excl dividend)	
£5,000 × 20%	1,000
Tax Liability	2,008
Less: PAYE	(1,000)
Tax suffered on building society interest	(1,000)
Tax payable	8

The building society interest falls within the basic rate band so it is taxed at 20%.

Note that both tax suffered on building society interest and tax suffered under the PAYE system are deducted from the tax liability to arrive at tax payable. If these amounts had exceeded the tax liability, the excess could have been repaid.

Activity 1.7

	Dividend income £
Dividends (× 100/90)	38,000
Less personal allowance	(4,745)
Taxable income	33,255

Tax on dividend income

	£
£31,400 × 10%	3,140
£1,855 × 32.5%	603
	3,743
Less: Tax credit on dividend (max)	(3,743)
Tax payable	–

The dividend income that falls within the starting and basic rate thresholds is taxed at 10%. Dividend income over the threshold of £31,400 is taxed at 32.5%. The tax credit suffered on the dividend income, £3,800, can be offset against the tax liability to reduce it to £nil. However, the excess tax credit, £57 (£3,800 – £3,743) cannot be repaid. The tax credit is offsettable but not repayable.

Activity 1.8

	£
Patent royalty (£3,900 × 100/78)	5,000
Copyright royalty	1,000
Total to deduct income tax computation	6,000

Copyright royalties are paid gross. The patent royalties are paid net of 22% tax but Harriet will deduct the gross amounts in her income tax computation.

Activity 1.9

	Non-savings Income £	Savings(excl dividend) income £	Dividend income £	
Schedule D Case I	8,000			
Building society interest (× 100/80)		17,500		
Dividends (× 100/90)			500	
Patent royalty (× 100/78)	(8,000)	(4,000)		
	–	13,500	500	14,000
Less personal allowance	–	(4,745)	–	
	–	8,755	500	9,255

Income tax on savings (excl dividend) income	£
£2,020 × 10%	202
£6,735 × 20%	1,347
Dividend income £500 × 10%	50
Add: Tax retained on charge (£12,000 × 22%)	1,599
	2,640
Income tax liability	4,239

Activity 1.10

	Non-savings £
Salary	58,000
Less: personal allowance	(4,745)
Taxable income	53,255

Income tax	£	£
Starting rate band	2,020 × 10%	202
Basic rate band	29,380 × 22%	6,464
Basic rate band (extended)	10,000 × 22%	2,200
Higher rate band	11,855 × 40%	4,742
	53,255	13,608

The basic rate band is extended by the gross amount of the gift aid donation (£7,800 × 100/78).

Activity 1.11

	2003/04 £	2004/05 £
Salary	39,000	20,000
Less: personal allowance	(4,755)	(4,745)
Taxable income	34,255	15,255
Tax		
£2,020 × 10%	202	202
£29,380/£13,235 × 22%	6,464	2,912
£2,855 × 22%	628	
	7,294	3,114

Income is below the higher rate threshold in 2004/05, so even if no claim were made no additional relief would be given on the gift aid donation in 2004/05. The claim allows £2,855 of income in 2003/04 to be taxed at 22% rather than 40%, saving tax of £514 [(40% - 22%) x £2,855]. The basic rate band could be extended by up to £10,000 (£7,800 × $^{100}/_{78}$) in 2003/04.

Activity 1.12

	Non-savings £	Savings (excl. dividend)	Dividend £	Total £
Earnings	24,200			
Building society interest £1,600 × 100/80		2,000		
Dividends £14,625 × 100/90			16,250	
	24,200	2,000	16,250	42,450
Less personal allowance	(4,745)			
Taxable income	19,455	2,000	16,250	37,705

Non-savings income		£
£2,020 × 10%		202
£17,435 × 22%		3,836
Savings (excl. dividend) income		
£2,000 × 20%		400
Dividend income		
£9,945 × 10%		994
£800 × 10% (Note)		80
£5,505 × 32.5%		1,789

Tax liability			7,301
Less tax suffered:	Tax credit on dividend income	1,625	
	Building society interest	400	
	PAYE	4,750	
			(6,775)
Tax payable			526

Note. The basic rate band is extended by the **gross** amount of the gift aid donation. Did you read the question properly; you were given the gross amount of the gift aid donation in the question. You did not need to gross this figure up again!

Activity 1.13

Mr Pink	Non-savings £	Savings (excl. dividends) £	Dividends £	Total £
Earnings	36,000			
Dividends × 100/90			1,211	
Bank deposit interest × 100/80		250		
Building society interest × 100/80		179		
STI	36,000	429	1,211	37,640
Less personal allowance	(4,745)			
Taxable income	31,255	429	1,211	32,895

	£	£
Non-savings income		
£2,020 × 10%		202
£29,235 × 22%		6,432
Savings (excluding dividend) income		
£145 × 20%		29
£284 × 40%		114
Dividend income		
£1,211 × 32.5%		393
		7,170
Less: tax credit on dividend	121	
tax suffered on savings income	86	
PAYE	6,000	
		(6,207)
Tax payable		963

	Non-savings £	Savings (excl. dividends) £	Dividends £	Total £
Mrs Pink				
Earnings	30,000			
Dividends × 100/90			2,820	
Bank deposit interest × 100/80		95		
Building society interest × 100/80	–	525		
STI	30,000	620	2,820	33,440
Less personal allowance	(4,745)			
Taxable income	25,255	620	2,820	28,695

	£	£
Non-savings income		
£2,020 × 10%		202
£23,235 × 22%		5,112
Savings (excluding dividend) income		
£620 × 20%		124
Dividend income		
£2,820 × 10%		282
Tax liability		5,720
Less: tax credit on dividends	282	
tax suffered on savings income	124	
PAYE	4,800	
		(5,206)
Tax payable		514

Premium bond prizes are tax free

The gift aid donation is paid net of basic rate tax, so it does not affect the personal tax computation.

If Mrs Pink was a higher rate taxpayer in the previous year, it would have been advantageous to carry the gift aid donation back in order to obtain additional relief in the previous year.

Chapter 2: Calculation of employment income

Activity 2.1

(a)   31 January 2005
(b)   30 April 2005

Activity 2.2

Molly is not an excluded employee. For this purpose Molly's earnings are taken to be £9,500 (£6,500 + £3,000)

Activity 2.3

	£
Annual value	1,600
Additional benefit £(420,000 – 75,000) × 5%	17,250
Taxable benefit	18,850

Activity 2.4

	£	£
Salary		27,400
Net emoluments		
Accommodation benefits		
Annual value: exempt (job related)		
Ancillary services		
Electricity	550	
Gas	400	
Gardener	750	
Redecorations	1,800	
	3,500	
Restricted to 10% of £27,400	2,740	
Less employee's contribution	(600)	
		2,140
Employment income		29,540

Activity 2.5

The CO_2 emissions of the car are 225g/km (rounded down to the nearest five below).

Amount over baseline figure 225 – 145 = 80g/ km

Divide by 5 = 16

The taxable percentage is 15% + 16% = 31%

So the benefit is 31% × £10,000 × 9/12 = £2,325.

Tutorial note: The benefit is multiplied by 9/12 as the car was only available for nine months in the tax year.

Activity 2.6

Round CO_2 emissions figure down to the nearest 5, ie 195 g/km.

Amount by which CO_2 emissions exceed the baseline:
(195 – 145) = 50 g/km
Divide by 5 = 10
Taxable percentage = 15% + 10% = 25%

	£
Car benefit £15,000 × 25%	3,750
Fuel benefit £14,400 × 25%	3,600
	7,350
Less contribution towards use of car	(270)
	7,080

If the contribution of £270 had been towards the petrol the benefit would have been £7,350.

Activity 2.7

	£
Mileage allowance received (15,400 × 35p)	5,390
Less: tax free [(10,000 × 40p) + (5,400 × 25p)]	(5,350)
Taxable benefit	40

£5,350 is tax free and the excess amount received of £40 is a taxable benefit.

Activity 2.8

	£
Mileage allowance received (12,000 × 25p)	3,000
Less: statutory allowance (10,000 × 40p + 2,000 × 25p)	(4,500)
	(1,500)

£3,000 is tax free. Tax relief can be claimed on £1,500, the excess of the statutory allowance over the amount received.

Activity 2.9

Average method

	£
$5\% \times \dfrac{30,000 + 10,000}{2}$	1,000
Less interest paid	(250)
Benefit	750

Alternative method (strict method)

	£
£30,000 × $\frac{246}{365}$ (6 April – 6 December) × 5%	1,011
£10,000 × $\frac{119}{365}$ (7 December – 5 April) × 5%	163
	1,174
Less interest paid	(250)
Benefit	924

The Revenue might opt for the alternative method.

Activity 2.10

Interest: no benefit because loan not over £5,000.

Loan written off: £4,000 × 35% = £1,400 taxable benefit.

Activity 2.11

	£
Salary	30,000
Season ticket loan £2,300 × 5%	115
Loan to buy yacht £54,000 × (5 –3 = 2%)	1,080
Earnings	31,195
Less personal allowance	(4,745)
Taxable income	26,450

As the total of the cheap loans provided to Anna exceeds £5,000, a taxable benefit arises in respect of both loans.

Activity 2.12

£3,800 x 20% − £500 = £260

Activity 2.13

Zoe is not entitled to tax relief for the costs incurred in travelling between Wycombe and Chiswick since these are normal commuting costs. However, relief is available for all costs that Zoe incurs when she travels from Wycombe to Wimbledon to visit her client.

Activity 2.14

Although Philip is spending all of his time at the Morpeth branch it will not be treated as his normal work place because his period of attendance will be less than 24 months. Thus Philip can claim relief in full for the costs of travel from his home to the Morpeth branch.

Activity 2.15

	£	£
Salary		36,000
Car £20,000 × 22%		4,400
Fuel £14,400 × 22% (partial contribution gives no reduction)		3,168
Mobile telephone		0
Use of video camera £600 × 20%		120
Loan: does not exceed £5,000		0
Childminder		4,000
		47,688
Less: professional subscriptions	180	
cost of business telephone calls	45	
		(225)
Earnings		47,463

Tutorial notes

1. The CO_2 emissions of the car are rounded down to 180g/km.
    The baseline figure for CO_2 emissions given in the tax rates and allowances tables is 145g/km at which the % is 15%.
    The excess over the baseline is 180 − 145 = 35g/km.
    Divide this by 5, $\frac{35}{5}$ = 7, so the taxable % is 22% (15% + 7%).
    The % increases by 1% for each 5g/km that this figure is exceeded.

2. The telephone line rental and the golf club subscription do not qualify for a deduction because they are not paid wholly, exclusively and necessarily for employment purposes.

Chapter 3: Employment income – additional aspects

Activity 3.1

£102,000 (the earnings cap) × 15% – £3,500 = £11,800.

Activity 3.2

Tax year	Age at start of yr	% of NRE	Basis year	Maximum contribution
2004/05	45	20	2004/05(N1)	£30,000 × 20% = £6,000
2005/06	46	25(N2)	2004/05	£30,000 × 25% = £7,500
2006/07	47	25	2004/05	£30,000 × 25% = £7,500
2007/08	48	25	2004/05	£30,000 × 25% = £7,500
2008/09	49	25	2004/05	£30,000 × 25% = £7,500
2009/10	50	25	2004/05	£30,000 × 25% = £7,500
2010/11	51	30	2007/08(N3)	£28,000 × 30% = £8,400
2011/12	52	30	2011/12(N4)	£34,000 × 30% = £10,200

Notes

1. The basis year for 2004/05 will apply for 2004/05 to 2009/10 (maximum).

2. The relevant percentage is determined by the age of the individual at the start of the *contribution* year. The basis year used is irrelevant.

3. In 2010/11, any year from 2005/06 to 2010/11 inclusive can be chosen as the basis year. 2007/08 has been chosen as it gives the highest NRE. This does not affect the contributions made in 2007/08 to 2009/10 because the basis year for those years (2004/05) has higher NRE.

4. In 2011/12, any year from 2006/07 to 2011/12 inclusive can be chosen as the basis year. 2011/12 has been chosen as it gives the highest NRE.

Activity 3.3

	Non savings income
	£
Earnings/STI	46,000
Less: PA	(4,745)
Taxable income	41,255

Tax

	£
£2,020 × 10%	202
£29,380 × 22%	6,464
£9,000 (7,020 × 100/78) × 22%	1,980
£855 × 40%	342
41,255	8,988

The basic rate band is extended by the gross amount of the pension contributions.

Activity 3.4

(a) A form P45 is given to an employee leaving employment.

(d) Form P14 is used to inform the Revenue of an employee's total tax and NI.

(c) Form P35 summarises the above forms.

(d) Forms P14 and P35 must be submitted to the Revenue by 19 May following the end of the tax year.

(e) Form P9D details benefits for employees earning less than £8,500 per annum.

(f) P9D must be submitted to the Revenue by 6 July following the tax year.

Chapter 4: Investments and land

Activity 4.1

	£
NSB easy access account	80
Interest from Natwest Bank £80 × 100/80	100
Interest on $3\frac{1}{2}$ % War loan	50
Interest assessable 2004/05	230

National Savings Certificates and ISA – exempt

The interest on the 3½ % war loan and on the National Savings Bank Easy Access Savings account is received gross.

Activity 4.2

	Savings (excl. dividend) £
STI (bank deposit interest) £9,600 × 100/80	12,000
Less personal allowance	(4,745)
Taxable income	7,255

Income tax	£
£2,020 × 10%	202
£5,235 × 20%	1,047
Tax liability	1,249
Tax suffered £12,000 × 20%	(2,400)
Repayment due	(1,151)

The tax suffered on bank and building society interest can be repaid if it exceeds the individual's tax liability.

Activity 4.3

	Dividend income £
Dividend (× 100/90)	14,000
Less: PA	(4,745)
Taxable income	9,255
	£
£9,255 × 10%	925
Less: Tax credit	(925)
Tax payable / repayable	Nil

Note: The tax credit on dividend income cannot be repaid.

Activity 4.4

Dividend income	
(10,000 × 18p) = 1,800 × 100/90	£2,000
Interest on loan stock	
(20,000 × 5%) = 1,000 × 100/80	£1,250

Activity 4.5

	£
Rental (9 months) 9 × £500	4,500
Less: agent's fees £4,500 × 15%	(675)
insurance (7 months)	
7/12 × £360	(210)
Wear and tear £4,500 × 10%	(450)
Schedule A	3,165

Activity 4.6

2004/05

	£
Rental (6 months) 6 × £300	1,800
Less: cleaning 6 × £50	(300)
water rates 6 × £20	(120)
interest on loan 6 × £210	(1,260)
wear and tear (1,800 – 120) × 10%	(168)
Schedule A loss carried forward	(48)

2005/06

	£
Rental 1 month × £300	300
11 months × £350	3,850
	4,150
Less: cleaning 12 × £50	(600)
water rates 12 × £20	(240)
interest on loan 12 × £210	(2,520)
wear and tear (4,150 – 240) × 10%	(391)
Profit	399
Less: loss b/f	(48)
Schedule A profit	351

Activity 4.7

(a)

	£	£
Rent		
House 1: first letting £600 × 6		3,600
House 1: second letting £6,000 × 3/12		1,500
House 2 £5,000 × 8/12		3,333
House 3 £7,800 × 8/12		5,200
		13,633
Expenses		
House 1: new roof, disallowable because capital	0	
House 1: loft insulation	1,200	
House 1: water rates	320	
House 1: buildings insurance £480 × 10/12	400	
House 2: water rates	240	
House 2: furniture £(3,333 – 240) × 10%	309	
House 3: redecoration	1,200	
House 3: water rates	360	
House 3: buildings insurance £440 × 9/12	330	
House 3: contents insurance £180 × 8/12	120	
House 3: furniture £(5,200 – 360) × 10%	484	
		(4,963)
Schedule A income from 3 houses		8,670

Note: The loft insulation is a capital expense but it is specifically allowable up to £1,500.

(b) If the cottages are to be treated as furnished holiday lettings, the first condition is that the lettings must be made on a **commercial basis with a view to the realisation of profit**.

Each property must be **available for letting** to the public for not less than 140 days in a tax year. Between them, the properties **must be let for at least 70 days each** in the 140 day period. For example, if the first cottage is let for 90 days in the year, the second cottage must be let for at least 50 days in the year to give an average of 70 days. If one of the cottages satisfies the 70 day test but the aggregation of the other cottage would pull the average down to below 70 days, the landlord can choose to treat the cottage which satisfies the 70 days test as furnished holiday accommodation.

In addition, **for at least 7 months** (including the 70 days) **each property must not normally be in the same occupation for more than 31 days**.

If the cottages satisfies these conditions, **the income from the lettings is taxed under Schedule A but as if the landlord was carrying on a trade under Schedule D Case I** (except for the basis period rules). **This means that any losses are treated as trading losses instead of Schedule A losses, capital allowance are available on furniture (instead of either the renewals basis or the 10% wear and tear allowance) and the income qualifies as net relevant earnings for the purposes of personal pension relief.**

Chapter 5: An outline of capital gains tax

Activity 5.1

	£
Gains	26,100
Less losses	(8,000)
	18,100
Less annual exemption	(8,200)
Taxable gains	9,900

Activity 5.2

The tax bands are initially allocated to income. Gains are then taxed as though they were an additional slice of savings (excl dividend) income.

	Total	Income	Gains
Starting rate	2,020	2,020	0
Basic rate	29,380	26,195	3,185
Higher rate	2,100	0	2,100
		28,215	5,285

The CGT payable is as follows.

	£
£3,185 × 20%	637
£2,100 × 40%	840
Total CGT payable	1,477

Activity 5.3

TAXABLE INCOME AND GAINS

	£
Gross bank interest	24,500
Less: personal allowance	(4,745)
Taxable income	19,755

	£
Gains	35,000
Less annual exemption	(8,200)
Taxable gains	26,800

£11,645 (£31,400 – £19,755) of the gains fall within the basic rate band and are taxed at 20%. The remaining gains are taxed at 40%.

The capital gains tax liability is as follows.

	£
£11,645 × 20%	2,329
£15,155 × 40%	6,062
£26,800	8,391

Activity 5.4

	£
Current year gains	15,000
Less: Current year losses	(3,000)
	12,000
Less: loss b/f	(3,800)
	8,200
Less: annual exemption	(8,200)
	NIL

The loss carried forward to 2005/06 is £5,200 (£9,000 – £3,800).

The set off of the brought forward loss is restricted to ensure that the annual exemption is not wasted.

Activity 5.5

The £10,000 net loss which arises in 2004/05 will be carried back. We must set off the loss against the 2004/05 gains first even though the gains are more than covered by the 2004/05 annual exemption.

£200 of the loss will be used in 2003/04. None of the loss will be used in 2002/03 (because the gains for that year are covered by the annual exemption), and so the remaining £9,800 will be used in 2001/02. Repayments of CGT will follow.

Activity 5.6

The current year loss must be deducted in full from the gain before taper relief is applied:

	£
Gain	14,000
Loss	(1,300)
Net gain	12,700

The asset was owned for 7 years (including the additional year) so:

	£
Gain after taper relief (75%)	9,525
Less: Annual exemption	(8,200)
Taxable gain	1,325

Activity 5.7

	£
Gain	17,500
Loss	(6,000)
Current net gains	11,500
Less: brought forward loss	(3,300)
Gains before taper relief	8,200
Gains after taper relief (7 years ownership) £8,200 × 75%	6,150
Less: annual exemption	(8,200)
Taxable gains	Nil

Note that the benefit of the taper relief is effectively wasted since the brought forward loss reduces the gain down to the annual exemption amount but the taper is then applied to that amount reducing it further.

The loss carried forward is £6,700 (£10,000 − £3,300).

Activity 5.8

	£	£
Non-business asset owned for 2 years	20,000	
Less: loss b/f	(10,000)	
Net gain after taper relief (100%)		10,000
Non-business asset owned since 1993 (75%)		37,500
		47,500
Less: annual exemption		(8,200)
Taxable gain		39,300

The loss brought forward is set against the gain that attracts the least taper relief (ie where the highest percentage of the gain remains taxable).

Activity 5.9

No: motor cars are exempt assets.

Activity 5.10

Motor cars are exempt assets, so the loss brought forward from 2003/04 is £6,300.

The position for 2004/05 is as follows.

	£
Gains	
Shares (no taper relief)	7,800
Picture (no taper relief)	3,000
	10,800
Less loss on shares	(2,000)
	8,800
Less loss brought forward	(600)
	8,200
Less annual exemption	(8,200)
Chargeable gains	0

Gilt-edged securities are exempt assets. Losses brought forward are (unlike current year losses) only used to bring net gains down to the annual exempt amount.

The loss carried forward at the end of 2004/05 is £(6,300 − 600) = £5,700.

Chapter 6: The computation of gains and losses

Activity 6.1

No: it is not reflected in the state or nature of the asset at the time of disposal.

Activity 6.2

The indexation allowance is computed as follows.

	£
0.960 × £5,000	4,800
0.834 × £2,000	1,668
	6,468

Activity 6.3

	£
Proceeds	24,000
Less cost	(97,000)
Allowable loss	(73,000)

Indexation cannot increase a loss.

Activity 6.4

	£
Deemed disposal proceeds (connected person)	50,000
Less: Cost	(60,000)
Allowable loss	(10,000)

This loss will only be available to set against chargeable gains that Holly makes on other disposals to Emily.

Activity 6.5

	£
No gain/no loss transfer	
Cost for Nicholas	
Cost 1991	18,000
Indexation 0.085 × 18,000	1,530
	19,530

Sale by Nicholas	£
Proceeds	50,000
Less: cost	(19,530)
	30,470
Less: indexation 0.151 × 19,530	(2,949)
Indexed gain	27,521

Activity 6.6

The amount of the original cost attributable to the part sold is

$$\frac{18,000}{18,000 + 36,000} \times £27,000 = £9,000$$

	£
Proceeds	18,000
Less cost (see above)	(9,000)
Unindexed gain	9,000
Less indexation allowance (March 1984 to April 1998)	
$0.859 \times £9,000$	(7,731)
Gain before taper relief	1,269

Gain after taper relief (6.4.98 – 5.4.04 = 6 years plus additional year = 7 years)

$75\% \times £1,269$ <u>£952</u>

Activity 6.7

Cost: £150,000 × 190/(190 + 327) = £55,126

Incidental costs of disposal: £3,000

Total: £58,126

Activity 6.8

(a)   The vase

	£
Proceeds	100,000
Less cost	(65,000)
	35,000
Less indexation allowance (July 1988 to April 1998)	
$0.524 \times £65,000$	(34,060)
Chargeable gain before taper relief	940

(b)   The plot of land

	£
Proceeds	47,000
Less: cost	(20,000)
expenditure July 1992	(5,000)
expenditure July 1999	(4,000)
	18,000
Less: indexation allowance	
On cost $0.361 \times £20,000$	(7,220)
On enhancement $0.171 \times £5,000$	(855)
Chargeable gain before taper relief	9,925

(c)   The house

	£
Proceeds	173,000
Less: cost	(65,000)
	108,000
Less: indexation allowance 0.485 × £65,000	(31,525)
Chargeable gain before taper relief	76,475

Tutorial note. For CGT purposes the house is deemed to be disposed of on the date of exchange of contracts not on the date or completion.

(d)   The table was disposed of between spouses living together, so there is no chargeable gain or allowable loss.

(e)

	£
Proceeds (market value)	32,000
Less: cost	(35,000)
Loss	(3,000)

Tutorial note. A loss arises on the sale of the bungalow, but because the bungalow was sold to a connected person, the loss can only be set against gains on disposals in the same year or future years to the same connected person while he or she remains connected. A brother cannot, of course, cease to be connected, but a connection by marriage could cease.

(f)

	£
Vase £940 (W1) × 75%	705
Plot of land (W2) £9,925 × 75%	7,444
House £76,475 (W3) × 75%	57,356
	65,505
Less annual exemption	(8,200)
Taxable gains	57,305

All the assets were owned for seven complete years after 6.4.98 (including the additional year), so 75% of the gains are taxable.

(g)   Capital gains tax of £57,305 × 40% = £22,922

Tutorial Note: You are told that Hardup pays income tax at the rate of 40%. This means that the starting and basic rate bands have all been used by income and therefore all capital gains will be subject to 40% CGT.

BPP
PROFESSIONAL EDUCATION

Chapter 7: Shares and securities

Activity 7.1

Match post April 1998 acquisitions on a LIFO basis

1 March 2003

	£
Disposal proceeds (£14,000 × $\frac{1,000}{1,600}$)	8,750
Less: cost	(1,260)
Gain	7,490

15 May 2002

	£
Disposal proceeds (£14,000 × $\frac{600}{1,600}$)	5,250
Less: cost (1,900 × $\frac{600}{1,800}$)	(633)
Gain	4,617

The total chargeable gain on the sale of June's shares is £12,107 (£7,490 + £4,617). No taper relief is due in respect of either of the disposals.

Activity 7.2

	No of shares	Cost £	Indexed cost £
Value at 6.4.85	2,000	6,000	6,289
Indexed rise			
0.029 × £6,289			182
	2,000	6,000	6,471
Acquisition	2,000	4,000	4,000
Value at 10.7.86	4,000	10,000	10,471

Activity 7.3

	No of shares	Cost £	Indexed cost £
10 July 1986	4,000	10,000	10,471
Index to April 1998 0.667 × 10,471			6,984
Value of pool at 6.4.98	4,000	10,000	17,455

Activity 7.4

		No of shares	Cost £
1.5.02	Purchase	10,000	42,000
1.12.03	Bonus issue	2,000	–
		12,000	42,000

	£
Disposal proceeds	15,000
Less: Cost $\dfrac{4,000}{12,000} \times £42,000$	(14,000)
Gain	1,000

No taper relief available

Activity 7.5

(a) *Post 5.4.98 holding*

	Number	Cost £
Shares acquired 11.9.01	2,000	5,000
Shares acquired 1.2.02 (rights) 1:2 @ £2.75	1,000	2,750
	3,000	7,750

Gain

	£
Proceeds $\dfrac{3,000}{5,000} \times £15,000$	9,000
Less: cost	(7,750)
Gain	1,250

Taper relief (based on ownership of original holding 11.9.01 – 10.9.04)

95% (Three years: non business asset) × £1,250   £1,188

(b) *FA 1985 pool*

	Number	Cost £	Indexed cost £
1.10.95	10,000	15,000	15,000
IA to 4.98 0.085 × £15,000			1,275
Pool at 5.4.98	10,000	15,000	16,275
Rights issues 1.2.02	5,000	13,750	13,750
	15,000	28,750	30,025
14.10.04 Sale	(2,000)	(3,833)	(4,003)
c/f	13,000	24,917	26,022

Gain

	£
Proceeds $\frac{2,000}{5,000} \times £15,000$	6,000
Less: cost	(3,833)
Unindexed gain	2,167
Less: indexation £(4,003 − 3,833)	(170)
Indexed gain	1,997

Taper relief (based on original holding 6.4.98 − 5.4.04)

75% (Seven years: non business asset) × £1,997	£1,498

(c)   Total gains (after taper relief)

£(1,188 + 1,498)	£2,686

Activity 7.6

Post 6.4.98 acquisitions: match on a LIFO basis.

17.1.02

	£
Proceeds $\frac{2,000}{6,000} \times £24,000$	8,000
Less: cost	(6,000)
Chargeable gain	2,000

No taper relief

12.12.01

	£
Proceeds $\frac{2,000}{6,000} \times £24,000$	8,000
Less: cost	(5,500)
Chargeable gain	2,500

No taper relief

The FA 1985 pool

	Shares	Cost £	Indexed cost £
Acquisition 19.9.85	2,000	1,700	1,700
Indexation to April 1998 (Pool closes)			
0.704 × £1,700			1,197
Value when pool closes (5.4.98)	2,000	1,700	2,897
Disposal 17.5.04	(2,000)	(1,700)	(2,897)
	0	0	0

	£
Proceeds $\dfrac{2,000}{6,000} \times £24,000$	8,000
Less cost	(1,700)
	6,300
Less indexation allowance £(2,897 − 1,700)	(1,197)
Chargeable gain	5,103

Taper relief is available for this non-business asset with seven complete years of ownership (including the additional year) post 5 April 1998. Gain after taper relief £3,827

The total gains are £(2,000 + 2,500 + 3,827) = £8,327.

Chapter 8: CGT – additional aspects

Activity 8.1

	£
Proceeds	7,000
Less incidental costs of sale	(700)
Net proceeds	6,300
Less cost	(1,458)
Gain before taper relief	4,842

The maximum gain is $5/3 \times £(7,000 - 6,000) = £1,667$

The chargeable gain before taper relief is the lower of £4,842 and £1,667, so it is £1,667.

Gain after taper relief £1,667 × 95%	£1,584

Note. Taper relief is available to reduce this gain on a non-business asset with three years post 5.4.98 ownership.

Activity 8.2

	£
Proceeds (assumed)	6,000
Less incidental costs of disposal (£2,700 x 10/90)	(300)
	5,700
Less cost	(8,000)
Allowable loss	(2,300)

Activity 8.3

(a) *The vase*

	£
Proceeds	7,000
Less selling expenses	(350)
	6,650
Less cost	(800)
Gain	5,850

The chargeable gain before taper relief is the lower of £5,850 and £(7,000 – 6,000) × 5/3 = £1,667, so it is £1,667. No taper relief is due as the chattel had only been owned for one complete year.

(b) The sideboard

	£
Proceeds (deemed)	6,000
Less selling expenses	(250)
	5,750
Less: cost	(7,000)
Loss	(1,250)

Activity 8.4

No gain/loss arises. The gain on the disposal of a principal private residence is exempt. Any loss is not allowable.

Activity 8.5

	£
Sales proceeds	450,000
Less: cost	(150,000)
	300,000
Less Private Residence Exemption (£300,000 × 5/6)	(250,000)
Chargable gain	50,000

The last three years of ownership are treated as a period of occupation even though Nitin owned another house at the time.

Activity 8.6

(a)   Exempt and chargeable periods

Period		Exempt months	Chargeable months
(i)	April 1982 – June 1982 (occupied)	3	0
(ii)	July 1982 – June 1984 (working abroad)	24	0
(iii)	July 1984 – December 1997 (occupied)	162	0
(iv)	January 1998 – December 2001 (see below)	0	48
(v)	January 2002 – December 2004 (last 36 months)	36	0
		225	48

No part of the period from January 1998 to December 2001 can be covered by the exemption for three years of absence for any reason because it is not followed at any time by actual occupation.

(b)   The chargeable gain

	£
Proceeds	150,000
Less cost	(50,000)
Unindexed gain	100,000
Less indexation allowance (March 1982 to April 1998)	
1.047 × £50,000	(52,350)
Indexed gain	47,650
Less exempt under PPR provisions	
$\frac{225}{273}$ × £47,650	(39,272)
Chargeable gain	8,378

Gain after taper relief (7 years including additional year) 75% × £8,378   £6,284

Activity 8.7

(a)

		Total (months)	Exempt (months)
1.4.00 – 30.9.00	Actual residence	6	6
1.10.00 – 31.9.01	House let	12	
1.10.01 – 30.9.04	Actual residence	36	34
		54	42

Therefore chargeable months = 12

(b)

	£	£
Proceeds		300,000
Less costs of disposal: estate agent's fees	5,000	
legal fees	1,200	
		(6,200)
Net proceeds		293,800
Less cost		(120,000)
Unindexed gain		173,800
Less principal private residence exemption		
£173,800 × $\frac{42}{54}$		(135,178)
Chargeable gain		38,622
Less letting exemption		
Lower of		
(i) £40,000		(38,622)
(ii) £135,178		
(iii) £38,622		
Chargeable gain before taper relief		Nil

Activity 8.8

	£
Proceeds	340,000
Less: cost	(90,000)
Unindexed gain	250,000

Less indexation allowance (March 1992 to April 1998)

	£
0.189 × £90,000	(17,010)
Indexed gain	232,990

Less PPR exemption

$$£232,990 \times \frac{33(1.4.92-31.12.94)+36(1.9.01-31.8.04)}{149(1.4.92-31.8.04)}$$ 107,895

$$£232,990 \times \frac{80(1.1.95-31.8.01)}{149(1.4.82-31.8.04)} \times 40\%$$ 50,038

	(157,933)
	75,057

Less letting exemption
    Lowest of:

(a)   gain attributable to letting $£232,990 \times \dfrac{80}{149} \times 60\% = £75,057$

(b) £40,000	(40,000)
(c) gain exempt under PPR rules £157,933	
Gain left in charge	35,057

Gain after taper relief (7 years including additional year)

75% × £35,057	£26,293

Working

Period	Ownership months	Notes
1.4.92 – 31.12.94	33	100% of house occupied
1.1.95 – 31.8.01	80	40% of house occupied 60% of house let
1.9.01 – 31.8.04	36	Last 36 months treated as 100% of house occupied
	149	

Note. The gain on the 40% of the house always occupied by Miss Coe is fully covered by PPR relief. The other 60% of the house has not always been occupied by Miss Coe and thus any gain on this part of the house is taxable where it relates to periods of time when Miss Coe was not actually (or deemed to be) living in it.

As a further point if Miss Coe had reoccupied the lower floors (60% part) of the house prior to the sale then 3 years worth of the non-occupation period between 1.1.95 and 31.8.01 could have been treated as deemed occupation under the special 3 years absence for any reason rule.

Chapter 9: Administration

Activity 9.1

£4,200. The return was due on 31 January 2005. It was therefore over 12 months late and the maximum penalty is £200 plus 100% of the tax liability.

Activity 9.2

	£
Income tax:	
Total income tax charged for 2004/05	9,200
Less: tax deducted for 2004/05	(3,200)
Relevant amount'	6,000
Payments on account for 2005/06:	
31 January 2006 £6,000 × ½	3,000
31 July 2006 As before	3,000

There is no requirement to make payments on account of capital gains tax.

Activity 9.3

Income tax: £18,000 − £2,750 − £6,500 − £6,500 = £2,250. CGT = £5,120.

Final payment due on 31 January 2006 for 2004/2005 £2,250 + £5,120 = £7,370

Activity 9.4

Herbert made an excessive claim to reduce his payments on account, and will therefore be charged interest on the reduction. The payments on account should have been £4,500 each based on the 2003/04 liability (not £5,000 each based on the 2004/05 liability). Interest will be charged as follows:

(a) First payment on account

   (i) On £3,500 – nil – paid on time
   (ii) On £1,000 from due date of 31 January 2005 to day before payment, 18 February 2006

(b) Second payment on account

   (i) On £3,500 from due date of 31 July 2005 to day before payment, 11 August 2005
   (ii) On £1,000 from due date of 31 July 2005 to day before payment, 18 February 2006

(c) Balancing payment

   (i) On £3,500 from due date of 31 January 2006 to day before payment, 18 February 2006

Activity 9.5

Tim's Payments on Account for 2004/05 were based on the excess of his 2003/04 tax liability over amounts deducted under the PAYE system, amounts deducted at source and tax credits on dividends:

	£
2003/04 tax liability	16,800
Less: PAYE	(7,200)
Tax deducted at source	(800)
Tax credit on dividends	(200)
Total payments on account for 2004/05	8,600

Two equal payments on account of £4,300 (£8,600 / 2) were required. The due dates for these payments were 31 January 2005 and 31 July 2005 respectively.

The final payment in respect of Tim's 2004/05 tax liability was due on 31 January 2006 and was calculated as follows:

	£
2004/05 tax liability	22,000
Less: PAYE	(7,100)
Tax deducted at source	(900)
Tax credit on dividends	(250)
	13,750
Less: Payments on account	(8,600)
Final payment due 31.1.06	5,150

P A R T E

Practice activities

BPP
PROFESSIONAL EDUCATION

chapter 1

An outline of Income Tax

Activity checklist

This checklist shows which performance criteria are covered by each activity in this chapter. Full details of the performance criteria are shown on page (xiv) onwards. Tick off each activity as you complete it.

Activity

1		Performance Criteria 19.3A, B and C
2		Performance Criteria 19.3A, B and C
3		Performance Criteria 19.3A, B and C
4		Performance Criteria 19.3A, B and C
5		Performance Criteria 19.3A, B and C
6		Performance Criteria 19.3A, B and C
7		Performance Criteria 19.3A, B and C

All of these activities cover Knowledge and Understanding points 2, 3, 4, 10 and 11.

1 Income tax computation

Selina received the following income in 2004/05:

Salary	£18,900
Building society interest received	£800
Dividends received	£298

PAYE tax of £2,100 was withheld from the gross salary stated above.

Tasks

(a)	Prepare a schedule of income for 2004/05 clearly showing the distinction between non-savings, savings (excluding dividend) income and dividend income. Selina's personal allowance should be deducted as appropriate.

(b)	Calculate the income tax liability for 2004/05.

(c)	Calculate the income tax payable for 2004/05.

Guidance notes

1	The major part of this question requires you to calculate an individual's overall tax position for 2004/05. Start with non-savings income.

2	Insert the savings (excl. dividend) income, remembering that income is always included gross in the tax computation even if the amounts are actually received net.

3	Insert the dividend income, remembering that dividends are received net of a 10% tax credit and they must be grossed up before inclusion in the tax computation.

4	After deducting the personal allowance to find the taxable income, you need to calculate tax payable. It is best to calculate tax on non-savings, savings (excl. dividend) and dividend income separately.

5	Finally, deduct the tax credit on dividend income and tax suffered at source.

Savings	non Savings	Dividends

18,900

1,000	331.

474J
13255	1,000	331

2020	202
11235	2471.70
1000	200
20%
331 10	33.10
2906.80 —
(2100.00)
(20.w)
(33)

573 40

2 Mr Betteredge

Mr Betteredge has the following income:

	£
Salary for the year to 5 April 2005	15,065
Interest received (cash received shown):	
National Westminster Bank plc	457
National Savings Bank investment account	26
Mini cash ISA account	180
Nationwide Building Society ordinary account	400
National Savings Certificates	173

Tasks

(a)   Prepare a Schedule of income for 2004/05 clearly showing the distinction between non-savings, savings and dividend income. Mr Betteredge's personal allowance should be deducted as appropriate.

(b)   Calculate the income tax liability of Mr Betteredge for 2004/05.

3 John Smith

John Smith has the following income and outgoings for the tax year 2004/05.

		£	
(i)	Salary (£9,200 tax deducted under PAYE)	45,000	(gross amount)
(ii)	Interest on a deposit account with the Scotia Bank	800	(net)
(iii)	Donation under the gift aid scheme made on 1 September 2004	5,132	(amount paid)
(iv)	Interest on a National Savings Bank investment account	496	
(v)	Dividends received on UK shares	900	(net)

Tasks

(a)   Prepare a schedule of income for 2004/05, clearly showing the distinction between non-savings, savings and dividend income. John Smith's personal allowance should be deducted as appropriate.

(b)   Calculate the net income tax payable for 2004/05.

(c)   Explain how you have dealt with the gift aid donation in your computation.

4 Mrs Rogers

Mrs Rogers has the following income:

Salary (PAYE deducted £3,000)	£17,776 (gross)

Investment income (cash received):

	£
Building society interest received on ordinary deposit account	1,500
Interest received on an individual savings account	300
National Savings Bank:	
Investment account interest	150

Dividend income (cash received)

Dividend of £1.35 per share on 10,000 quoted ordinary shares.

Tasks

(a) Prepare a schedule of income for 2004/05, clearly showing the distinction between non-savings, savings and dividend income. Mrs Rogers' personal allowance should be deducted as appropriate.

(b) Calculate Mrs Rogers' income tax payable/repayable for the year to 5 April 2005.

5 Mrs Butcher

Mrs Butcher, is aged 62. Her income in the year ended 5 April 2005 was as follows.

	£
Pension (no tax deducted before receipt)	7,204
Rent from let cottage	5,776
Interest on Government stock (received gross)	490
Dividends received from UK companies	270
Building society interest received	4,000
Premium bond prizes	250

Tasks

(a) Prepare a schedule for 2004/05 clearly showing the distinction between non savings, savings and dividend income. Mrs Butcher's personal allowance should be deducted as appropriate.

(b) Compute the income tax payable for 2004/05.

6 Eric Wright

Eric Wright, aged 55, is a partner in a firm of architects. His taxable profits for 2004/05 are £26,060.

Eric has a bank account with the Halifax Bank. His account was credited with interest of £1,600 on 31 March 2005.

Eric made a gift aid donation of £390 to Oxfam on 1 December 2004.

Eric is married to Doreen. Doreen, who is 61, received a taxable state pension of £4,027 in 2004/05. She also received dividends of £1,818.

Tasks

(a) Prepare a Schedule for 2004/05 clearly showing the distinction between non-saving, savings and dividend income for Eric Wright. Eric Wright's personal allowance should be deduced as appropriate.

(b) Compute the income tax payable by Eric Wright for 2004/05.

(c) Prepare a schedule for 2004/05 clearly showing the distinction between non-savings, savings and dividend income for Doreen.

(d) Compute the income tax payable by Doreen for 2004/05.

7 Melanie Wong

Melanie is employed as a head teacher in a local primary school. In 2004/05 she had earnings of £40,000. PAYE of £8,429 was deducted from these earnings.

Melanie received dividends of £4,500 during 2004/05. She also cashed in National Savings Certificates and received £250 interest in addition to the repayment of the capital invested.

Melanie made a gift aid donation of £1,170 to the RSPCA on 1 February 2005.

Tasks

(a) Prepare a schedule for Melanie Wong clearly showing the distinction between non-savings, savings (excl) dividend and dividend income for 2004/05. Melanie Wong's personal allowance should be deducted as appropriate.

(b) Compute the tax payable by/repayable to Melanie Wong for 2004/05.

chapter 2

Calculation of employment income

Activity checklist

This checklist shows which performance criteria are covered by each activity in this chapter. Full details of the performance criteria are shown on page (xiv) onwards. Tick off each activity as you complete it.

Activity

8		Performance Criteria 19.1A.
9		Performance Criteria 19.1A.
10		Performance Criteria 19.1A.
11		Performance Criteria 19.1A.
12		Performance Criteria 19.1A.
13		Performance Criteria 19.1B.

8 Cars and lunches

Mr William Sherman's remuneration package is as follows.

Annual salary £50,000.

Luncheon vouchers worth £5 per day for the 50 days each year that he will spend working away from the office. During the remaining 180 days that he will be in the office, he will be able to eat free of charge in the employee canteen which is open to all staff. It is likely that the cost of his meals will be £900 per year.

The company provides him with the use of a company car together with all petrol for both business and private use. The list price of the car was £25,000. The car emits 195g/km of CO_2.

Task

Calculate the total taxable benefits.

Guidance notes

1   There is a small exemption in relation to meal vouchers such as luncheon vouchers.

2   The car and fuel benefits depend on the level of the cars CO_2 emissions.

9 Directors

You act for a number of directors.

The following benefits are enjoyed by the various directors.

(a)   A director has had the use of a private house bought by the company for £120,000 in 2002. The director paid all of the house expenses plus the agreed open market annual rental of £2,000. The annual value of the house is £2,000.

(b)   A television video system, which had been provided at the start of 2000/01 for the use of a director and which had cost the company £3,500, was taken over by the director on 6 April 2004 for a payment of £600 (its market value at that date).

(c)   On 6 April 2004 a director had a loan of £40,000 at 4% interest. On 6 December 2004, £10,000 of this loan was repaid. This is the only loan he had taken out.

(d)   Medical insurance premiums were paid for a director and his family, under a group scheme, at a cost to the company of £800. Had the director paid for this as an individual the cost would have been £1,400.

(e)   On 6 September 2004 a director was given the use of a Mercedes car which had cost £24,000. The CO_2 emissions of the car were 245g/km. The director used the Mercedes for both business and private purposes. He was required to make good the cost of any petrol used for private mileage.

(f)   On 6 April 2004 the company lent a director a computer costing £3,900 for use at home. The director used the computer for both business and private purposes.

Task

Show how each of the above benefits would be quantified for tax purposes. Assume that the official rate of interest is 5%. Make all time apportionments on a monthly basis.

Guidance notes

1   Work through each benefit separately. Calculate its value before you move on to the next benefit. Watch out for exempt benefits.

2   Remember that any benefit that is only available for part of a year must be time apportioned. This is often the case in exam questions with car and fuel benefits. Is it relevant here?

10 Taxable and exempt benefits

During 2004/05, the following benefits were provided to employees of a company. All the employees earn more than £8,500 per year.

(a)   An interest free loan of £3,000 was made to Zoë Dexter on 6 April 2004. This was used to finance her daughter's wedding. *non taxable benefit - under £5k*

(b)   Throughout 2004/05 Victoria Eustace was provided with a computer and printer which she uses at home for both private and business purposes. The computer equipment cost the company £2,000. *£400 taxable benefit*

✱ _(c)   Amanda Valentine was provided with a petrol engined car on 6 June 2004. The company had acquired the car new on 1 March 2001 at a cost of £17,250. The market value of the car on 6 June 2004 was estimated to be £13,000. The car emits 145g/km of CO_2. The company pays all the running costs of the car including fuel.

✱ (d)   Throughout 2004/05 Catherine Crawley was provided with a petrol engined car which cost £16,000. The car emits 220g/km of CO_2. The company provided her with petrol for business and private motoring but she paid £500 to the company as a partial reimbursement of the cost of private fuel.

(e)   Emma Forbes was provided with a mobile telephone throughout 2004/05. Emma used the phone for business and private calls. Stowe Ltd paid total charges in respect of the phone during 2004/05 of £300. *non taxable benefit*

(f)   Stella was paid £2 a week towards her costs of working at home. *allowable deduction .* *upto £co*

Task

State the amounts, if any, that are taxable benefits. Explain why any benefits are exempt benefits.

(✱ - 15% of 17,250 = 2587.50 × 10/12 = 2156.25
15% of 14,400 = 2160.00   12
1800.00
3956

d ✱   30% of 16,000 = 4800
30% of 14,400 = 4320   9120

11 Accommodation

Mr Ford, the managing director of the company you work for, is provided with the exclusive private use of a flat in London. The flat is not job related accommodation for Mr Ford. The company acquired the flat for £100,000 in 2003 and Mr Ford has used it since then. The flat was fully furnished at a cost of £5,000 and the council tax paid by the company amounted to £500. The rateable value is £900. The running costs of the flat amounting to £1,200 for 2004/05 were paid directly by Mr Ford.

One of your company's other employees, Charles Rainer, was relocated on 6 April 2004 and required to live in an unfurnished company house; the annual value of this job-related accommodation was £4,000. The company had bought the house in March 2004 for £80,000. The company paid the council tax in respect of the house of £800. Mr Rainer paid all the running costs in respect of the house himself.

Tasks

(a) Show the taxable amounts for 2004/05 in respect of the accommodation provided to Mr Ford.

(b) Show the taxable amounts for 2004/05 in respect of the accommodation provided to Charles Rainer.

Assume the official rate of interest is 5%.

$(100-75) \times 5\%$ 1250
900
$5000 \times 20\%$ 1,000
Tax   500

12 Rita

Rita, a fashion designer for Daring Designs Ltd, was re-located from London to Manchester on 6 April 2004. Her annual salary is £48,000. She was immediately provided with a house with an annual value of £4,000 for which her employer paid an annual rent of £3,500. Rita was re-imbursed relevant re-location expenditure of £12,000. Rita's employer provided ancillary services for the house in 2004/05 as follows.

	£
Electricity	700
Gas	1,200
Water	500
Council tax	1,300
Property repairs	3,500

The house has been furnished by Daring Designs Limited prior to Rita's occupation at a cost of £30,000. On 6 October 2004 Rita bought all of the furniture from Daring Designs Ltd for £20,000 when its market value was £25,000.

Daring Designs Limited had made an interest free loan to Rita in 2003 of £10,000. The loan is not being used for a 'qualifying purposes'. No part of the loan has been repaid. $10000 \times 5\% = 500$

Tasks

(a) Compute the taxable benefit arising in respect of the accommodation provided for Rita.

(b) Compute the taxable benefit arising in respect of the relocation expenses.

(c) Compute the taxable benefit arising in respect of the interest free loan.

13 Sally

Sally, a company's marketing director earning £90,000 a year, incurs the following expenses in 2004/05.

(i)   An annual first class rail season ticket costing £2,700. She uses the ticket to travel between her home and her place of work. She used to walk to work, but then her company relocated to a new site 40 miles from her home. A standard class season ticket would cost £1,800 a year.

(ii)   Her telephone bill for the telephone at her home, which is as follows (for the whole year).

	£
Line rental	100
Private calls	130
Business calls	270
	500

(iii)   Her subscription of £50 to the Chartered Institute of Marketing. She needs to keep up with developments in marketing so as to put herself in a position to perform her duties.

(iv)   Subscriptions to various professional journals, totalling £130. Regular reading of these journals significantly improves her skill in her job.

(v)   A subscription of £230 to a London club. She uses the club's bar and restaurant to meet business contacts.

Tasks

(a)   Prepare a schedule to accompany Sally's tax return, setting out the deductible expenses.

(b)   Prepare a memorandum for Sally explaining the tax treatment of the various items above.

£90,000 Salary

a)

i) Rail ticket not deductible

ii) Business calls £270.00 deductible expenses

iii) £50 deductible for subscription as she is a professional & belongs to C.I.M.

iv) £130, not deductible,

v) London club is private hence not deductible.

chapter 3

Employment income: additional aspects

Activity checklist

This checklist shows which performance criteria are covered by each activity in this chapter. Full details of the performance criteria are provided on page (xiv) onwards. Tick off each activity as you complete it.

Activity

14		Performance Criteria 19.1A and 19.1B.
15		Performance Criteria 19.1B.
16		Performance Criteria 19.1B.
17		Performance Criteria 19.1B.
18		Performance Criteria 19.1B.
19		Performance Criteria 19.1B.
20		Performance Criteria 19.1A, 19.1B, 19.1D, 19.3A, 19.3B, 19.3C.
21		Performance Criteria 19.2A, 19.3A, 19.3B, 19.3C, 19.3E.

14   Bill Wilson

Bill Wilson, a 35 year old married man, was employed as a works manager in a large UK resident company. He was made redundant on 1 January 2005.

During the year 2004/05 he had the following income.

	£	
Salary	33,750	(to 31 December 2004)
Job Seeker's Allowance	723	(from 1 January 2005)
Dividends	1,350	(from UK companies)
	1,600	(from ISA investments) Ex
Interest	360	(from UK building societies)
	240	(from ISA) Ex
	110	(from a National Savings Bank easy access account) Ex
	250	(from 3.5% War Loan)

All the dividends and interest receipts are stated at the actual amounts received. The other items are stated at the gross amounts.

The Job Seekers allowance is a taxable state benefit.

During his employment he was provided with a BMW car which had a list price of £20,000. The CO_2 emissions of the car were 182 g/km. The company paid for all of the petrol.

Following the cessation of his employment Bill was provided with

- Cash of £20,000 — non taxable
- Use of the car until 5 April 2005.

The company was not contractually obliged to provide this.

Bill paid £400 (gross) to a registered charity under the Gift Aid scheme on 1 December 2004.

Tasks

(a)   Calculate Bill's taxable income for the tax year 2004/05.

(b)   Calculate Bill's income tax payable (prior to PAYE deductions) for the tax year 2004/05.

(c)   Give reasons where you have left any amounts out of the calculations.

(d)   List FOUR types of expenses that Bill could deduct from his employment income.

$(15+7)\% \times 20,000 = 4,400 \times 9/12 =$
$22\% \times 14,400 = 3168 \times 9/12 =$

£20,000 not included as up to £30k can be tax free.

15 Ian Warburton

Ian Warburton works as a consultant for a company supplying computer systems. Ian's monthly salary was increased by 5% to £1,365 from 1 August 2004. He contributes 3% of this salary to the company's occupational pension scheme, the company adding a further 9%.

Ian had a company car which was available to him throughout the year. The car was registered in 2003 and cost the company £11,000. The car emits CO_2 of 198g/km. The company provided all petrol for Ian although he did reimburse them £200 in respect of petrol for his summer vacation. Other costs in respect of the car, all paid by the company, were insurance £800, repairs £490 and new tyres £100.

Ian was paid a Christmas bonus of £1,000 with his December 2004 salary.

Task

Calculate Ian Warburton's earnings for 2004/05.

[handwritten: 195-145=50, 10+5=25, 14460 ×25, 11,000 = 6350]

[handwritten: 1300×4 = 5200, 1365×8 = 10920, = 1,000, 17120, 6350]

[handwritten: 17120.00, 513.60, 16606.40, 6350 = 22956.40]

16 David

David Rogers, aged 36, and his wife Sue, aged 34, are personal tax clients of your firm. David, who is employed as a designer, has always paid tax at the basic rate. Sue, who stays at home looking after the couples' two children, does not have any earnings of her own. David has not previously made any pension contributions but would like to consider contributing to a stakeholder pension scheme.

Task

Draft a letter to David setting out the rules governing personal pension contributions.

17 Stakeholder pensions

Bill, who was born on 18 August 1961, became employed by ABC plc on 1 June 2004. His employer does not provide an occupational pension scheme. Bill forecasts that he will have the following net relevant earnings from 2004/05.

	£
2004/05	25,000
2005/06	80,000
2006/07	60,000
2007/08	70,000
2008/09	75,000
2009/10	66,000
2010/11	70,000
2011/12	60,000

Bill has decided to contribute to a stakeholder pension scheme. He has not previously made any pension provision and has never earned more than £20,000 per annum previously.

[handwritten table:]

Tax Yr	Age	%	Base Yr	Max Cont		
4|5	42	20	25k	20% × 25	=	5,000
5|6	43	20	80k	20% × 80	=	16,000
6|7	44	20	80k	"	=	16,000
7|8	45	20	80k	"	=	16,000
8|9	46	25	80k	25% × 80	=	20,000
9|10	47	25	80k	"	=	20,000
10|11	48	25	80k	"	=	20,000
11|12	49	25	75k 8|9	25% × 75k	=	18,750

Tasks

(a) Calculate the maximum amount of gross pension contributions for which Bill will be entitled to tax relief in 2004/05 to 2011/12.

(b) Explain how tax relief is given for personal pension payments.

Assume the relevant rules and allowances in 2004/05 remain unchanged.

No Tax impli~~Tax relief~~ as deducted at source
cation

Guidance notes

1   First choose a basis year for each year. The basis year can be the year concerned or any one of the five previous tax years.

2   The relevant percentage depends on the taxpayer's age at the start of the tax year concerned.

18 Roger Thesaurus

Roger Thesaurus, aged 46 on 1 June 2004, has the following income and outgoings for the tax year 2004/05.

		£
(a)	Profits from sole trade	67,000
(b)	Interest on a deposit account with the Scotia Bank	*1496* 1,197 (net)
(c)	Copyright royalty paid	6,000 *gross*
(d)	Personal pension contributions. Roger joined a stakeholder pension scheme on 6.4.04. Roger chose 1999/00 as his basis year in 2004/05. In 1999/00 his profits were £80,000	11,700 (amount paid)
(e)	Dividends received on UK shares	900 (amount received)

Tasks

(a) Calculate the income tax payable by Mr Thesaurus for 2004/05.

(b) Explain how you have dealt with the personal pension contribution and the copyright royalty.

67000   1496
(6000)   1000

19 PAYE forms

An employer has certain responsibilities under the PAYE system to provide the Revenue and employees with various forms.

Tasks

(a) State what PAYE forms an employer must send to the Revenue following the tax year end. State the date(s) by which these forms must be provided.

(b)   State what PAYE forms an employer must provide to an employee following the tax year end. State the date(s) by which these forms must be provided.

(c)   State which PAYE form must be provided in respect of an employee who is leaving an employment and to whom this should be provided.

20 Frederick Fuse

You have just received the following letter from Mr Frederick Fuse. Mr Frederick Fuse is the managing director of a company called Nuts and Bolts Ltd.

Hammer, Wrench and Co   25 Town Road
Accountants   Lanchester
Credit Street
Lanchester   31 May 2005

Dear Ms Drill,

Income tax year ended 5 April 2005

The information you require to calculate my income tax liability for 2004/05, is as follows.

1   I receive a gross salary of £41,000 from my employment as Managing Director of Nuts and Bolts Limited. Income tax of £13,600 was deducted under the PAYE (Pay As You Earn) scheme, according to my form P60 for the tax year 2004/05.

2   Throughout 2004/05 I had the use of a company car with CO_2 emissions of 196g/km. The list price of the car was £14,000. The company supplied me with all petrol for business and private use.

3   The company reimbursed me with entertaining expenses of £3,000. I had incurred £2,900 of this amount on business entertaining. The company also reimbursed me with £700 in respect of home telephone expenses. £100 of this was for line rental and £600 was for calls. 50% of the calls were for business purposes.

4   From 6 December 2004, I had a company computer at home which I use for both private and business use. The computer cost £10,000.

5   The only other benefit I received from the company was private medical insurance. In 2004/05 this cost the company £965. If I had paid for the private medical insurance myself it would have cost me £1,265.

6   My dividend vouchers show that I received dividends of £3,330 in 2004/05. The tax credits attaching to these dividends were £370. In addition, I received £1,100 of interest on my bank account with the Nat west plc, £4,500 of interest on a high interest account with the Lanchester Building Society, £630 of interest on an individual Savings account and £95 of interest on a National Savings Bank investment account.

7   I paid £165 a month into my stakeholder pension scheme.

If you need further information please contact me.

Yours sincerely

Frederick Fuse

Task 1

Calculate Mr Fuse's taxable earnings including benefits for 2004/05.

Task 2

Prepare a schedule of income for 2004/05, clearly showing the difference between non-savings, savings and dividend income. Mr Fuse's personal allowance should be deducted as appropriate.

Task 3

Calculate the net income tax payable for 2004/05.

Task 4

The accountant of Nuts and Bolt Limited wants Mr Fuse to contribute towards some of the benefits he has received. He has suggested the following payments for 2005/06:

Payments towards the private use of the car   £100 per month
Payments towards the cost of private petrol   £10 per month (a contribution only, the full cost of private petrol would be approximately £1,000 for the year)

State how the above contributions will affect the benefits that Mr Fuse will be taxed on for 2005/06. You may assume the rules for taxing benefits in 2005/06 will be the same as they were in 2004/05.

21 The Benns

Benn, aged 51 on 1 January 2004, is married to Mrs Benn, aged 44. The following information relates to the year ended 5 April 2005.

(i) Mr Benn's salary was £40,720. His benefits have been agreed at £5,000.

(ii) During the year he paid a personal pension contribution of £8,700.

(iii) He also had the following income.

	£
Bank deposit account interest (net)	107
Building society interest (net)	320
Dividends (including tax credits)	1,230
Interest on mini cash ISA account	195

(iv) Mrs Benn owns a business that manufactures window frames. Her agreed profits taxable in 2004/05 are £9,800.

(v) Mrs Benn paid a patent royalty of £780 (net) in 2004/05.

(vi) Mrs Benn's dividends received totalled £100 (including tax credits).

Tasks

(a) Prepare a schedule for 2004/05 clearly showing the distinction between non savings, savings and dividend income for Mr Benn. Mr Benn's personal allowance should be deducted as appropriate.

(b) Compute Mr Benn's income tax liability for 2004/05.

(c) and (d)   Repeat the above tasks for Mrs Benn.

chapter 4

Investments and land

22 Tax rates

You have received the following letter from a client.

> 23 Charles Street
> Anytown
> AN1 4BQ
>
> H Jones
> Technicians & Co
> 14 Duke Street
> Notown
> NT4 5AZ
>
> 1 October 2004
>
> Dear Hilary
>
> You have always been very helpful in answering my tax queries, and I hope you will not mind my troubling you with this one. I heard recently that dividends are paid net of a 10% tax credit and that building society interest is paid net of 20% tax. However, I thought you told me that I won't need to pay any extra tax on my dividend or interest income. How can this be, since my marginal rate of tax is 22%?
>
> Yours sincerely
>
> *Anthony Smith*
>
> Anthony Smith

23 Nitin

Nitin starts to let out property on 1 July 2004. He has the following transactions.

(a)   On 1 July 2004, he lets a house which he has owned for several years. The tenant is required to pay annual rent of £8,000, quarterly in advance. The house is let unfurnished.

(b)   On 1 October 2004 he buys a badly dilapidated house for £350,000. During October, he spends £40,000 on making the house habitable. He lets it furnished for £3,600 a month from 1 November 2004, but the tenant leaves on 31 January 2005. A new tenant moves in on 1 March 2005, paying £21,000 a quarter in arrears. Water rates are £390 a year, payable by Nitin. Nitin also pays buildings insurance of £440 for the period from 1 October 2004 to 31 August 2005. He financed the purchase (but not the repairs) with a bank loan at 10% interest. Nitin decides to claim the renewals basis. He replaces some furniture on 1 May 2005, at a cost of £3,500. The tenant is responsible for all repair costs and council tax.

Task

Compute Nitin's Schedule A income for 2004/05.

Income - $\frac{9}{12} \times 8,000 = 6,000$

Total Income = 23,800
Less deductable = 17,935
Exp
5865

House 2
$3 \times 3600 = 10,800$
$\frac{1}{3} \times 21000 = 7,000$

Water = (~~390~~) 195
Ins 6×440 = (~~440~~) 240
Interest $350,000 \times 10\% \times \frac{5}{12}$ = (17500)

BPP
PROFESSIONAL EDUCATION

24 William Wiles

William Wiles acquired three houses on 6 April 2004. Houses 1 and 2 were acquired freehold, and are let as furnished holiday accommodation. House 3 was acquired on a 25 year lease, and is let furnished. During 2004/05 the houses were let as follows.

House 1 was available for letting for 42 weeks during 2004/05, and was actually let for 14 weeks at £375 per week. During the 10 weeks that the house was not available for letting, it was occupied rent free by William's sister. Running costs for 2004/05 consisted of business rates £730, insurance £310, and advertising £545.

House 2 was available for letting for 32 weeks during 2004/05, and was actually let for eight weeks at £340 per week. The house was not available for letting for 20 weeks due to a serious flood. As a result of the flood, £6,250 was spent on repairs. The damage was not covered by insurance. The other running costs for 2004/05 consisted of business rates £590, insurance £330, and advertising £225.

House 3 was unoccupied from 6 April 2004 until 31 December 2004. On 1 January 2005 the house was let on at a rent of £8,600 pa payable annually in advance. During 2004/05 he paid interest on a loan to purchase the property of £3,200 and spent £710 on redecorating the property during June 2004.

Immediately after their purchase, William furnished the three houses at a cost of £5,200 per house. He claimed a capital allowance of 50% (ie £2,600) where relevant. With the exception of the 10 week rent-free letting of house 1, all the lettings are at a full rent.

Tasks

(a) Briefly explain why both house 1 and house 2 qualify to be treated as a trade under the furnished holiday letting rules. State the tax advantages of the houses being so treated.

(b) Calculate William's allowable Schedule A loss for 2004/05, and advise him as to the possible ways of relieving the loss.

House 1   House 2   House

5250
730
310
545

chapters 5 and 6

Capital gains tax

This checklist shows which performance criteria are covered by each activity in this chapter. Full details of the performance criteria are provided on page (xiv) onwards. Tick off each activity as you complete it.

Activity

25		Performance Criteria 19.4A, 19.4C, 19.4D, 19.4E.
26		Performance Criteria 19.4A, 19.4C, 19.4D, 19.4E.
27		Performance Criteria 19.4A, 19.4C, 19.4D, 19.4E.
28		Performance Criteria 19.4D.
29		Performance Criteria 19.4C, 19.4D, 19.4E.

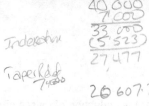
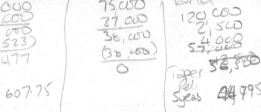

25 Oregon

Oregon disposed of assets in 2004/05 as follows.

(i)   On 6 June 2004, he sold an antique table for £40,000. He had bought it on 15 December 1984 for £7,000.

(ii)   On 18 July 2004 he sold a picture for £75,000. He had bought it for £37,000 in March 1982.

(iii)   On 12 November 2004 he sold a plot of land for £120,000, before expenses of sale of £2,500. He had bought the land as an investment in May 1999 for £57,000. In 2001 he spent £4,000 on new permanent drainage, and in May 2003 he spent £3,800 defending his title to the land.

Oregon's taxable income for 2004/05 is £80,000.

Tasks

(a)   Calculate the taxable gain or loss made on the disposal of the table after taper relief, if applicable.

(b)   Calculate the taxable gain or loss made on the disposal of the picture after taper relief, if applicable.

(c)   Calculate the taxable gain or loss made on the disposal of the plot of land after taper relief, if applicable.

(d)   Compute Oregon's total taxable gains after deduction of the annual exemption for 2004/05.

(e)   Compute Oregon's capital gains tax liability for 2004/05.

Assume the following indexation factors:

December 1984 to April 1998	0.789
March 1982 to April 1998	1.047

26 John Lewis

John Lewis carried out the following disposals of assets during 2004/05.

(a)   On 6 June 2004 he sold 4 acres of a 16 acre field he owned for £125,000. Expenses of the sale amounted to £300. John had acquired the entire field in December 2002 on the death of his uncle when it had been valued for probate at £500,000. The value of the remaining 12 acres on 6 June 2004 was £375,000.

(b)   On 2 October 2004 he sold his 1959 motor car to a friend for £2,000. He had purchased the car in December 1999 for £300 and had spent many hours restoring it as a hobby.

(c)   On 30 January 2005 he sold for £60,000 an investment property, which had been acquired in July 2001 for £25,000.

John Lewis had unused capital losses carried forward at 5 April 2002 of £2,500 and transactions in the following two years gave rise to gains and losses as follows.

	Gains £	Losses £	Annual exemption £
2002/03	8,000	1,000	7,700
2003/04	10,900	2,000	7,900

No taper relief was available to reduce the gains in either of the above years.

Tasks

(a) Compute John Lewis's net taxable gains for 2004/05 after the deduction of losses but before taper relief.

(b) Compute John Lewis's taxable gains for 2004/05 after the deduction of taper relief and the annual exemption.

(c) Compute John Lewis's capital gains tax liability for 2004/05 assuming that his income before the personal allowance is:

    (i)   £6,000
    (ii)   £34,480

27 Wyoming

In 2004/05, Wyoming made the following disposals.

	Gain/(loss) before taper relief
Asset	£
Motor car	(3,000) ✓
Picture	14,500
Gilt-edged securities	45,000 ✗
Quoted shares	20,000

All assets were sold for their market values and had been owned since 1997. The quoted shareholding was a non-business asset for taper relief purposes.

Wyoming'a statutory total income for 2004/05 was £20,150 (all non-savings).

Tasks

(a) Compute Wyoming's taxable income for 2004/05.
(b) Calculate Wyoming's income tax liability for 2004/05.
(c) Calculate Wyoming's total taxable gains for 2004/05 after deduction of taper relief and the annual exemption.
(d) Calculate Wyoming's capital gains tax liability for 2004/05.

28 Washington

Washington died on 5 October 2004. His gains and losses in recent years had been as follows.

Year	Gains	Losses	Annual exemption	
	£	£	£	
2001/02	2,000	10,000 (8,000)	7,500	~~select of~~ loss 0
2002/03	32,500	4,500 (8,500)	7,700	12,300
2003/04	10,100	2,000 ~~use 2000 loss~~ 7,900		200
2004/05	15,000	27,000 (12000)	8,200	0

Washington had no gains or losses in earlier years.

12,000 loss left over

Task

Compute the original and final taxable gains for each of the years 2001/02 to 2004/05.

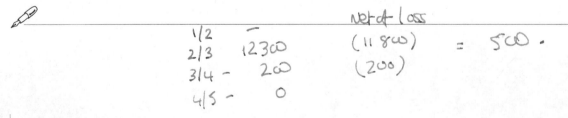

Net of loss
1/2   —
2/3   12300   (11 800)   = 500 .
3/4 -   200   (200)
4/5 -   0

BPP PROFESSIONAL EDUCATION

29 Alison Garry

Alison Garry sold two holiday cottages in 2004/05 as follows:

Cottage 1

	£
Proceeds of sale	95,000
Legal fees	(1,321)
Estate agent's fees	(1,597)
Net proceeds paid to client	92,082

Date of sale: 10 March 2005

Purchase price (June 1983): £41,000

Cottage 2

The solicitors paid Alison £85,000. She paid their fee of £850 and the estate agent's fee of £1,500 (date of sale 19 August 2004).

The cottage had cost £30,000 in March 1982. An extension had been added in June 1983 at a cost of £10,000.

Task 1

Compute the chargeable gain arising before taper relief on the disposal of cottage 1.

Task 2

Compute the chargeable gain arising before taper relief on the disposal of cottage 2.

Task 3

Compute Alison Garry's capital gains liability for 2004/05. You may assume that Alison Garry is a higher rate taxpayer.

Assume indexation factors

March 1982 to April 1998	1.047
June 1983 to April 1998	0.917

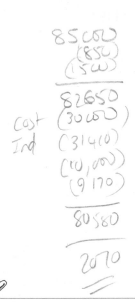

BPP
PROFESSIONAL EDUCATION

chapter 7

Shares and securities

Activity checklist

This checklist shows which performance criteria are covered by each activity in this chapter. Full details of the performance criteria are covered on page (xiv) onwards. Tick off each activity as you complete it.

Activity

30		Performance Criteria 19.4B, 19.4C and 19.4D.
31		Performance Criteria 19.4B, 19.4C and 19.4D.
32		Performance Criteria 19.4A, 19.4B, 19.4C, 19.4D and 19.4E.
33		Performance Criteria 19.4A, 19.4B, 19.4C and 19.4D.

30 Eleanor

Eleanor sold 11,000 ordinary shares in Biggs plc on 17 May 2004 for £66,000. She had bought ordinary shares in the company on the following dates.

	No of shares	Cost £
19 September 1982	2,000	1,700
17 January 1985	2,000	6,000
12 December 1985	2,000	5,500
29 June 2001	3,000	17,500
3 November 2002	2,000	12,800

Task

Calculate, after taper relief but before the annual exemption, the capital gain for 2004/05. The shares are not a business asset for taper relief purposes.

Assume the following indexation factors

September 1982 to April 1985	0.158
January 1985 to April 1985	0.039
April 1985 to December 1985	0.013
December 1985 to April 1998	0.693

Guidance notes

1 Disposals are matched with post April 1998 acquisitions on a LIFO basis before they are matched with the FA 1985 pool.

2 We must build up the FA 1985 pool (including all the first three acquisitions). Indexation is first given up to April 1985, and then up to each later purchase or sale. Remember that the FA 1985 pool closes on 5 April 1998 so the final indexation allowance calculation will be to that date.

3 Losses are set against gains before taper relief. They should be set against the gains that suffer the lowest rate of taper relief (ie the highest percentage of the gain remains taxable).

31 Yvonne

Yvonne had the following transactions in the shares of Scotia plc. The shares are a non business asset for taper relief purposes.

		Shares	£
18 August 1995	bought	3,000	6,000
19 September 2002	bought	2,000	5,000
13 March 2005	sold	5,000	23,000
28 March 2005	bought	1,000-	4,400

6000
510
6510

(Indexation factor August 1995 – April 1998 is 0.085)

Task

Calculate Yvonne's capital gain for 2004/05 after taper relief, but before the annual exemption.

4600
4400
200

9200
5000
4200

9200
6510
2690

7090

32 James Ramesty

James Ramesty, managing director of Beech Limited, has sold some shares, a car and a freehold holiday home during 2004/05. James Ramesty pays income tax at the 40% rate. The details of the disposals are as follows:

- **Sale of a holiday cottage**

  The solicitor's statement of the account was as follows: £

Proceeds of sale	160,000
Legal fees	(2,000)
Estate agent's fees	(1,000)
Net proceeds paid to client	157,000

Date of sale:	1 June 2004	Address of property:	The Coppice
Date of purchase:	1 October 1983		12 Green Lane
Purchase price:	£30,000		Torquay
			Devon SL6 1JH

- **Sale of shares in N and T plc**

  Transactions in these quoted shares have been as follows:

  Shares purchased

Date	Number of shares	Cost
		£
12 March 1989	200	400
04 May 1991	2,000	10,000
07 June 2001	3,000	15,000
12 July 2002	1,000	5,000

  There was also a bonus issue of shares on 21 June 1994. 1 bonus share was issued for every 2 shares held on that date. The shares are not a business asset for taper relief purposes.

  Shares sold

  James Ramesty sold all his shares in N and T plc for £41,010 on 10 January 2005.

- **Sale of car**

	£
Proceeds of sale	5,400
Purchase price	12,000
Date of purchase	12.6.00
Date of sale	3.3.05

James Ramesty had capital losses brought forward from 2003/04 of £1,000.

Task

(a) Calculate any chargeable gains arising on the disposals before taper relief.
(b) Calculate net taxable gains after deducting taper relief and the annual exemption.
(c) Calculate any capital gains tax payable for 2004/05.

Assume indexation factors

October 1983 to April 1998	0.883
March 1989 to May 1991	0.189
May 1991 to April 1998	0.218

Proceeds 3160
cost 3160 ×40,000   12 200
3160+   1940
72000   820
1120

33 Kay and Shirley

(a) Kay purchased 20 acres of land as an investment in February 1992 for £40,000. In March 2005 she sold part of the land for £31,600 when the value of the remainder was £72,000. Kay had made no other capital disposals in 2004/05.

Task

Calculate the capital gains chargeable on Kay, after the annual exemption for 2004/05.

(b) Shirley had the following dealings in the shares of Wingfield plc, a UK quoted company.

	Number of shares	£
January 1997 – bought	4,000	18,000
March 2001 – rights issue 1 for 4	1,000	7,000
November 2004 – bought	3,000	24,000
January 2005 – bonus issue 1 for 2	4,000	–
March 2005 – sold	7,000	56,000

The shares were not a business asset for taper relief purposes.

Task

Calculate Shirley's capital gain for 2004/05, before the annual exemption.

Assume indexation factors

May 1991 to April 1998	0.218
February 1992 to April 1998	0.193
January 1997 to April 1998	0.053

chapter 8

CGT: Additional aspects

Activity checklist

This checklist shows which performance criteria are covered by each activity in this chapter. Further details of the performance criteria are provided on page (xiv) onwards. Tick off each activity as you complete it.

Activity

Activity		Performance Criteria
34		Performance Criteria 19.4A, 19.4C and 19.4D.
35		Performance Criteria 19.4A, 19.4B, 19.4C, 19.4D and 19.4E.
36		Performance Criteria 19.4A, 19.4C and 19.4D.
37		Performance Criteria 19.4A, 19.4C, 19.4D and 19.4E.
38		Performance Criteria 19.4A, 19.4C and 19.4D.
39		Performance Criteria 19.4A, 19.4C, 19.4D and 19.4E.
40		Performance Criteria 19.4A, 19.4C, 19.4D and 19.4E.

34 Michelle

Michelle purchased an antique vase in March 1982 for £4,000 and sold it in November 2004 for £10,000. 10% sales commission was deducted from this sale price.

Task

Calculate Michelle's gain for 2004/05 (after taper relief but before the annual exemption).

Assume Indexation factor

March 1982 to April 1998 = 1.047

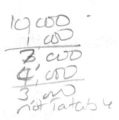

35 A cottage, shares and a chattel

John Hammond has an annual salary of £21,000. He had the following capital transactions in the year ended 5 April 2005.

(i)   On 5 May 2004 he sold his holiday cottage in Scotland for £100,000. The legal and advertising expenses of the sale were £800.

John had purchased the property on 31 March 1982 for £25,000 and had incurred costs of £8,000 on 1 December 1983 for the building of an extension.

The property had never been John's main residence.

(ii) On 14 September 2004 he sold 4,000 shares in JVD Products plc for £20,000, his previous transactions being as follows.

1 May 1997 purchased 2,000 shares cost £1,500
6 June 2001 purchased 500 shares cost £400
10 March 2002 purchased 500 shares cost £800
2 August 2004 purchased 2,800 shares cost £13,900

The shares are not a business asset for taper relief purposes.

(iii) On 27 October 2004 he sold an oil painting to his sister for £5,000. The market value at the date of sale was £7,000. Hammond had purchased the painting on 18 May 1997 for £10,000.

Tasks

(a)   Compute the taxable gain or loss arising on the disposal of the holiday cottage, after the deduction of taper relief if appropriate.

(b)   Compute the taxable gain or loss arising on disposal of the shares, after the deduction of taper relief, if appropriate.

(c)   Compute the taxable gain or loss arising on the disposal of the oil painting, after deducting taper relief if appropriate.

(d)   Compute the income tax and capital gains tax liabilities of John Hammond for the year 2004/05.

Assume indexation factors

March 1982 to April 1998	1.047
December 1983 to April 1998	0.871
May 1997 to April 1998	0.036

Guidance notes

1 The key date to remember in any CGT question is 5 April 1998.

2 All the assets were sold after 5 April 1998. Remember that the indexation allowance can only be calculated to April 1998 and not beyond that date.

3 Remember that shares acquired after 5.4.98 are treated as disposed of on a LIFO basis.

4 Calculations for disposals to connected persons proceed in the same way as normal transactions, but remember the relevance of market value and the restriction on setting off losses.

5 When you come to work out the tax liabilities, remember that the starting and basic rate bands must be used for both income and gains.

36 Geoff Williams

Geoff Williams made the following disposals of assets during the year 2004/05.

(i) On 14 April 2004 he sold a Ming vase for £10,000. This he had purchased on 8 July 1992 for £2,400 plus expenses of purchase of £100. Expenses of selling amounted to £500.

(ii) On 19 September 2004 a 25% share of a painting was sold for £20,000. The remaining 75% had a value of £90,000. The painting had originally been purchased for £40,000 in May 1987.

(iii) Another picture, which had cost £3,000 in August 1993, was sold for £5,500 in December 2004.

Task $1000 - 8000 \times \frac{1}{3} = 6667$

Calculate the chargeable gains for the tax year 2004/05.

Indexation factors

July 1992 – April 1998	0.171	
May 1987 – April 1998	0.596	index
August 1993 – April 1998	0.156	

(handwritten annotations)

10,000
cost 2,400
600
——
7,000
410
——
6590

Proceeds   20,000
7272
Costs = 20 × 40
———
20+90

PROFESSIONAL EDUCATION

37 Miss Wolf

Miss Wolf carried out the following capital transactions:

(a) On 30 June 2004 she sold a building originally acquired as an investment for £30,750. The building had cost £6,383 in January 1996.

(b) On 5 August 2004 she sold a picture for £9,000 at auction. The auctioneer's costs were 10% of the sale price. Miss Wolf had acquired the painting for £2,200 on 10 September 2000.

Miss Wolf had allowable losses of £2,203 brought forward to 2004/05. Miss Wolf's rate of income tax for the year was 40%.

Task

Prepare a statement showing Miss Wolf's capital gains tax payable for 2004/05.

Assume indexation factor: January 1996 to April 1998 = 0.083

38 Mr Fox

Mr Fox bought a house on 1 August 1985 for £50,000. He lived in the house until 31 July 1988. He then went abroad to work as a self-employed engineer until 31 July 1993.

Mr Fox went back to live in the house until 31 January 1994. He then moved in with his sister.

Mr Fox sold the house on 31 July 2004 for £180,000.

Task

Calculate the gain on sale after all reliefs.

Assume indexation factor: August 1985 to April 1998 = 0.703

39 John Harley

John Harley purchased a property on 1 August 1984 for £40,000 and lived in it until 31 May 1985 when he moved overseas to take up an offer of employment. He returned to the UK on 1 August 1989 and took employment in Scotland until 31 October 1995. During these periods he lived in rented accommodation. On 1 November 1995 he moved back into his own house until he moved out permanently on 30 June 1996. The house was then put up for sale and was finally sold on 30 November 2004 for £120,000. At all times when John was not in the house it remained empty.

Task

Calculate the chargeable gain on the sale of the house. A schedule of periods of exemption and non-exemption should be given, together with the reasons for exemption where applicable.

Assume indexation August 1984 – April 1998 = 0.808.

40 Peter Robinson

Peter Robinson made the following disposals of non-business assets during the tax year 2004/05.

1 September 2004:

His flat for £370,000. This Peter had purchased on 1 September 1990 for £21,000. Peter lived in the flat continuously until the date of sale.

1 February 2005:

A crystal chandelier for £7,500. This he had purchased in January 2003 for £4,000.

5 March 2005

A rare stamp for £20,000. This was acquired on 1 June 2004 at a stamp auction for £545

Task

Calculate Peter's capital gains tax payable for the year 2004/05. Peter's taxable income (after personal allowances) for income tax purposes was £27,500.

Proceeds - 370,000
Costs   - (21,000)
            349,000

14 years

A Nil
B 2500
C 19455
   21955
   8200
   13755

3900 × 20% = 780
9855 × 40% = 3942

          4722

7500
4000
3500

$\frac{5}{3}$ × (7500 - 6000) = 2500

20,000
  545
19,455

$\frac{5}{3}$ × (2900 - 600)

= 23,333

hence 19455

chapter 9

Administration and completion of tax return

Activity checklist

This checklist shows which performance criteria are covered by each activity in this chapter. Full details of the performance criteria are covered on page (xiv) onwards. Tick off each activity as you complete it.

Activity

41		Performance Criteria 19.3E, 19.3G, 19.4G and 19.4I.
42		Performance criteria 19.1D, 19.1F, 19.2F, 19.2H, 19.3E, 19.3G, 19.4G and 19.4I.
43		Performance criteria 19.2A, 19.2B, 19.2E, 19.2F, 19.2H, 19.3A, 19.3B, 19.3C, 19.3D, 19.3E and 19.3G.
44		Performance criteria 19.1A, 19.1B, 19.1C, 19.1D, 19.2A, 19.2C, 19.3A, 19.3B, 19.3C, 19.3D and 19.3E.

41 Mr Brown

Mr Brown's income tax liability for 2003/04 was £16,000. He had suffered tax by deduction at source of £4,000 and paid two payments on account of £6,000 each on the due dates. He submitted his 2003/04 return on 31 January 2005. Mr Brown made a claim to reduce his payments on account for 2004/05 on the basis that this total liability for 2004/05 would be £14,000 with tax suffered of £5,000. He made the payments on account of £4,500 on 28 February and 14 August 2005. Finally, on 13 March 2006 he submitted his return for 2004/05 which showed total tax due of £17,000 and tax deducted at source of £4,000. He therefore paid a further £4,000 on the same date.

Tasks

(a) Outline the time limits for submission of returns and payments of tax under self assessment and detail the provisions for failure to comply.

(b) Calculate the interest on overdue tax chargeable in respect of Mr Brown's tax payments for 2004/05. You are not required to compute any surcharges payable.

Note. Assume interest is charged at 6.5% per annum.

42 John Jefferies

John Jefferies is a senior manager working for a large UK resident trading company. He has an annual salary of £48,000 and has a company car, provided for the whole year.

The car is a petrol driven Ford with a list price of £18,000 (although the company only paid £16,000 for it under a group scheme). The CO_2 emissions of the car are 229 g/km. All the running costs, including fuel, are paid for by the company.

He pays 10% of his gross salary (not including the value of the car) to a personal pension plan. This amount represents the gross amount of premiums due.

He also pays £140 per year to the Institute of Management (which his employers insist upon), and £300 per year membership to a local sports club that his employers require him to be a member of. This, they say, will enable him to maintain good relations with possible customers.

During the year ended 5 April 2005 he also received the following income.

	£
Dividends	1,800
National Savings Bank easy access account interest	300
Child benefit (Not taxable)	1,260
Rental income	5,400

All the above amounts represent the actual cash figure received.

Expenses relating to the rental income were as follows.

	£
Council tax	700
Water rates	350
Agents fees	600
New window frames	2,400
Boiler repairs	350

He has also spent £400 on new furniture. He claims the standard wear and tear allowance allowed by the Revenue.

A Schedule A loss of £1,130 was made in the year 2003/04.

John paid £390 (net) to a national charity in November 2004.

Tasks

(a)   Calculate the taxable income of John Jefferies for 2004/05.

(b)   Calculate the income tax payable by John Jefferies for 2004/05.

(c)   Mr Jefferies has received his annual self-assessment return and requires advice on the system. Acting as Mr Jefferies' tax advisor write to him explaining the following.

(i)   How long he needs to keep details of tax information.

(ii)   What deadlines he needs to meet.

(iii)   How and by when any payment should be made.

Mr Jefferies did not receive the new Short Tax return.

43 Kitty Bennett

Miss Bennett owns her own business: 'Longbourn Gift Shop'. Schedule D Case I profits have been calculated as £18,716 for 2004/05.

Miss Bennett made the following payments on account of her 2004/05 tax liability

31 January 2005	£500
31 July 2005	£500

Miss Bennett's other income is as follows.

1   **Rented property – Pemberley Court (flat)**

Rented from 1 January 2004 to 30 September 2004 at an annual rental of £4,000.

Rented from 1 October 2004 to date at an annual rental of £5,000.

Expenses 2004/05	£
Property management fees	800
Interest on £35,000 loan to purchase the flat	2,450
Repairs to roof	400

2   **Dividend Vouchers – shares held**

Wickham plc

Final dividend for the year ended 31 December 2003 – Paid 31 October 2004

Tax credit	Net dividend received
£400	£3,600

Interim dividend for the year ended 31 December 2004 – Paid 31 March 2005

Tax credit	Net dividend received
£300	£2,700

3   **Building society interest**

Date	Gross interest £	Tax deducted at source £	Net interest £
30.06.04	2,500.00	500.00	2,000.00
31.12.04	2,100.00	420.00	1,680.00

4   **Bank interest**

Date	Gross interest £	Tax deducted at source £	Net interest £
30.09.04	800.00	160.00	640.00
31.03.05	1,190.00	238.00	952.00

Task 1

Prepare a calculation of Schedule A income for 2004/05.

Task 2

Prepare schedules of Kitty Bennett's dividend and interest income for 2004/05.

Task 3

Compute Miss Bennett's income tax payable for 2004/05.

Task 4

Explain how much income tax is outstanding for 2004/05 and what payments of account must be made for 2005/06.

Task 5

Complete the supplementary property pages which will need to accompany Miss Bennett's tax return form.

Income for the year ended 5 April 2005

Inland Revenue

LAND AND PROPERTY

Name

Fill in these boxes first

Tax reference

If you want help, look up the box numbers in the Notes.

Are you claiming Rent a Room relief for gross rents of £4,250 or less?
(Or £2,125 if the claim is shared?)
Read the Notes on page LN2 to find out
- whether you can claim Rent a Room relief; and
- how to claim relief for gross rents over £4,250

Yes | If 'Yes', tick box. If this is your only income from UK property, you have finished these Pages

Is your income from furnished holiday lettings?
If not applicable, please turn over and fill in Page L2 to give details of your property income

Yes | If 'Yes', tick box and fill in boxes 5.1 to 5.18 before completing Page L2

Furnished holiday lettings

- Income from furnished holiday lettings | **5.1** £

- *Expenses* (furnished holiday lettings only)

- Rent, rates, insurance, ground rents etc. | **5.2** £
- Repairs, maintenance and renewals | **5.3** £
- Finance charges, including interest | **5.4** £
- Legal and professional costs | **5.5** £
- Costs of services provided, including wages | **5.6** £
- Other expenses | **5.7** £

total of boxes 5.2 to 5.7
5.8 £

Net profit (put figures in brackets if a loss)

box 5.1 *minus* box 5.8
5.9 £

- *Tax adjustments*

- Private use | **5.10** £
- Balancing charges | **5.11** £

box 5.10 + box 5.11
5.12 £

- Capital allowances | **5.13** £

- Tick box 5.13A if box 5.13 includes enhanced capital allowances for environmentally friendly expenditure | **5.13A**

boxes 5.9 + 5.12 minus box 5.13
5.14 £

Profit for the year (copy to box 5.19). If loss, enter '0' in box 5.14 and put the loss in box 5.15

boxes 5.9 + 5.12 *minus* box 5.13
5.15 £

Loss for the year (if you have entered '0' in box 5.14)

- *Losses*

- Loss offset against 2004-05 total income | **5.16** £

see Notes, page LN4
- Loss carried back | **5.17** £

see Notes, page LN4
- Loss offset against other income from property (copy to box 5.38) | **5.18** £

SA105

BPP PROFESSIONAL EDUCATION

Other property income

■ Income

copy from box 5.14

- Furnished holiday lettings profits **5.19** £

Tax deducted

- Rents and other income from land and property **5.20** £   **5.21** £

- Chargeable premiums **5.22** £

boxes 5.19 + 5.20 + 5.22 + 5.22A

- Reverse premiums **5.22A** £   **5.23** £

■ Expenses (do not include figures you have already put in boxes 5.2 to 5.7 on Page L1)

- Rent, rates, insurance, ground rents etc. **5.24** £

- Repairs, maintenance and renewals **5.25** £

- Finance charges, including interest **5.26** £

- Legal and professional costs **5.27** £

- Costs of services provided, including wages **5.28** £

total of boxes 5.24 to 5.29

- Other expenses **5.29** £   **5.30** £

box 5.23 minus box 5.30

Net profit (put figures in brackets if a loss)   **5.31** £

■ Tax adjustments

- Private use **5.32** £

box 5.32 + box 5.33

- Balancing charges **5.33** £   **5.34** £

- Rent a Room exempt amount **5.35** £

- Capital allowances **5.36** £

- Tick box 5.36A if box 5.36 includes a claim for 100% capital allowances for flats over shops **5.36A**

- Tick box 5.36B if box 5.36 includes enhanced capital allowances for environmentally friendly expenditure **5.36B**

- 10% wear and tear **5.37** £

boxes 5.35 to box 5.38

- Furnished holiday lettings losses (from box 5.18) **5.38** £   **5.39** £

boxes 5.31 + 5.34 minus box 5.39

Adjusted profit (if loss enter '0' in box 5.40 and put the loss in box 5.41)   **5.40** £

boxes 5.31 + 5.34 minus box 5.39

Adjusted loss (if you have entered '0' in box 5.40)   **5.41** £

- Loss brought forward from previous year   **5.42** £

box 5.40 minus box 5.42

Profit for the year   **5.43** £

■ Losses etc

- Loss offset against total income (read the note on page LN8)   **5.44** £

- Loss to carry forward to following year   **5.45** £

- Tick box 5.46 if these Pages include details of property let jointly   **5.46**

- Tick box 5.47 if **all** property income ceased in the year to 5 April 2005 **and** you don't expect to receive such income again, in the year to 5 April 2006   **5.47**

Now fill in any other supplementary Pages that apply to you.
Otherwise, go back to page 2 of your Tax Return and finish filling it in.

BS 12/04net   TAX RETURN ■ LAND AND PROPERTY: PAGE L2

44 Mr Watson

You have received a copy of the following letter from John Watson.

25 Abbey Grange
Boscombe Valley

Doyle and Co
Three Gables Road
Boscombe Valley   1.5.2005

Dear Sirs,

Income tax return

Further to your recent letter I can give you the following information needed to complete my tax return for the year ended 5 April 2005.

1   Pay: £30,250, tax deducted £9,059.

2   Benefits

    Car, cost £15,850, supplied new from 1 January 2004
    The car emits 160g/km of CO_2
    My contribution for private use for the year: £600
    Petrol provided for all use

Medical insurance	£656
Travel costs reimbursed	£1,255
Entertaining costs reimbursed	£1,254
Telephone costs reimbursed – rental	£125
– calls	£595

    Video, cost £650 on 6 April 2004 and lent to me for private use from that date.

Please note that 40% of my telephone calls were for business purposes and that all of the travel and entertaining costs were for business purposes.

3   Dividend vouchers for my shares are enclosed.

4   Interest statements from my building society and bank accounts are enclosed.

I hope this is all you need to complete the return, but if you need any further information, please do not hesitate to contact me.

Yours faithfully

John Watson

John Watson

The Red Headed League plc

Final dividend for the year ended 31 March 2004
Paid 31 October 2004

Gross dividend	Tax credit	Net dividend
£2,000	£200	£1,800

The Red Headed League plc

Interim dividend for the year ended 31 March 2005
Paid 31 March 2005

Gross dividend	Tax credit	Net dividend
£1,000	£100	£900

STRAND BUILDING SOCIETY
INTEREST STATEMENT 2004/05
HIGH INTEREST ACCOUNT
MR JOHN WATSON
ACCOUNT NUMBER 44332211A

Date	Gross interest	Tax deducted at source	Net interest
	£	£	£
30.06.04	5,960.00	1,192.00	4,768.00
31.12.04	6,110.00	1,222.00	4,888.00

BANK OF WALES
INTEREST STATEMENT 2004/05
INVESTMENT ACCOUNT
MR JOHN WATSON
ACCOUNT NUMBER 55667788B

Date	Gross interest	Tax deducted at source	Net interest
	£	£	£
30.09.04	550.00	110.00	440.00
31.03.05	630.00	126.00	504.00

Task 1

Prepare a calculation of taxable earnings for 2004/05.

Task 2

Prepare a schedules showing John Watson's dividend and interest income for 2004/05.

Task 3

Compute income tax payable for Mr Watson for 2004/05.

Task 4

Complete Mr Watson's supplementary employment pages that will accompany Mr Watson's income tax return form.

Task 5

John Watson is considering changing jobs in the near future. State, for any particular activity, whether he can choose between employed and self employed status, If not, state the main considerations to be made in determining whether an individual is self employed or employed.

Income for the year ended 5 April 2005

Inland Revenue

EMPLOYMENT

Fill in these boxes first

Name

Tax reference

If you want help, look up the box numbers in the Notes.

Details of employer

Employer's PAYE reference - may be shown under 'Inland Revenue office number and reference' on your P60 or 'PAYE reference' on your P45

1.1

Employer's name

1.2

Date employment started
(only if between 6 April 2004 and 5 April 2005)

1.3 / /

Employer's address

1.5

Date employment finished
(only if between 6 April 2004 and 5 April 2005)

1.4 / /

Tick box 1.6 if you were a director of the company

1.6

and, if so, tick box 1.7 if it was a close company

1.7

Postcode

Income from employment

■ *Money - see Notes, page EN3*

Before tax

● Payments from P60 (or P45) **1.8** £

● Payments not on P60, etc. - tips **1.9** £

- other payments (excluding expenses entered below and lump sums and compensation payments or benefits entered overleaf) **1.10** £

Tax deducted

● **Tax deducted** in the UK from payments in boxes 1.8 to 1.10 **1.11** £

■ *Benefits and expenses - see Notes, pages EN3 to EN6. If any benefits connected with termination of employment were received, or enjoyed, after that termination and were from a former employer you need to complete Help Sheet IR204, available from the Orderline. Do not enter such benefits here.*

Amount

● Assets transferred/ payments made for you **1.12** £

Amount

● Vans **1.18** £

Amount

● Vouchers, credit cards and tokens **1.13** £

Amount

● Interest-free and low-interest loans see Note for box 1.19, page EN5 **1.19** £

Amount

● Living accommodation **1.14** £

box 1.20 is not used

Amount

● Excess mileage allowances and passenger payments **1.15** £

Amount

● Private medical or dental insurance **1.21** £

Amount

● Company cars **1.16** £

Amount

● Other benefits **1.22** £

Amount

● Fuel for company cars **1.17** £

Amount

● Expenses payments received and balancing charges **1.23** £

SA101

BS 12/04net

TAX RETURN ■ EMPLOYMENT: PAGE E1

Please turn over

PROFESSIONAL EDUCATION

Income from employment continued

■ *Lump sums and compensation payments or benefits including such payments and benefits from a former employer*
Note that 'lump sums' here includes any contributions which your employer made to an unapproved retirement benefits scheme

*You must read page EN6 of the Notes **before** filling in boxes 1.24 to 1.30*

Reliefs

- £30,000 exception **1.24** £
- Foreign service and disability **1.25** £
- Retirement and death lump sums **1.26** £

Taxable lump sums

- From box B of *Help Sheet IR204* **1.27** £
- From box K of *Help Sheet IR204* **1.28** £
- From box L of *Help Sheet IR204* **1.29** £
- Tax deducted from payments in boxes 1.27 to 1.29 - *leave blank if this tax is included in the box 1.11 figure and tick box 1.30A.* Tax deducted **1.30** £
- Tick this box if you have left box 1.30 blank because the tax is included in the box 1.11 figure **1.30A**

■ *Foreign earnings not taxable in the UK in the year ended 5 April 2005 - see Notes, page EN6* **1.31** £

■ *Expenses you incurred in doing your job - see Notes, pages EN7 to EN8*

- Travel and subsistence costs **1.32** £
- Fixed deductions for expenses **1.33** £
- Professional fees and subscriptions **1.34** £
- Other expenses and capital allowances **1.35** £
- Tick box 1.36 if the figure in box 1.32 includes travel between your home and a permanent workplace **1.36**

■ *Seafarers' Earnings Deduction* **1.37** £

■ *Foreign tax for which tax credit relief not claimed* **1.38** £

Student Loans

■ *Student Loans repaid by deduction by employer - see Notes, page EN8* **1.39** £

- Tick box 1.39A if your income is under Repayment of Teachers' Loans Scheme **1.39A**

1.40 *Additional information*

Now fill in any other supplementary Pages that apply to you.
Otherwise, go back to page 2 in your Tax Return and finish filling it in.

PART F

Full Exam based Assessments

PRACTICE EXAM PAPER 1

TECHNICIAN STAGE – NVQ4

Unit 19

Preparing personal tax computations (PTC)

DO NOT OPEN THIS PAPER UNTIL YOU ARE READY TO START
UNDER EXAM CONDITIONS

INSTRUCTIONS

This examination paper is in TWO sections.

You have to show competence in BOTH sections.

You should therefore attempt and aim to compete EVERY task in EACH section.

You should spend about 90 minutes on Section 1 and 90 minutes on Section 2.

COVERAGE OF PERFORMANCE CRITERIA

The following performance criteria are covered in this exam.

Element	PC Coverage
19.1	**Calculate income from employment**
A	Prepare accurate computations of emoluments, including benefits
B	List allowable expenses and deductions
C	Record relevant details of income from employment accurately and legibly in the tax return
D	Make computations and submissions in accordance with current tax law and take account of current Revenue practice
19.2	**Calculate property and investment income**
B	Prepare schedules of property income and determine profits and losses
D	Apply deductions and reliefs and claim loss set-offs
E	Record relevant details of property and invest income accurately and legibly in the tax return
F	Make computations and submissions are made in accordance with current tax law and take account of current Inland Revenue practice
19.3	**Prepare Income Tax Computations**
A	List general income, savings income and dividend income and check for completeness
B	Calculate and deduct charges and personal allowance
C	Calculate Income Tax payable
D	Record income and payments legibly and accurately in the tax return
E	Make computations and submissions are made in accordance with current tax law and take account of current Revenue practice
19.4	**Prepare capital gains tax computations**
A	Identify and value disposed-of chargeable assets
C	Calculate chargeable gains and allowable losses
D	Apply reliefs and exemptions correctly
E	Calculate Capital Gains Tax payable
F	Record details of gains and the Capital Gains Tax payable legibly and accurately in the tax return
G	More computations and submissions are made in accordance with current tax law and take account of current Revenue practice

Section 1

DATA

Mrs Austen has been one of Mole and Co's clients for a number of years. She is employed as a director of a local company and also has rental income. Mrs Austen has provided you with the attached P60, P11D and property income statement for 2004/05.

Mrs Austen had given you the following additional information.

Date of birth: 31 March 1969

Employment: Director of Book Supplies Limited

In receipt of salary (see Form P60) and benefits (see Form P11D). Note that some of the information that would normally be on the P11D (cash equivalent of benefits) has been omitted for exam purposes.

Entertaining expenditure is generally all deductible as an employment expense.

Task 1.1

Prepare a calculation of taxable earnings for 2004/05.

Task 1.2

Prepare a computation of Schedule A rental income for 2004/05.

Task 1.3

Complete the employment and the land and property pages that will accompany Mrs Austen's income tax return for 2004/05.

Task 1.4

Calculate Mrs Austen's taxable income for 2004/05.

Task 1.5

Calculate income tax payable for 2004/05. Mrs Austen did not make any payments on account in respect of her 2004/05 tax.

Section 2

DATA

Mrs Austen sold two of her rental properties on 30 April 2004. Mrs Austen held the freehold interest in both properties. The sale proceeds, costs of sale and original cost of both properties were as follows:

	Property 1	Property 2
Sale Proceeds	£300,000	£100,200
Costs of sale (Toad & Co's fees)	£1,500	£2,000
Original cost of building on 31 March 1982/25 June 1994	£125,000	£25,000

In 2003/04 Mrs Austen had capital losses of £10,000, unused and available to carry forward against future capital gains.

Tasks to be completed on Mrs Jane Austen's capital gains tax liability.

Task 2.1

Calculate the capital gains before taper relief on the two disposals for 2004/05.

Task 2.2

Calculate the capital gains tax payable for 2004/05.

Task 2.3

Write a covering letter to Mrs Austen, enclosing the income tax computation, capital gains tax computation and self assessment return, and advising her of the amount of tax to be paid and of the due date by which payment should be made.

300,000
1 500
298,500 0
Cost (125,000)
Indexation (130 875)
42 625

100 200
2,000
98,200
Cost 25,000
Index 3 100
70,100

Total Gain 112725
B/f Loss 10,000
102725

Taper Relief 75%
less 87043.75
8200.00
68 843.75

22   40%x7634375   37537.50

P60 End of Year Certificate

Tax Year to 5 April | 2005

To the employee:

Please keep this certificate in a safe place as you will not be able to get a duplicate. **You will need it if you have to fill in a Tax Return.**

You can also use it to check that your employer is deducting the right rate of National Insurance contributions for you and using your correct National Insurance number.

By law you are required to tell the Inland Revenue about any income that is not fully taxed, even if you are not sent a Tax Return.

INLAND REVENUE

Employee's details

Surname

Forenames or initials

National Insurance number

Works/payroll number

Pay and Income Tax details

	Pay £ p	Tax deducted £ p
In previous employment(s)		

	Pay	Tax deducted *if refund mark 'R'*
In this employment	41,000 00	15,000 00

Figures shown here should be used for your Tax Return, if you get one

Final tax code

Employee's Widows & Orphans/Life Assurance contributions in this employment

£ p

National Insurance contributions in this employment

NIC table letter	Earnings up to and including the Earnings Threshold (where earnings are equal to or exceed the Lower Earnings Limit) £	Earnings above the Earnings Threshold, up to and including the Upper Earnings Limit £	Employee's **contributions payable** on earnings in previous column £ p

Employee's contributions above to be reduced by this amount of NIC rebate £ p

This applies only to employees in contracted-out occupational pension schemes

Employee's contributions are payable on earnings above the 'Earnings Threshold', up to and including the 'Upper Earnings Limit'

Other details

Student Loan Deductions in this employment £

Tax Credits in this employment £ p

To Employee

Employer's full name and address (including Postcode)

Employer's PAYE reference

Certificate by Employer/Paying Office:

This form shows your total pay for Income Tax purposes in this employment for the year. Any overtime, bonus, commission etc, statutory sick pay or statutory maternity pay is included. It also shows, for this employment, total Income Tax and National Insurance contributions deducted (less any refunds), Student Loan deductions made, and Tax Credits paid to you.

Revenue

P11D EXPENSES AND BENEFITS 2004-05

Note to employer
Complete this return for a director, or an employee who earned at a rate of £8,500 a year or more during the year 6 April 2004 to 5 April 2005. Do not include expenses and benefits covered by a dispensation or PAYE settlement agreement. Read the P11D Guide and booklet 480, Chapter 24, before you complete the form. Send the completed P11D and form P11D(b) to the Inland Revenue office by 6 July 2005. You must give a copy of this information to the director or employee by the same date. The term employee is used to cover both directors and employees throughout the rest of this form.

Note to employee
Your employer has filled in this form. Keep it in a safe place as you may not be able to get a duplicate. You will need it for your tax records and to complete your 2004-05 Tax Return if you get one. Your tax code may need to be adjusted to take account of the information given on this P11D. The box numbers on this P11D have the same numbering as the Employment Pages of the Tax Return, for example, 1.12. Include the total figures in the corresponding box on the Tax Return, unless you think some other figure is more appropriate.

Employer's details
Employer's name: Book Supplies Ltd
PAYE tax reference: B452

Employee's details
Employee's name: Jane Austen
If a director tick here ✓
Works number/department:
National Insurance number: NB 40 20 30 E

Employers pay Class 1A National Insurance contributions on most benefits. These are shown in boxes which are brown and have a **1A** indicator

A Assets transferred (cars, property, goods or other assets)
Cost/Market value £ – Amount made good or from which tax deducted £ = Cash equivalent **1.12** £ **1A**
Description of asset

B Payments made on behalf of employee
Description of payment **1.12** £
Tax on notional payments not borne by employee within 30 days of receipt of each notional payment **1.12** £

C Vouchers or credit cards
Value of vouchers and payments made using credit cards or tokens
Gross amount £ – Amount made good or from which tax deducted £ = Cash equivalent **1.13** £

D Living accommodation
Cash equivalent of accommodation provided for employee, or his/her family or household **1.14** £ **1A**

E Mileage allowance
Car and mileage allowances paid for employee's car
Gross amount £ – Amount made good or from which tax deducted £ = Taxable payment **1.15** £

F Cars and car fuel If more than two cars were made available, either at the same time or in succession, please give details on a separate sheet

	Car 1	Car 2
Make and Model	Vauxhall Vectra	
Dates car was available	From / / to / /	From / / to / /
Enter CO₂ emissions data for the car	195 g/km	g/km
Tick type of fuel	Petrol ✓ Diesel	Petrol Diesel
List price of car	£ 19,000	£
Price of optional accessories fitted when car was first made available to the employee	£	£
Price of accessories added after the car was first made available to the employee	£	£
Capital contributions (maximum £5,000) the employee made towards the cost of car or accessories	£	£
Amount paid by employee for private use of the car	£ 600	£
Cash equivalent of each car	£	£

Total cash equivalent of all cars available in 2004-05 **1.16** £ **1A**
Cash equivalent of fuel for each car £ £
Total cash equivalent of fuel for all cars available in 2004-05 **1.17** £ **1A**

 223

G | **Vans**
Cash equivalent of all vans made available for private use | **1.18** £ | 1A

H | **Interest-free and low interest loans**
If the total amount outstanding on all loans does not exceed £5,000 at any time in the year, there is no need for details in this section.

	Loan 1	Loan 2
Number of joint borrowers *(if applicable)*		
Amount outstanding at 5 April 2004 or at date loan was made if later	£	£
Amount outstanding at 5 April 2005 or at date loan was discharged if earlier	£	£
Maximum amount outstanding at any time in the year	£	£
Total amount of interest paid by the borrower in 2004-05 – *enter "NIL" if none was paid*	£	£
Date loan was made in 2004-05 if applicable	/ /	/ /
Date loan was discharged in 2004-05 if applicable	/ /	/ /
Cash equivalent of loans after deducting any interest paid by the borrower	**1.19** £ 1A	**1.19** £ 1A

I | **Private medical treatment or insurance**

	Cost to you	Amount made good or from which tax deducted	Cash equivalent
Private medical treatment or insurance	£ 965	– £	= **1.21** £ 965	1A

J | **Qualifying relocation expenses payments and benefits**
Non-qualifying benefits and expenses go in N and O below

Excess over £8,000 of all qualifying relocation expenses payments and benefits for each move | **1.22** £ | 1A

K | **Services supplied**

	Cost to you	Amount made good or from which tax deducted	Cash equivalent
Services supplied to the employee	£	– £	= **1.22** £	1A

L | **Assets placed at the employee's disposal**

		Annual value plus expenses incurred	Amount made good or from which tax deducted	Cash equivalent
Description of asset	*Video recorder (made available 1.7.04 - cost £1,500)*	£	– £	= **1.22** £ 1,500	1A

M | **Shares**
Tick the box if during the year there have been share-related benefits for the employee | ☐

N | **Other items (including subscriptions and professional fees)**

		Cost to you	Amount made good or from which tax deducted	Cash equivalent
Description of other items		£	– £	= **1.22**	1A
Description of other items		£	– £	= **1.22** £

	Tax paid
Income tax paid but not deducted from director's remuneration	**1.22**

O | **Expenses payments made to, or on behalf of, the employee**

		Cost to you	Amount made good or from which tax deducted	Taxable payment
Travelling and subsistence payments		£	– £	= **1.23** £
Entertainment *(trading organisations read P11D Guide and then enter a tick or a cross as appropriate here)*	☐	£ 3,500	– £	= **1.23** £ 3,500
General expenses allowance for business travel	✓	£	– £	= **1.23** £
Payments for use of home telephone		£	– £	= **1.23** £
Non-qualifying relocation expenses *(those not shown in sections J or N)*		£	– £	= **1.23** £
Description of other expenses		£	– £	= **1.23** £

Property Rental Agencies Limited

Rental income and expenditure statement

Client: Mrs Jane Austen
Dates: 6 April 2004 to 5 April 2005

Furnished property let	1	2	3	4
Rental Income	4,000	3,000	2,000	6,500
Less expenses				
Management fees	400	300	200	650
Buildings insurance	100	100	100	100
Contents insurance	50	50	50	50
Cleaning	260	260	260	260
Repairs	100	250	3,000	50
Council Tax	450	350	200	350
Total remitted to client in year	2,640	1,690	(1,810)	5,040
Total				£7,560

Please note: all properties were fully let all year and are fully furnished.

Property Rental Agencies Limited
12 Another Street
Anytown

Margaret Jones
Tax Manager
Mole and Co Chartered Accountants
24 Main Street
Anytown

Dear Ms Jones

Mrs Jane Austen – Property rental statement for 2004/05

Further to your recent letter concerning the repairs expenditure shown on the above statement, we are able to provide the following additional information:

Property	Amount	Description
1	£100	Repainting the doors and windows
2	£250	Repairing a chimney damaged by bad weather
3	£3,000	Building a kitchen extension
4	£50	Repainting the front door

I hope this is enough information, but should you require any more details please contact us.

Yours sincerely

John Smith

Property Letting Consultant

TAXATION TABLES

Capital gains tax

Annual Exemption

2004/05   £8,200

Indexation factors:

March 1982 to April 1998   1.047
June 1994 to April 1998   0.124

Income tax – 2004/05

Personal allowance	£4,745
Taxed at 10%	£2,020
Taxed at 22% (next)	£29,380
Taxed at 40%	The balance

Savings (excl. dividend) income that falls in the basic rate band is taxed at 20%. Any dividend income in the starting or basic rate band is taxed at 10% and dividend income that exceeds the higher rate threshold is taxed at 32.5%.

Fuel benefit

Flat rate, £14,400

Car benefit

Baseline CO_2 emissions 145 g/km.

Tapering reliefs for capital gains tax

The percentage of the gain chargeable is as follows

No of complete tax years after 5 April 1998	Gains on Non-business assets
0	100.0
1	100.0
2	100.0
3	95.0
4	90.0
5	85.0
6	80.0
7	75.0
8	70.0
9	65.0
10 or more	60.0

Income for the year ended 5 April 2005

Inland Revenue

EMPLOYMENT

Fill in these boxes first

Name	Tax reference

If you want help, look up the box numbers in the Notes.

Details of employer

Employer's PAYE reference - may be shown under 'Inland Revenue office number and reference' on your P60 or 'PAYE reference' on your P45

1.1

Employer's name

1.2

Date employment started
(only if between 6 April 2004 and 5 April 2005)

1.3 / /

Date employment finished
(only if between 6 April 2004 and 5 April 2005)

1.4 / /

Employer's address

1.5

Postcode

Tick box 1.6 if you were a director of the company

1.6

and, if so, tick box 1.7 if it was a close company

1.7

Income from employment

■ *Money - see Notes, page EN3*

Before tax

● Payments from P60 (or P45) — **1.8** £

● Payments not on P60, etc. - tips — **1.9** £

- other payments (excluding expenses entered below and lump sums and compensation payments or benefits entered overleaf) — **1.10** £

Tax deducted

● **Tax deducted** in the UK from payments in boxes 1.8 to 1.10 — **1.11** £

■ *Benefits and expenses - see Notes, pages EN3 to EN6. If any benefits connected with termination of employment were received, or enjoyed, after that termination and were from a **former** employer you need to complete Help Sheet IR204, available from the Orderline. Do not enter such benefits here.*

	Amount			Amount
● Assets transferred/ payments made for you	**1.12** £		● Vans	**1.18** £
● Vouchers, credit cards and tokens	**1.13** £		● Interest-free and low-interest loans *see Note for box 1.19, page EN5*	**1.19** £
● Living accommodation	**1.14** £		*box 1.20 is not used*	
● Excess mileage allowances and passenger payments	**1.15** £		● Private medical or dental insurance	**1.21** £
● Company cars	**1.16** £		● Other benefits	**1.22** £
● Fuel for company cars	**1.17** £		● Expenses payments received and balancing charges	**1.23** £

SA101

BPP PROFESSIONAL EDUCATION

Income from employment continued

■ *Lump sums and compensation payments or benefits including such payments and benefits from a former employer*
Note that 'lump sums' here includes any contributions which your employer made to an unapproved retirement benefits scheme

You must read page EN6 of the Notes before filling in boxes 1.24 to 1.30

Reliefs

- £30,000 exception **1.24** £
- Foreign service and disability **1.25** £
- Retirement and death lump sums **1.26** £

Taxable lump sums

- From box B of *Help Sheet IR204* **1.27** £
- From box K of *Help Sheet IR204* **1.28** £
- From box L of *Help Sheet IR204* **1.29** £

- Tax deducted from payments in boxes 1.27 to 1.29 - *leave blank if this tax is included in the box 1.11 figure and tick box 1.30A.* Tax deducted **1.30** £

- Tick this box if you have left box 1.30 blank because the tax is included in the box 1.11 figure **1.30A**

■ *Foreign earnings not taxable in the UK in the year ended 5 April 2005* - see Notes, page EN6 **1.31** £

■ *Expenses you incurred in doing your job* - see Notes, pages EN7 to EN8

- Travel and subsistence costs **1.32** £
- Fixed deductions for expenses **1.33** £
- Professional fees and subscriptions **1.34** £
- Other expenses and capital allowances **1.35** £
- Tick box 1.36 if the figure in box 1.32 includes travel between your home and a permanent workplace **1.36**

■ *Seafarers' Earnings Deduction* **1.37** £

■ *Foreign tax for which tax credit relief not claimed* **1.38** £

Student Loans

■ *Student Loans repaid by deduction by employer* - see Notes, page EN8 **1.39** £

- Tick box 1.39A if your income is under Repayment of Teachers' Loans Scheme **1.39A**

1.40 *Additional information*

*Now fill in any other supplementary Pages that apply to you.
Otherwise, go back to page 2 in your Tax Return and finish filling it in.*

BS 12/04net TAX RETURN ■ EMPLOYMENT: PAGE E2

BPP
PROFESSIONAL EDUCATION

Income for the year ended 5 April 2005

Inland Revenue

LAND AND PROPERTY

Name

Tax reference

Fill in these boxes first

If you want help, look up the box numbers in the Notes.

Are you claiming Rent a Room relief for gross rents of £4,250 or less?
(Or £2,125 if the claim is shared?)
Read the Notes on page LN2 to find out
- whether you can claim Rent a Room relief; and
- how to claim relief for gross rents over £4,250

| Yes | |

If 'Yes', tick box. If this is your only income from UK property, you have finished these Pages

Is your income from furnished holiday lettings?
If not applicable, please turn over and fill in Page L2 to give details of your property income

| Yes | |

If 'Yes', tick box and fill in boxes 5.1 to 5.18 before completing Page L2

Furnished holiday lettings

- Income from furnished holiday lettings — **5.1** £

■ *Expenses* (furnished holiday lettings only)

- Rent, rates, insurance, ground rents etc. — **5.2** £
- Repairs, maintenance and renewals — **5.3** £
- Finance charges, including interest — **5.4** £
- Legal and professional costs — **5.5** £
- Costs of services provided, including wages — **5.6** £
- Other expenses — **5.7** £

total of boxes 5.2 to 5.7
5.8 £

Net profit (put figures in brackets if a loss)

box 5.1 minus box 5.8
5.9 £

■ *Tax adjustments*

- Private use — **5.10** £
- Balancing charges — **5.11** £

box 5.10 + box 5.11
5.12 £

- Capital allowances — **5.13** £

- Tick box 5.13A if box 5.13 includes enhanced capital allowances for environmentally friendly expenditure — **5.13A**

boxes 5.9 + 5.12 minus box 5.13
5.14 £

Profit for the year (copy to box 5.19). If loss, enter '0' in box 5.14 and put the loss in box 5.15

boxes 5.9 + 5.12 *minus* box 5.13
5.15 £

Loss for the year (if you have entered '0' in box 5.14)

■ *Losses*

- Loss offset against 2004-05 total income — **5.16** £

see Notes, page LN4
- Loss carried back — **5.17** £

see Notes, page LN4
- Loss offset against other income from property (copy to box 5.38) — **5.18** £

SA105

BS 12/04net

TAX RETURN ■ LAND AND PROPERTY: PAGE L1

Please turn over

Other property income

■ Income

		copy from box 5.14		
● Furnished holiday lettings profits	5.19 £			

Tax deducted

● Rents and other income from land and property | **5.20** £ | | **5.21** £ |

● Chargeable premiums | **5.22** £ |

boxes 5.19 + 5.20 + 5.22 + 5.22A
● Reverse premiums | **5.22A** £ | | **5.23** £ |

■ Expenses (do not include figures you have already put in boxes 5.2 to 5.7 on Page L1)

● Rent, rates, insurance, ground rents etc. | **5.24** £ |

● Repairs, maintenance and renewals | **5.25** £ |

● Finance charges, including interest | **5.26** £ |

● Legal and professional costs | **5.27** £ |

● Costs of services provided, including wages | **5.28** £ |

total of boxes 5.24 to 5.29
● Other expenses | **5.29** £ | | **5.30** £ |

box 5.23 minus box 5.30
Net profit (put figures in brackets if a loss) | **5.31** £ |

■ Tax adjustments

● Private use | **5.32** £ |

box 5.32 + box 5.33
● Balancing charges | **5.33** £ | | **5.34** £ |

● Rent a Room exempt amount | **5.35** £ |

● Capital allowances | **5.36** £ |

● Tick box 5.36A if box 5.36 includes a claim
for 100% capital allowances for flats over shops | **5.36A** |

● Tick box 5.36B if box 5.36 includes enhanced
capital allowances for environmentally
friendly expenditure | **5.36B** |

● 10% wear and tear | **5.37** £ |

boxes 5.35 to box 5.38
● Furnished holiday lettings losses
(from box 5.18) | **5.38** £ | | **5.39** £ |

boxes 5.31 + 5.34 minus box 5.39
Adjusted profit (if loss enter '0' in box 5.40 and put the loss in box 5.41) | **5.40** £ |

boxes 5.31 + 5.34 minus box 5.39
Adjusted loss (if you have entered '0' in box 5.40) | **5.41** £ |

● Loss brought forward from previous year | **5.42** £ |

box 5.40 minus box 5.42
Profit for the year | **5.43** £ |

■ Losses etc

● Loss offset against total income (read the note on page LN8) | **5.44** £ |

● Loss to carry forward to following year | **5.45** £ |

● Tick box 5.46 if these Pages include details of property let jointly | **5.46** |

● Tick box 5.47 if **all** property income ceased in the year to 5 April 2005 **and**
you don't expect to receive such income again, in the year to 5 April 2006 | **5.47** |

Now fill in any other supplementary Pages that apply to you.
Otherwise, go back to page 2 of your Tax Return and finish filling it in.

PRACTICE EXAM PAPER 2

TECHNICIAN STAGE – NVQ4

Unit 19

Preparing personal tax computations (PTC)

DO NOT OPEN THIS PAPER UNTIL YOU ARE READY TO START UNDER EXAM CONDITIONS

COVERAGE OF PERFORMANCE CRITERIA

The following performance criteria are covered in this exam.

Element	PC Coverage
19.1	**Calculate income from employment**
A	Prepare accurate computations of emoluments, including benefits
B	List allowable expenses and deductions
C	Record relevant details of income from employment accurately and legibly in the tax return
D	Make computations and submissions are made in accordance with current tax law and take account of current Revenue practice
G	Maintain client confidentiality at all times
19.2	**Calculate property and investment income**
A	Prepare schedules of dividends and interest received on all shares and securities
B	Prepare schedules of property income and determine profits and losses
D	Apply deductions and reliefs and claim loss set offs
E	Record relevant details of property and investment income accurately and legibly in the tax return
F	Make computations and submissions are made in accordance with current tax law and take account of current Revenue practice
I	Maintain client confidentiality at all times
19.3	**Prepare income tax computations**
A	List general income, savings income and dividend income and check for completeness
B	Calculate and deduct charges and personal allowances
C	Calculate Income Tax payable
D	Record income and payments legibly and accurately in the tax return
E	Make computations and submissions in accordance with current tax law and take account of current Revenue practice
H	Maintain client confidentiality

Element	PC Coverage
19.4	**Prepare capital gains tax computations**
A	Identify and value disposed-of chargeable personal assets
B	Identify shares disposed of by individuals
C	Calculate chargeable gains and allowable losses
D	Apply reliefs and exemptions correctly
E	Calculate capital gains tax payable
G	Make computations and submissions in accordance with current tax law and take account of current Revenue practice
J	Maintain client confidentiality at all times

INSTRUCTIONS

This examination paper is in TWO sections.

You have to show competence in BOTH sections.

You should therefore attempt and aim to compete EVERY task in BOTH sections.

You should spend about 90 minutes on Section 1 and 90 minutes on Section 2.

Section 1

DATA

E-MAIL

To: Accounting Technician
From: Mr Smith, Production Director
Date: 31 August 2004

I am in the process of obtaining a mortgage and the bank has requested that I provide them with full details of my income and gains for the tax year 2004/05. They have suggested that I provide them with a copy of my tax return for that year.

Background

My income comprises my salary of £40,000 per annum and benefits from employment together with dividends and interest which I receive from investments which I hold. I also receive rental income from a furnished flat which I let out through a letting agent. Tax of £8,114 was deducted from my salary in 2004/05 under the PAYE system.

The following benefits were received from my employment during 2004/05.

- I was provided with a space in a multi-storey car park next to the office. The season ticket costs Global plc £2,000 for the year. *exempt*

- I do not have a company car nor am I provided with any fuel. I am permitted, however to submit a claim for business mileage undertaken in my Mercedes. I submitted a claim for 15,000 business miles and was reimbursed at a flat rate of 50p per mile. I make a claim for tax purposes using the statutory mileage rates. ✓

- Throughout the year I had use of a home entertainment system which was bought by Global plc at a cost of £10,000. ✓

- I am provided with a mobile phone which I use for both business and personal purposes.

- Some years ago I received a loan from Global plc in the amount of £20,000. The loan is interest free. The loan was outstanding throughout the year. ✓

- The company paid my subscription of £225 to the Institute of Production Management. This is an Revenue approved Institute. ✓

- I often work from home and during 2004/05 I received £104 from my employer towards the costs of working from home. ✓

INCOME FROM INVESTMENTS

	£
Interest received	
£20,000 10% Exchequer Stock 2007	
Cash received 30.04.2004	800.00
Cash received 31.10.2004	800.00
Total cash received	1,600.00

	£
Building Society Account	
Per statement:	
Gross interest	1,200.00
Tax deducted	240.00
Net interest	960.00

	£
Dividends received	
Body Shack Enterprises plc	
Cash received 30.06.2004	270.00
Cash received 30.12.2004	450.00
Total cash received	720.00

RENTAL INCOME AND EXPENSES

The furnished flat, which I acquired during March 2004, was let out throughout the year. I changed tenant mid-way through the year but there was no gap in letting and the rent from each tenant was unchanged at £24,000 per annum.

I used a letting agent who provided me with the following statement for the year ended 5 April 2005:

THE PROPERTY AGENCY
'We will let you if you will let us'

Statement for Mr Smith
Year ended 5 April 2005

Rental income received		£24,000
Expenses incurred:		
Letting Agent's Commission	2,400 ✓	
Advertising for tenant	250 ✓	
Repair kitchen	125	
Council tax	900 ✓	
		(3,675)
Net Rental Income due to you		20,325

EXTRACT FROM PERMANENT FILE

Robert Smith

Date of birth:	18 June 1960
Employment details:	Production director of Global plc
General:	Mr Smith pays £3,900 (net) into a personal pension scheme each year.
	He pays £1,560 per annum (net) to his local church under the gift aid scheme.
	He has had no underpayments of tax up to and including the tax year 2003/04. No payments on account of tax were made for 2004/05

Tasks

Task 1.1

Prepare a calculation of taxable earnings for 2004/05.

Task 1.2

Prepare schedules showing taxable dividend and interest income for 2004/05.

Task 1.3

Prepare a calculation of rental income for 2004/05.

Task 1.4

Prepare Mr Smith's income tax computation for 2004/05.

Task 1.5

Complete the supplementary employment and land and property pages that will accompany Mr Smith's income tax return for 2004/05.

Task 1.6

State the latest date by which the 2004/05 tax return can be submitted together with details of the due dates for payment of the tax. Mr Smith has not received a short tax return. Please also advise of any other payments of income tax which Mr Smith has to make on any of the dates.

Mr Smith is aware that you correspond with the Revenue on his behalf. He is a bit concerned that others may be able to obtain his details from the Revenue – state whether this could happen.

Section 2

DATA

Another client, Mr Jones, made three capital disposals during the year as follows:

1   **£20,000 10% Exchequer Stock 2008**

Date sold	31.01.2005
Proceeds received	£28,000
Date purchased	30.09.2002
Purchase cost	£20,000

The shares are a non-business asset for taper relief purposes.

2   **15,000 £1 Ordinary shares in Body Shack Enterprises plc**

Date sold	31.12.2004
Proceeds received (15,000 @ £1.60)	£24,000

Dates of costs and acquisition:

Date	No. of shares	Cost
30.06.03	10,000	9,000
30.11.92	15,000	15,000

The shares are a non business asset for taper relief purposes.

3   **10,000 £1 Ordinary shares in JOL plc**

Mr Jones gave shares in JOL plc to his sister on 31 December 2004 at which time they had a market value of £50,000. He subscribed for these shares at their nominal value of £1 per share on 30 June 1990. These shares are a non-business asset for the purposes of taper relief.

Mr Jones had a capital loss of £13,500 brought forward from 2003/04.

Tasks

Task 2.1

Calculate any chargeable gains arising on the disposals.

Task 2.2

Calculate any capital gains tax payable for 2004/05 and state the payment date. Assume that Mr Jones is a higher rate tax payer.

TAXATION TABLES

Income tax

Tables

Starting rate	£1 – 2,020	10%
Basic rate	£2,021 – £31,400	22%
Higher rate	£31,401 and above	40%

Note: Savings (excl. dividend) income that falls in the basic rate band is taxed at 20%. UK dividends are taxed at 10% when they fall within the starting and basic rate bands and at 32.5% thereafter.

Personal allowances

Personal allowance   £4,745

Mileage allowances – Authorised mileage rates

Up to 10,000 miles	40p
Over 10,000 miles	25p

Official rate of interest

Throughout the year ended 5 April 2005   5%

Capital gains tax

Indexation Factors

November 1992 to April 1998	0.164
June 1990 to April 1998	0.283

Tapering reliefs for capital gains tax

The percentage of the gain chargeable is as follows

No of complete tax years after 5 April 1998	Gains on Non-business assets
0	100.0
1	100.0
2	100.0
3	95.0
4	90.0
5	85.0
6	80.0
7	75.0
8	70.0
9	65.0
10 or more	60.0

Annual exemption

Individuals   £8,200

Inland Revenue

Income for the year ended 5 April 2005

EMPLOYMENT

Fill in these boxes first

Name MR SMITH

Tax reference

If you want help, look up the box numbers in the Notes.

Details of employer

Employer's PAYE reference - may be shown under 'Inland Revenue office number and reference' on your P60 or 'PAYE reference' on your P45

1.1

Employer's name

1.2

Date employment started
(only if between 6 April 2004 and 5 April 2005)

1.3 / /

Employer's address

1.5

Date employment finished
(only if between 6 April 2004 and 5 April 2005)

1.4 / /

Tick box 1.6 if you were a director of the company

1.6

and, if so, tick box 1.7 if it was a close company

1.7

Postcode

Income from employment

■ *Money - see Notes, page EN3*

Before tax

- Payments from P60 (or P45) **1.8** £

- Payments not on P60, etc.   - tips **1.9** £

  - other payments (excluding expenses entered below and lump sums and compensation payments or benefits entered overleaf) **1.10** £

Tax deducted

- **Tax deducted** in the UK from payments in boxes 1.8 to 1.10 **1.11** £

■ *Benefits and expenses - see Notes, pages EN3 to EN6. If any benefits connected with termination of employment were received, or enjoyed, after that termination and were from a **former** employer you need to complete Help Sheet IR204, available from the Orderline. Do not enter such benefits here.*

	Amount			Amount
• Assets transferred/ payments made for you	**1.12** £		• Vans	**1.18** £
• Vouchers, credit cards and tokens	**1.13** £		• Interest-free and low-interest loans *see Note for box 1.19, page EN5*	**1.19** £
• Living accommodation	**1.14** £		box 1.20 is not used	
• Excess mileage allowances and passenger payments	**1.15** £		• Private medical or dental insurance	**1.21** £
• Company cars	**1.16** £		• Other benefits	**1.22** £
• Fuel for company cars	**1.17** £		• Expenses payments received and balancing charges	**1.23** £

SA101

BS 12/04net

TAX RETURN ■ EMPLOYMENT: PAGE E1

Please turn over

BPP PROFESSIONAL EDUCATION

Income from employment continued

■ *Lump sums and compensation payments or benefits including such payments and benefits from a former employer*
Note that 'lump sums' here includes any contributions which your employer made to an unapproved retirement benefits scheme

*You must read page EN6 of the Notes **before** filling in boxes 1.24 to 1.30*

Reliefs

● £30,000 exception   **1.24** £

● Foreign service and disability   **1.25** £

● Retirement and death lump sums   **1.26** £

Taxable lump sums

● From box B of *Help Sheet IR204*   **1.27** £

● From box K of *Help Sheet IR204*   **1.28** £

● From box L of *Help Sheet IR204*   **1.29** £

● Tax deducted from payments in boxes 1.27 to 1.29 - *leave blank if this tax is included in the box 1.11 figure and tick box 1.30A.*   Tax deducted   **1.30** £

● Tick this box if you have left box 1.30 blank because the tax is included in the box 1.11 figure   **1.30A**

■ *Foreign earnings not taxable in the UK in the year ended 5 April 2005 - see Notes, page EN6*   **1.31** £

■ *Expenses you incurred in doing your job - see Notes, pages EN7 to EN8*

● Travel and subsistence costs   **1.32** £

● Fixed deductions for expenses   **1.33** £

● Professional fees and subscriptions   **1.34** £

● Other expenses and capital allowances   **1.35** £

● Tick box 1.36 if the figure in box 1.32 includes travel between your home and a permanent workplace   **1.36**

■ *Seafarers' Earnings Deduction*   **1.37** £

■ *Foreign tax for which tax credit relief not claimed*   **1.38** £

Student Loans

■ *Student Loans repaid by deduction by employer - see Notes, page EN8*   **1.39** £

● Tick box 1.39A if your income is under Repayment of Teachers' Loans Scheme   **1.39A**

1.40 *Additional information*

Now fill in any other supplementary Pages that apply to you.
Otherwise, go back to page 2 in your Tax Return and finish filling it in.

Income for the year ended 5 April 2005

Inland Revenue

LAND AND PROPERTY

Fill in these boxes first

Name

Tax reference

If you want help, look up the box numbers in the Notes.

Are you claiming Rent a Room relief for gross rents of £4,250 or less?
(Or £2,125 if the claim is shared?)

Read the Notes on page LN2 to find out
- whether you can claim Rent a Room relief; and
- how to claim relief for gross rents over £4,250

Yes ☐

If 'Yes', tick box. If this is your only income from UK property, you have finished these Pages

Is your income from furnished holiday lettings?
If not applicable, please turn over and fill in Page L2 to give details of your property income

Yes ☐

If 'Yes', tick box and fill in boxes 5.1 to 5.18 before completing Page L2

Furnished holiday lettings

- Income from furnished holiday lettings — **5.1** £

- *Expenses* (furnished holiday lettings only)

- Rent, rates, insurance, ground rents etc. — **5.2** £
- Repairs, maintenance and renewals — **5.3** £
- Finance charges, including interest — **5.4** £
- Legal and professional costs — **5.5** £
- Costs of services provided, including wages — **5.6** £
- Other expenses — **5.7** £

total of boxes 5.2 to 5.7
5.8 £

Net profit (put figures in brackets if a loss)

box 5.1 *minus* box 5.8
5.9 £

- *Tax adjustments*

- Private use — **5.10** £
- Balancing charges — **5.11** £

box 5.10 + box 5.11
5.12 £

- Capital allowances — **5.13** £

- Tick box 5.13A if box 5.13 includes enhanced capital allowances for environmentally friendly expenditure — **5.13A** ☐

Profit for the year (copy to box 5.19). If loss, enter '0' in box 5.14 and put the loss in box 5.15

boxes 5.9 + 5.12 *minus* box 5.13
5.14 £

Loss for the year (if you have entered '0' in box 5.14)

boxes 5.9 + 5.12 *minus* box 5.13
5.15 £

- *Losses*

- Loss offset against 2004-05 total income — **5.16** £

see Notes, page LN4
- Loss carried back — **5.17** £

see Notes, page LN4
- Loss offset against other income from property (copy to box 5.38) — **5.18** £

SA105

BS 12/04net

TAX RETURN ■ LAND AND PROPERTY: PAGE L1

Please turn over ➤

BPP PROFESSIONAL EDUCATION

Other property income

■ Income

	copy from box 5.14		
● Furnished holiday lettings profits	**5.19** £		
		Tax deducted	
● Rents and other income from land and property	**5.20** £	**5.21** £	
● Chargeable premiums	**5.22** £		
			boxes 5.19 + 5.20 + 5.22 + 5.22A
● Reverse premiums	**5.22A** £		**5.23** £

■ Expenses (do not include figures you have already put in boxes 5.2 to 5.7 on Page L1)

● Rent, rates, insurance, ground rents etc.	**5.24** £	
● Repairs, maintenance and renewals	**5.25** £	
● Finance charges, including interest	**5.26** £	
● Legal and professional costs	**5.27** £	
● Costs of services provided, including wages	**5.28** £	
		total of boxes 5.24 to 5.29
● Other expenses	**5.29** £	**5.30** £

	box 5.23 minus box 5.30
Net profit (put figures in brackets if a loss)	**5.31** £

■ Tax adjustments

● Private use	**5.32** £	
		box 5.32 + box 5.33
● Balancing charges	**5.33** £	**5.34** £
● Rent a Room exempt amount	**5.35** £	
● Capital allowances	**5.36** £	
● Tick box 5.36A if box 5.36 includes a claim for 100% capital allowances for flats over shops	**5.36A**	
● Tick box 5.36B if box 5.36 includes enhanced capital allowances for environmentally friendly expenditure	**5.36B**	
● 10% wear and tear	**5.37** £	
		boxes 5.35 to box 5.38
● Furnished holiday lettings losses (from box 5.18)	**5.38** £	**5.39** £

	boxes 5.31 + 5.34 minus box 5.39
Adjusted profit (if loss enter '0' in box 5.40 and put the loss in box 5.41)	**5.40** £

	boxes 5.31 + 5.34 minus box 5.39	
Adjusted loss (if you have entered '0' in box 5.40)	**5.41** £	
● Loss brought forward from previous year		**5.42** £

	box 5.40 minus box 5.42
Profit for the year	**5.43** £

■ Losses etc

● Loss offset against total income (read the note on page LN8)	**5.44** £
● Loss to carry forward to following year	**5.45** £
● Tick box 5.46 if these Pages include details of property let jointly	**5.46**
● Tick box 5.47 if **all** property income ceased in the year to 5 April 2005 **and** you don't expect to receive such income again, in the year to 5 April 2006	**5.47**

Now fill in any other supplementary Pages that apply to you.
Otherwise, go back to page 2 of your Tax Return and finish filling it in.

BS 12/04net   TAX RETURN ■ LAND AND PROPERTY: PAGE L2

PRACTICE EXAM PAPER 3

(December 2003 Exam paper)

TECHNICIAN STAGE – NVQ4

Unit 19

Preparing personal tax computations (FA 2004) (PTC)

DO NOT OPEN THIS PAPER UNTIL YOU ARE READY TO START UNDER EXAM CONDITIONS

INSTRUCTIONS

This examination paper is in TWO sections.

You have to show competence in BOTH sections.

You should therefore attempt and aim to compete EVERY task in EACH section.

You should spend about 80 minutes on Section 1 and 100 minutes on Section 2.

COVERAGE OF PERFORMANCE CRITERIA

The following performance criteria are covered in this exam.

Element	PC Coverage
19.1	**Calculate income from employment**
A	Prepare accurate computations of emoluments, including benefits
B	List allowable expenses and deductions
C	Record relevant details of income from employment accurately and legibly in the tax return
D	Make computations and submissions in accordance with current tax law and take account of current Revenue practice
19.2	**Calculate property and investment income**
B	Prepare schedules of property income and determine profits and losses
D	Apply deductions and reliefs and claim loss set-offs
E	Record relevant details of property and investment income accurately and legibly in the tax return
F	Make computations and submissions are made in accordance with current tax law and take account of current Revenue practice
19.3	**Prepare Income Tax Computations**
A	List general income, savings income and dividend income and check for completeness
B	Calculate and deduct charges and personal allowance
C	Calculate Income Tax payable
D	Record income and payments legibly and accurately in the tax return
E	Make computations and submissions are made in accordance with current tax law and take account of current Revenue practice
19.4	**Prepare capital gains tax computations**
A	Identify and value disposed-of chargeable assets
C	Calculate chargeable gains and allowable losses
D	Apply reliefs and exemptions correctly
E	Calculate Capital Gains Tax payable
F	Record details of gains and the Capital Gains Tax payable legibly and accurately in the tax return
G	More computations and submissions are made in accordance with current tax law and take account of current Revenue practice

TAXATION TABLES

Tax rates and bands:

	%	£
Starting rate	10	first 2,020
Basic rate	22	next 29,380
Higher rate	40	over 31,400

Savings income taxed at 10%, 20% and 40%.
Dividends are taxed at 10% and 32.5%

Personal allowances:

Personal allowance	£4,745

Car fuel benefit:

Scale charge	£14,400

Car benefit

Baseline for CO_2 emissions 145 g/km

Inland revenue official rate – 5%

Capital gains tax:

Annual exemption	£8,200

Indexation factors:

July 1989 to August 1993	0.223
August 1993 to April 1995	0.054
April 1995 to April 1998	0.091
December 1985 to April 1998	0.693
January 1990 to April 1998	0.361

Tapering relief for non-business assets:

Number of years held after 05/04/98	% of gain
2 or less	100
3	95
4	90
5	85
6	80
7	75
8	70

SECTION 1

DATA

The date is 1 December 2005. You work as a trainee accountant in the tax department of a firm of Chartered Accountants.

One of your friends, Joanne, has asked you to help her sort out her tax return for 2004/05.
Joanne supplies you with the following information:

1. She has an annual salary of £40,000.

2. Throughout the year, she was provided with a 1,800cc diesel-engine company car that had a list price of £21,200 when new. It has an emission rating of 177g/km. The company pays all running costs. Joanne pays her company £75 per month as a contribution for the private use of the car.

3. In January 2004, she was provided with a company loan of £15,000 on which she pays interest at 2% per annum. No capital repayment of the loan has been made.

4. Joanne received £250 from her company as reimbursement of entertainment costs she had incurred.

5. Her employer provides a non-contributory pension scheme, with the employer paying 8% of her salary to the pension scheme.

6. She received other income of:

	£
Cheques for dividends	1,548
Interest credited to ISA	360

Task 1.1

Calculate the total taxable benefits for 2004/05.

Task 1.2

Prepare a computation of taxable income for 2004/05, clearly showing the distinction between the different types of income.

	NonSavings	Saving	Dividend
Salary	40000		
Benefits	8094		
Dividends			1720
Isa Exempt			
	48094	—	1720
less Personal All	4745		
	43349	—	1720
			45069 TOTAL

Task 1.3

Calculate the net income tax payable for 2004/05, before deducting PAYE.

Taxable Income

2020 × 10% =	202.00
29380 × 22% =	6463.60
11949 × 40% =	4779.60
1720 × 32.5%	559.00
	12,004.20
less Tax on Divi	(172.00)
	11832.20

BPP PROFESSIONAL EDUCATION

Task 1.4

Joanne does not know when she needs to complete her tax return for 2004/05. Joanne has not been issued with the new short tax return form.

Briefly explain:

- The key dates for completion of a tax return
- The implications, if any, of submitting a return during
  (i)   December 2005
  (ii)   February 2006

Tax return have to be completed & returned by 31st Jan 2006. If you want IR to self-assess your form, you have to submit by 30th Sept 05.

If already sent by dec 05 you are safe but February 2006 is far too late as you'll have to pay £100 fine.

Task 1.5

During June 2005, Joanne bought a flat with the prime intention of renting it out. She immediately decorated the flat and bought several items of furniture. The flat has been rented out to tenants since July 2005. Joanne does not know about the tax implications for this source of income.

Explain to Joanne how:

- her letting income is assessed
- expenditure is allowed
- any losses are relieved.

[You should assume the tax rules are the same in 2005/06 as 2004/05]

letting income will be treated exactly the same way.
as other income
Furniture.

Task 1.6

Complete the tax return on the following pages for Joanne's employment income.

Income for the year ended 5 April 2005

Inland Revenue

EMPLOYMENT

Name *Joanne Harper*

Fill in these boxes first

Tax reference

If you want help, look up the box numbers in the Notes.

Details of employer

Employer's PAYE reference - may be shown under 'Inland Revenue office number and reference' on your P60 or 'PAYE reference' on your P45

1.1

Employer's name

1.2 *Sunny Dials*

Date employment started
(only if between 6 April 2004 and 5 April 2005)

1.3 / /

Date employment finished
(only if between 6 April 2004 and 5 April 2005)

1.4 / /

Employer's address

1.5

Postcode

Tick box 1.6 if you were a director of the company

1.6

and, if so, tick box 1.7 if it was a close company

1.7

Income from employment

■ *Money - see Notes, page EN3*

● Payments from P60 (or P45)

Before tax

1.8 £ 40,000

● Payments not on P60, etc. - tips

1.9 £ —

- other payments (excluding expenses entered below and lump sums and compensation payments or benefits entered overleaf)

1.10 £ —

● **Tax deducted** in the UK from payments in boxes 1.8 to 1.10

Tax deducted

1.11 £

■ *Benefits and expenses - see Notes, pages EN3 to EN6. If any benefits connected with termination of employment were received, or enjoyed, after that termination and were from a **former** employer you need to complete Help Sheet IR204, available from the Orderline. Do not enter such benefits here.*

● Assets transferred/ payments made for you

Amount

1.12 £

● Vouchers, credit cards and tokens

Amount

1.13 £

● Living accommodation

Amount

1.14 £

● Excess mileage allowances and passenger payments

Amount

1.15 £

● Company cars

Amount

1.16 £ 4188

● Fuel for company cars

Amount

1.17 £ 3456

● Vans

Amount

1.18 £ —

● Interest-free and low-interest loans see Note for box 1.19, page EN5

Amount

1.19 £ 450

box 1.20 is not used

● Private medical or dental insurance

Amount

1.21 £ —

● Other benefits

Amount

1.22 £ —

● Expenses payments received and balancing charges

Amount

1.23 £ 250

SA101

BS 12/04net

TAX RETURN ■ EMPLOYMENT: PAGE E1

Please turn over

Income from employment continued

■ *Lump sums and compensation payments or benefits including such payments and benefits from a former employer*
Note that 'lump sums' here includes any contributions which your employer made to an unapproved retirement benefits scheme

*You must read page EN6 of the Notes **before** filling in boxes 1.24 to 1.30*

Reliefs

- £30,000 exception | **1.24** £

- Foreign service and disability | **1.25** £

- Retirement and death lump sums | **1.26** £

Taxable lump sums

- From box B of *Help Sheet IR204* | **1.27** £

- From box K of *Help Sheet IR204* | **1.28** £

- From box L of *Help Sheet IR204* | **1.29** £

- Tax deducted from payments in boxes 1.27 to 1.29 - *leave blank if this tax is included in the box 1.11 figure and tick box 1.30A.* | Tax deducted **1.30** £

- Tick this box if you have left box 1.30 blank because the tax is included in the box 1.11 figure | **1.30A**

■ *Foreign earnings not taxable in the UK in the year ended 5 April 2005 - see Notes, page EN6* | **1.31** £

■ *Expenses you incurred in doing your job - see Notes, pages EN7 to EN8*

- Travel and subsistence costs | **1.32** £

- Fixed deductions for expenses | **1.33** £

- Professional fees and subscriptions | **1.34** £

- Other expenses and capital allowances | **1.35** £ *250*

- Tick box 1.36 if the figure in box 1.32 includes travel between your home and a permanent workplace | **1.36**

■ *Seafarers' Earnings Deduction* | **1.37** £

■ *Foreign tax for which tax credit relief not claimed* | **1.38** £

Student Loans

■ *Student Loans repaid by deduction by employer - see Notes, page EN8* | **1.39** £

- Tick box 1.39A if your income is under Repayment of Teachers' Loans Scheme | **1.39A**

1.40 *Additional information*

*Now fill in any other supplementary Pages that apply to you.
Otherwise, go back to page 2 in your Tax Return and finish filling it in.*

SECTION 2

You should spend about 100 minutes on this section.

DATA

One of your firm's clients, George Green, has had the following capital transactions during the year 2004/05:

1.   *Shares*

In March 2005, George sold 2,000 of his shares in Crimson Ltd for £61,560. These shares do not qualify as business assets. His transactions in the shares of Crimson Ltd were as follows:

Date	Transaction	No of Shares	£
July 1989	Purchased	1,000	15,500
August 1993	Purchased	1,500	21,800
April 1995	Rights Issue	1 for 5	£10 each
May 2000	Sold	800	17,000
June 2002	Purchased	500	9,800

2.   *Table*

George had bought an antique table in December 1985 for £1,200. He sold the table in October 2004 for £5,900.

3.   *Land*

George bought 20 acres of land as an investment in January 1990 for £50,000. In November 2004, he sold 16 acres of this land to a property developer for £101,000. The remaining 4 acres were valued at £25,000 on the date of sale.

George has capital losses brought forward from 2003/04 of £20,000.

George also received the following income for 2004/05:

	£
Dividends from Crimson Ltd	7,650
Bank interest	720

Task 2.1

Calculate the taxable gain or loss made on the disposal of the shares in Crimson Ltd. Show the balance of shares to be carried forward for future disposal.

Task 2.2

Calculate the taxable gain or loss made on the disposal of the antique table, if applicable.

_____

_____

_____

_____

_____

_____

_____

_____

Task 2.3

Calculate the taxable gain or loss made on the disposal of the land.

_____

_____

_____

_____

_____

_____

_____

_____

_____

Task 2.4

Calculate the total of taxable gains for the year.

Task 2.5

Calculate George's total income tax and capital gains tax liability for 2004/05.

Task 2.6

You received the following e-mail from George Green:

From:	Ggreen@boxmail.net
To:	AATStudent@boxmail.net
Sent:	30 November 2005 9:12
Subject:	Concerned

I have an issue that I would like to raise. I have some friends who use the same firm of accountants that I do.

This means that some people within the firm have access to information that I would not like my friends to know about. I am concerned that my tax affairs will not stay private because of this.

Awaiting your response,

George Green

Reply to George Green's e-mail, giving your response to his concern.

From:	AATStudent@boxmail.net
To:	Ggreen@boxmail.net
Sent:	3 December 2005 14:57
Subject:	Concerned

PRACTICE EXAM PAPER 4

TECHNICIAN STAGE – NVQ4

Unit 19

Preparing personal tax computations (PTC)

DO NOT OPEN THIS PAPER UNTIL YOU ARE READY TO START
UNDER EXAM CONDITIONS

AAT SPECIMEN EXAM PAPER

NVQ/SVQ IN ACCOUNTING, LEVEL 4

UNIT 19

Preparing Personal Tax Computations

This examination paper is in TWO sections.

You have to show competence in BOTH sections.

You should therefore attempt and aim to complete EVERY task in EACH section.

You should spend about 70 minutes on Section 1 and 110 minutes on Section 2.

COVERAGE OF PERFORMANCE CRITERIA

The following performance criteria are covered in this exam.

Element	PC Coverage
19.1	**Calculate income from employment**
A	Prepare accurate computations of emoluments, including benefits
B	List allowable expenses and deductions
C	Record relevant details of income from employment accurately and legibly in the tax return
D	Make computations and submissions in accordance with current tax law and take account of current Revenue practice
G	Maintain client confidentiality at all times
19.2	**Calculate property and investment income**
A	Prepare schedules of dividends and interest received on shares and securities
F	Make computations and submissions in accordance with current tax law and take account of current Revenue practice
I	Maintain client confidentiality at all times
19.3	**Prepare income tax computations**
A	List general income, savings income and dividend income and check for completeness
B	Calculate and deduct charges and personal allowances
C	Calculate Income Tax payable
E	Make computations and submissions in accordance with current tax law and take account of current Revenue practice
H	Maintain client confidentiality at all times
19.4	**Prepare Capital Gains Tax computations**
A	Identify and value disposed-of chargeable personal assets
B	Identify shares disposed of by individuals
C	Calculate chargeable gains and allowance losses
D	Apply reliefs and exemptions correctly
E	Calculate Capital Gains Tax payable
G	Make computations and submissions in accordance with current tax law and take account of current Revenue practice
J	Maintain client confidentiality at all times

Section 1

DATA

The date is May 2005. You work for Autumn Jewels Ltd in its payroll department. One of the employees, Phil Bright, has asked if you could help him complete his 2004/05 tax return.

From the company records, you determine that his taxable earnings comprise:

1   Annual salary of £18,500

2   Throughout the year, he was provided with a 2,500cc petrol-engine company car that had a list price of £28,600 when new. It has an emission rating of 182g/km. The company pays all running costs.

3   In July 2003 he was provided with a company loan of £20,000 on which he pays interest at 2.5% per annum. No capital repayment of the loan has been made.

4   He pays pension contributions to the employer's pension scheme at 5% of his salary.

Phil Bright gives you the following additional information:

1   He is 42 years old

2   He received dividend cheques of £5,400 during 2004/05

3   He also received building society interest of £4,160, net

4   He paid an annual subscription to his professional organisation of £250.

Task 1.1 ^2015

Calculate the total assessable benefits for 2004/05.

Car Benefit = 22% x 28600 = 6292
22% x 14400 = 3168
loan Benefit 20,000x(5-2.5%) = 500
9960

180-
145
35÷5 = 7+15

Task 1.2

Prepare a schedule of income for 2004/05, clearly showing the distinction between non-savings, savings and dividend income. Phil Bright's personal allowances should be deducted, as appropriate.

	Non Savings	Savings	Dividends	TOTAL
Salary	18,500			18500
less Pension 5%	(925)			(925)
Dividends			6000	6000
Saving Int		5200		
less Benefit				
Subscription	(250)			
Plus Benefits	9960			
	27,285	5200	6000	
less P.A	4745			
	22,540	5200	6,000	

Task 1.3

Calculate the net income tax payable for 2004/05, before deducting PAYE.

10% of 2020	202.00
22% of 2~~9380~~	~~6468.60~~
20,520	4514.40
Savings 5200 x 20%	1040.00
Div 3660 x 10%	366.00
2340 x 32.5%	760.50
less deducted at source	6882.90
→	(1640.00)
	5242.90

8-860

Task 1.4

Another employee, Beryl Simmons, has heard that you are helping Phil Bright sort out his tax. She asks you what you have been doing for Phil, so that she can see if you can also help her.

Discuss how you should reply to this request.

....
....
....
....
....
....
....
....

Task 1.5

Complete the attached tax return for employment income of Phil Bright.

Income for the year ended 5 April 2005

Inland Revenue

EMPLOYMENT

Name

Tax reference

Fill in these boxes first

If you want help, look up the box numbers in the Notes.

Details of employer

Employer's PAYE reference - may be shown under 'Inland Revenue office number and reference' on your P60 or 'PAYE reference' on your P45

1.1

Employer's name

1.2

Date employment started
(only if between 6 April 2004 and 5 April 2005)

1.3 / /

Date employment finished
(only if between 6 April 2004 and 5 April 2005)

1.4 / /

Employer's address

1.5

Postcode

Tick box 1.6 if you were a director of the company

1.6

and, if so, tick box 1.7 if it was a close company

1.7

Income from employment

■ *Money* - *see Notes, page EN3*

Before tax

● Payments from P60 (or P45)

1.8 £ 17575

● Payments not on P60, etc. - tips

1.9 £

- other payments (excluding expenses entered below and lump sums and compensation payments or benefits entered overleaf)

1.10 £

Tax deducted

● **Tax deducted** in the UK from payments in boxes 1.8 to 1.10

1.11 £

■ *Benefits and expenses* - *see Notes, pages EN3 to EN6. If any benefits connected with termination of employment were received, or enjoyed, after that termination and were from a **former** employer you need to complete Help Sheet IR204, available from the Orderline. Do not enter such benefits here.*

	Amount			Amount
● Assets transferred/ payments made for you	**1.12** £		● Vans	**1.18** £
● Vouchers, credit cards and tokens	**1.13** £		● Interest-free and low-interest loans *see Note for box 1.19, page EN5*	**1.19** £
● Living accommodation	**1.14** £		*box 1.20 is not used*	
● Excess mileage allowances and passenger payments	**1.15** £		● Private medical or dental insurance	**1.21** £
● Company cars	**1.16** £		● Other benefits	**1.22** £
● Fuel for company cars	**1.17** £		● Expenses payments received and balancing charges	**1.23** £

SA101

BPP PROFESSIONAL EDUCATION

Income from employment continued

■ *Lump sums and compensation payments or benefits including such payments and benefits from a former employer*
Note that 'lump sums' here includes any contributions which your employer made to an unapproved retirement benefits scheme

*You must read page EN6 of the Notes **before** filling in boxes 1.24 to 1.30*

Reliefs

- £30,000 exception — **1.24** £
- Foreign service and disability — **1.25** £
- Retirement and death lump sums — **1.26** £

Taxable lump sums

- From box B of *Help Sheet IR204* — **1.27** £
- From box K of *Help Sheet IR204* — **1.28** £
- From box L of *Help Sheet IR204* — **1.29** £
- Tax deducted from payments in boxes 1.27 to 1.29 - *leave blank if this tax is included in the box 1.11 figure and tick box 1.30A.* — Tax deducted **1.30** £
- Tick this box if you have left box 1.30 blank because the tax is included in the box 1.11 figure — **1.30A**

■ *Foreign earnings not taxable in the UK in the year ended 5 April 2005* - see Notes, page EN6 — **1.31** £

■ *Expenses you incurred in doing your job* - see Notes, pages EN7 to EN8

- Travel and subsistence costs — **1.32** £
- Fixed deductions for expenses — **1.33** £
- Professional fees and subscriptions — **1.34** £
- Other expenses and capital allowances — **1.35** £
- Tick box 1.36 if the figure in box 1.32 includes travel between your home and a permanent workplace — **1.36**

■ *Seafarers' Earnings Deduction* — **1.37** £

■ *Foreign tax for which tax credit relief not claimed* — **1.38** £

Student Loans

■ *Student Loans repaid by deduction by employer* - see Notes, page EN8 — **1.39** £

- Tick box 1.39A if your income is under Repayment of Teachers' Loans Scheme — **1.39A**

1.40 *Additional information*

Now fill in any other supplementary Pages that apply to you.
Otherwise, go back to page 2 in your Tax Return and finish filling it in.

Section 2

DATA

You work for a firm of Chartered Accountants in the tax department. One of your clients, Jeanette Alsop, has had three capital transactions during the year 2004/05.

1   **Shares**

In January 2005, Jeanette sold all her shares in Purple Ltd for £45,000. These shares do not qualify as business assets. Your records show that her transactions in the shares of Purple Ltd were as follows:

Date	Transaction	No of Shares	£
April 1986	Purchased	300	3,000
May 1990	Purchased	500	8,500
June 1992	Bonus issue	1 for 5	
April 1995	Purchased	1,000	16,000
March 2001	Sold	400	7,600

2   **Motor car**

In November 2004, Jeanette sold a twenty-year old car that she has owned since April 1995. She originally paid £600 for the car, but sold it for £8,500.

3   **Land**

Jeanette bought 10 acres of land as an investment in August 1996 for £80,000. In February 2005, she sold 4 acres of this land to property developer for £71,000. The remaining 6 acres were valued at £95,000 on the date of sale.

Jeanette Alsop also owns a variety of properties that she rents out. The total rent receivable from these properties totalled £4,800 for 2004/05, of which she had received £4,000 by 5th April 2005. Of the remaining £800, £500 was deemed irrecoverable. She also had Schedule A losses brought forward from 2003/04 of £1,600.

Task 2.1

Calculate the taxable gain or loss, after any taper relief, made on the disposal of the shares in Purple Ltd, if applicable.

....
....
....
....
....
....
....
....
....
....
....
....
....
....
....
....
....
....
....
....
....
....
....
....
....
....

Task 2.2

Calculate the taxable gain or loss, after any taper relief, made on the disposal of the car, if applicable.

....

....

....

....

....

....

....

....

Task 2.3

Calculate the taxable gain or allowable loss, after taper relief, made on the disposal of the land, if applicable.

....

....

....

....

....

....

....

....

....

....

....

....

....

....

Task 2.4

Calculate the Schedule A income chargeable to tax for 2004/05.

....

....

....

....

Task 2.5

Assuming Jeanette Alsop has no other income, calculate her tax liability for 2004/05, assuming that she is only entitled to the basic personal allowance.

....

....

....

....

....

....

....

....

....

....

....

....

....

....

Task 2.6

Jeanette Alsop informs you that when she completed her 2003/04 income tax return,

- She failed to declare £800 received from a building society

- All her other income in that tax year was taxed at basic rate, and totalled £300 short of the 40% tax band.

- As the building society interest had already suffered tax at source, she thought that she did not need to declare it.

She has heard that this was not the right thing to do, and she has sought your advice.

Using the headed paper provided write a memo to Jeanette Alsop advising her of the best course of action to take with regard to her dealings with the Inland Revenue, and the penalties, surcharges and/or interest she may have to pay when her mis-declaration is notified. You do not need to calculate the tax implications of this mistake.

MEMO

To:	Jeanette Alsop
From:	Accounting Technician
Date:	1 June 2005
Ref:	Late declaration of income

TAXATION TABLES FOR PERSONAL TAX

Tax rates and bands

	%		£
Starting rate	10	first	2,020
Basic rate	22	next	29,380
Higher rate	40	over	31,400

Savings income taxed at 10%, 20% and 40%.

Dividends are taxed at 10% and 32.5%.

Personal allowances

Personal allowance   £4,745

Car fuel charge

Set figure £14,400

Car benefit

Baseline for CO_2 emissions   145 g/km

Inland revenue official rate

5%

Capital gains tax

Annual exemption   £8,200

Indexation factors:

April 1986 to May 1990	0.224
May 1990 to June 1992	0.111
June 1992 to April 1995	0.070
May 1990 to April 1995	0.181
April 1995 to April 1998	0.091
August 1996 to April 1998	0.062

Tapering relief for non-business assets:

Number of years held after 05/04/98	% of gain
2 or less	100
3	95
4	90
5	85
6	80
7	75
8	70

Answers to
Practice Activities

Chapter 1 An outline of Income Tax

1 Income tax computation

(a)

	Non-savings £	Savings (excl div) income £	Dividend £	Total £
Salary	18,900			
Building society interest × 100/80		1,000		
Dividends × 100/90			331	
STI	18,900	1,000	331	20,231
Less personal allowance	(4,745)			
	14,155	1,000	331	15,486

(b)

	£
Income tax on non-savings income	
£2,020 × 10%	202
£12,135 × 22%	2,670
Income tax on savings (excl dividend) income	
£1,000 × 20%	200
Income tax on dividend income	
£331 × 10%	33
Tax liability	3,105

(c)

	£
Income tax liability	3,105
Less tax credit on dividend income	(33)
Less tax suffered on interest	(200)
Less PAYE	(2,100)
Tax payable	772

2 Mr Betteredge

(a)

	Non-savings	Savings (excl dividend)	Total
	£	£	£
Earnings	15,065		
Schedule D Case III		26	
Bank deposit interest × 100/80		571	
Building society interest × 100/80		500	
National savings certificates: exempt			
Mini cash ISA: exempt			
STI	15,065	1,097	16,162
Less personal allowance	(4,745)		
Taxable income	10,320	1,097	11,417

(b)

	£
Income tax on non-savings income	
£2,020 × 10%	202
£8,300 × 22%	1,826
Income tax on savings (excl dividend) income £1,097 × 20%	219
Income tax liability	2,247

Tutorial note. It is important to recognise which types of income are exempt from tax.

3 John Smith

(a)   INCOME TAX COMPUTATION

	Non-savings	Savings (excl dividend)	Dividend	Total
	£	£	£	£
Salary	45,000			
Dividend £900 × 100/90			1,000	
Schedule D Case III		496		
Bank deposit interest £800 × 100/80		1,000		
	45,000	1,496	1,000	
Less personal allowance	(4,745)			
Taxable income	40,255	1,496	1,000	42,751

(b)

	£
Tax on non-savings income	
£2,020 × 10%	202
£29,380 × 22%	6,464
£6,579 (extended band: see part (c)) × 22%	1,447
£2,276 × 40%	910
Tax on savings (excl dividend) income £1,496 × 40%	598
Tax on dividend income £1,000 × 32.5%	325
Tax liability	9,946
Less tax credit on dividend income	(100)
Less tax suffered on bank interest (£1,000 × 20%)	(200)
Less PAYE	(9,200)
Tax payable	446

Tutorial note 1. National Savings Bank interest is received gross.

Tutorial note 2. The basic rate band must be extended by the gross amount of any gift aid donation.

(c) The payment under the gift aid scheme is treated as though it were paid net of basic rate tax. Additional relief is given though the income tax computation: the basic rate band is extended by the gross amount of the gift aid donation. The gross amount of the gift aid donation is £5,132 × 100/78 = £6,579.

4 Mrs Rogers

(a)

	Non-savings £	Savings (excl dividends) £	Dividends £	Total £
Salary	17,776			
Dividends (10,000 × £1.35 × 100/90)			15,000	
Interest on ISA – exempt				
Schedule D Case III		150		
Building society interest × 100/80		1,875		
STI	17,776	2,025	15,000	34,801
Less personal allowance	(4,745)			
Taxable income	13,031	2,025	15,000	30,056

Tutorial note. It is important to be aware of which items are exempt from income tax.

(b)

	£
Income tax on non-savings income	
£2,020 × 10%	202
£11,011 × 22%	2,422
Savings (excl dividend) income	
£2,025 × 20%	405
Dividend income	
£15,000 × 10%	1,500
Tax liability	4,529
Less Tax credit on dividends	(1,500)
Less BSI	(375)
Less PAYE	(3,000)
Income tax repayable	(346)

5 Mrs Butcher

(a)   INCOME TAX COMPUTATION

	Non-savings £	Savings £	Dividends £	Total £
Pension	7,204			
Schedule A	5,776			
Interest on government stock		490		
Dividends £270 × 100/90			300	
Building society Interest £4,000 × 100/80		5,000		
STI	12,980	5,490	300	18,770
Less personal allowance	(4,745)			
Taxable income	8,235	5,490	300	14,025

Tutorial note 1. Don't forget to gross up any amounts that are received net of tax.

Tutorial note 2. Premium bond prizes are tax free.

(b)

Income tax payable:

	£
Starting rate: £2,020 × 10%	202
Basic rate (non-savings): £6,215 × 22%	1,367
Basic rate (savings): £5,490 × 20%	1,098
Basic rate (dividends): £300 × 10%	30
Tax liability	2,697
Less tax suffered:	
Tax credit on dividend income (£300 × 10%)	(30)
Tax deducted at source on building society interest (£5,000 × 20%)	(1,000)
Tax payable	1,667

6 Eric Wright

(a) Eric

	Non-savings £	Savings (excl dividends) £	Dividends £	Total £
Sch DII	26,060			
BI £1,600 × 100/80		2,000		
STI	26,060	2,000	Nil	28,060
Less: PA	(4,745)			(4,745)
Taxable income	21,315	2,000	Nil	23,315

(b) *Tax on non-savings income*

	£
£2,020 × 10%	202
£19,295 × 22%	4,245
Tax on savings (excluding dividend) income	
£2,000 × 20%	400
Tax liability	4,847
Less: tax deducted at source	(400)
Tax due	4,447

Tutorial note. Eric will have paid the gift aid donation net of basic rate tax. As Eric is only a basic rate taxpayer the donation will have no further effect on the income tax computation.

(c) Doreen

	Non-savings £	Dividends £	Total £
Pension	4,027		
Dividends (×$^{100}/_{90}$)		2,020	
STI	4,027	2,020	6,047
Less: PA	(4,027)	(718)	(4,745)
Taxable income	Nil	1,302	1,302

(d)

	£
£1,302 × 10%	130
Less: Tax Credit on dividends	(130)
Income tax payable (repayable)	–

Tutorial note. The tax credit on the dividends can be deducted to bring the tax payable down to £nil. However the excess tax credit (£202 − £130 = £72) cannot be repaid.

7 Melanie Wong

(a)

	Non-savings £	Savings (excl dividends) £	Dividends £	Total £
Earnings	40,000			
Dividends £4,500 × 100/90			5,000	
NS Certificates interest – exempt				
STI	40,000	Nil	5,000	45,000
Less: PA	(4,745)			(4,745)
Taxable income	35,255	Nil	5,000	40,255

Tutorial note. Interest on the National Savings Certificate is exempt from income tax.

(b) *Tax on non-savings income*

	£
£2,020 × 10%	202
£29,380 × 22%	6,464
(£1,170 × 10/78) = £1,500 × 22% (gift aid)	330
£2,355 × 40%	942
Tax on dividend income	
£5,000 × 32$\frac{1}{2}$%	1,625
Tax liability	9,563
Less: PAYE	(8,429)
dividend tax credit	(500)
Tax due	634

Tutorial note. The basic rate band is extended by the gross amount of the gift aid donation.

Chapter 2 The taxation of employment income

8 Cars and lunches

TOTAL TAXABLE BENEFITS

	£
Luncheon vouchers 50 × (£5 – 15p)	243
Meals in staff canteen	0
Car £25,000 × 25%	6,250
Fuel £14,400 × 25%	3,600
Taxable benefits	10,093

Tutorial note. As the staff canteen is open to all employees there is no taxable benefit in respect of the meals taken there.

Working

1   *Taxable Percentage for car and fuel benefits*

Cars CO_2 emissions = 195g/km.

Amount above baseline 195 – 145 = 50g/km.

Divide by 5 = 10.

Taxable percentage = 15% + 10% = 25%.

9 Directors

(a)   **The use of a private house which cost £120,000**

Two calculations are required.

(i)   The living accommodation benefit

	£
Annual value	2,000
Less contribution by director	(2,000)
	0

(ii)   The additional charge for expensive accommodation

£(120,000 – 75,000) × 5%   £2,250

The total benefit is £2,250.

(b)   **The purchase of a company asset at an undervalue**

The **benefit is the greater** of:

(i)   The **asset's current market value**, and

(ii)   The **asset's market value when first provided, less the total benefits taxed during the period of use**.

The acquisition price paid by the director is deducted from whichever of (i) and (ii) is used.

	£	£
Market value when first provided		3,500
Less: taxed in 2000/01 (20% of market value)	700	
taxed in 2001/02 (20% of market value)	700	
taxed in 2002/03 (20%)	700	
taxed in 2003/04 (20%)	700	
		(2,800)
		700

The figure of £700 is taken (as greater than the current market value of £600).

Benefit taxed in 2004/05

	£
Initial market value minus benefits already taxed	700
Less amount paid by director	(600)
Benefit	100

(c) **Taxable cheap loan to a director**

Using the average method produces a taxable benefit of £350.

$$\frac{£40,000 + £30,000}{2} \times (5\% - 4\%) = £350$$

Using the strict method the benefit would be.

£40,000 × 8/12 (5% − 4%) + £30,000 × 4/12 (5% − 4%) = £367

The Revenue usually only insist on the strict method being used when the average method is being deliberately exploited

(d) **The provision of medical insurance**

The taxable amount of a benefit for an employee earning £8,500 or more a year or a director is the cost to the employer of providing it. The benefit is thus £800.

(e) **Mercedes car**

The car was available for only seven months of the year so the benefit must be on a time basis.

£24,000 × 35% (W) × 7/12 £4,900

As the director was required to make good the cost of all private fuel, no taxable benefit arises in respect of the fuel.

(f) **Computer**

	£
£3,900 × 20%	780
Less: de minimis	(500)
	280

BPP
PROFESSIONAL EDUCATION

Working

1   *Taxable percentage for car benefit*

CO_2 emissions = 245g/km
Emissions over baseline figure 245 − 145 = 100g/km
Divide by 5 = 20. Taxable % = 15 + 20 = 35%.

10 Taxable and exempt benefits

(a)   As the loan to Zoë Dexter does not exceed £5,000, this is not a taxable loan.

(b)   The annual value of the computer equipment lent to Victoria Eustace is 20% × £2,000 = £400. The first £500 of any annual benefit that would otherwise arise in respect of the private use of a computer by an employee is exempt. This means there is no taxable benefit.

(c)   The taxable benefit arising in respect of the car and fuel is:

	£
Car (£17,250 × 15%) × 10/12	2,156
Fuel (£14,400 × 15%) × 10/12	1,800
	3,956

Tutorial note 1. The car and fuel benefits are both multiplied by 10/12 as the car was available for only ten months throughout 2004/05.

Tutorial note 2. The car benefit is based on the original cost of the car, not the market value when first provided to Amanda.

Tutorial note 3. As the car emits CO_2 of 145g/km the taxable percentage used for calculating the car and fuel benefit is 15%.

(d)   The taxable amount in respect of the car and fuel is:

	£
Car (£16,000 × 30%)	4,800
Fuel (£14,400 × 30%)	4,320
	9,120

Tutorial note 1. The car emits 220g/km of CO_2, This is 75g/km above the baseline emissions of 145 g/km.

This means the taxable percentage is 15% + 75/5% = 30%.

Tutorial note 2. The fuel benefit is not reduced by partial reimbursements of the cost of private fuel.

(e)   The private use of a mobile telephone is an exempt benefit.

(f)   This benefit as an exempt benefit. An employer can pay up to £2 per week to an employee tax free without the need to keep any supporting evidence of the payment.

---

11 Accommodation

(a) The taxable benefit for Mr Ford will be equal to the annual value of the flat and of the furniture. The company's payment of the council tax will also be a taxable benefit:

	£
Basic accommodation benefit: Rateable value	900
Additional benefit £(100,000 – 75,000) × 5%	1,250
Furniture (20% × £5,000)	1,000
Council tax	500
	3,650

(b) As Charles Rainer's accommodation is job-related he is not taxable on either the accommodation or the council tax paid by the company.

Tutorial note. If accommodation is job related there is no taxable benefit in respect of the accommodation or of any council tax paid by the employer.

12 Rita

(a) *Accommodation*

	£
Annual value (higher than rent paid)	4,000
Electricity	700
Gas	1,200
Water	500
Council tax	1,300
Repairs	3,500
Furniture (20% × £30,000 × 6/12)	3,000
Purchase (W)	7,000
	21,200

Working

Purchase of furniture

Benefit is the higher of:

		£
(i)	Cost	30,000
	Less: taxed	(3,000)
		27,000
	Less: amount paid	(20,000)
		7,000
(ii)	Market value	25,000
	Less: amount paid	(20,000)
		5,000

ie £7,000

(b) Relocation (£12,000 – £8,000) = £4,000
(c) Loan (£10,000 × 5%) = 500

BPP)))
PROFESSIONAL EDUCATION

13 Sally

(a)   SCHEDULE: DEDUCTIBLE EXPENSES

   (i)   **Expenses other than professional subscriptions**

          Business calls on home telephone   £270

   (ii)   **Professional subscriptions**

          Chartered Institute of Marketing £50

(b)   MEMORANDUM

   To: Sally
   From: Richard
   Date: 12 April 2005
   Subject: Tax-deductibility of expenses

   The tax treatment of your expenses is as follows.

   (i)   Rail fare: no deduction, because the cost of travelling from home to work is the cost of your
          ordinary commuting to work. If you were only working at the new location on a temporary basis
          (up to 24 months), the cost would be deductible.

   (ii)   Telephone bill: the cost of business calls is deductible. However, it is not possible to apportion the
          line rental between business and private use and claim a deduction for the business proportion.

   (iii) Subscription to the Chartered Institute of Marketing: this is deductible under a special rule relating
          to subscriptions to professional bodies relevant to your job. The fact that you are a member in
          order to put yourself in a position to perform your duties better does not matter.

   (iv)   Subscriptions to professional journals: not deductible, because you read them in order to put
          yourself in a position to perform your duties better. You do not read them in performing your
          duties.

   (v)   Subscription to a London club: not deductible, because the subscription is not necessary in order
          to enable you to perform your duties.

Chapter 3 Employment income: Additional aspects

14 Bill Wilson

(a) **Bill Wilson – Taxable income**

	Non-savings income £	Savings (excl. dividends) income £	Dividend income £	Total income £
Salary	33,750			
Car benefit (W2)	3,300			
Fuel benefit (W3)	2,376			
Job seekers allowance	723			
Dividends £1,350 × 100/90			1,500	
Interest £360 × 100/80		450		
National Savings Bank – received gross		110		
3.5% War Loan – received gross		250		
STI	40,149	810	1,500	42,459
Less: PA	(4,745)			(4,745)
Taxable income	35,404	810	1,500	37,714

(b) **Tax payable**

	£
Non-savings income	
£2,020 × 10%	202
£29,380 × 22%	6,464
£400 × 22% (Gift Aid)	88
£(35,404 – 30,500 – 400) = £3,604 × 40%	1,442
Savings (excluding dividends) income	
£810 × 40%	324
Dividend income	
£1,500 × 32.5%	488
Tax liability	9,008
Less: tax on dividends £1,500 × 10%	(150)
tax on bank interest £450 × 20%	(90)
Tax payable (before PAYE)	8,768

Workings

1 *Taxable car and fuel %*

CO_2 emissions above baseline
180 g/km(rounded down to nearest below) – 145 g/km = 35 g/km
Divide by 5 = 35/5 = 7
% = 15% + 7% = 22%

2 *Car benefit*

22% (W1) × £20,000 × 9/12 =   £3,300

3 *Fuel benefit*

£14,400× 22% (W1) × 9/12 =   £2,376

(c) **Amounts left out of calculation**

(i) Dividends from ISA investments – not taxable.

(ii) Interest from ISA – not taxable.

(iii) Termination payment – not provided under a contractual obligation and less than £30,000.

(d) **Four expenses deductible from employment income**

Any four from:

(i) Contributions (within certain limits) to an approved occupational pension scheme

(ii) Subscriptions to professional bodies if relevant to occupation

(iii) Payments for certain liabilities and insurance against them

(iv) Mileage allowance relief

(v) Qualifying travel expenses

(vi) Other expenses incurred wholly, exclusively and necessarily in the performance of the duties of the employment

(vii) Amounts given under the payroll giving scheme.

15 Ian Warburton

	£
Salary (£1,365 × 100/105 × 4) + (£1,365 × 8)	16,120
Car benefit £11,000 × 25% (W)	2,750
Petrol benefit (partial contribution ignored) £14,400 × 25% (W)	3,600
Bonus	1,000
	23,470
Less pension contributions £16,120 × 3%	(484)
Taxable earnings	22,986

Tutorial note. Contributions to occupational pension schemes can be deducted in arriving at taxable income. Contributions to personal pension plans on the other hand, extend the basic rate income tax band.

Working

1 *Taxable percentage for car and fuel benefits*

CO_2 emissions = 195g/km (Rounded down to nearest 5 below)
Above baseline 195 – 145 = 50g/km
Divide by 5 = 10
Taxable percentage = 15% + 10% = 25%

16 David

David Rogers Esq
1 High Street
Marlow
Bucks

20 April 2005

Dear Mr Rogers

Personal pension contributions

Further to your query regarding personal pensions I have set out below the rules which now apply in respect of personal pension contributions.

With the exception of some members of company pension schemes, anyone who is under the age of 75 can make contributions to a stakeholder pension plan. Any individual can contribute up to £3,600 (gross) in any tax year to a pension scheme regardless of the level of their earnings. It is worth noting that, this means that £3,600 could be paid into a pension scheme for your wife Sue, regardless of the fact that she has no earnings. If contributions are to be higher than £3,600 (gross) per tax year the maximum contribution that can be paid depends on your age at the start of the tax year and, broadly, the level of your self employed earnings in the current tax year or any one of the five previous tax years as shown in the table below.

Age on 6 April in tax year	Maximum % of net relevant earnings that may be paid
35 or under	$17^{1}/_{2}$%
36 – 45	20%
46 – 50	25%
51 – 55	30%
56 – 60	35%
61 or over	40%

Any contributions made to a personal pension scheme are paid net of basic rate (22%) income tax. If you remain a basic rate income tax payer there will be no need for you to take any further action in respect of your pension contributions. If you become a higher rate (40%) taxpayer you will be able to claim additional tax relief on your pension contributions through your income tax return.

There is some flexibility in which year tax relief is claimed for a pension contribution. Provided you pay a contribution before 31 January in a tax year, and elect at the same time to carry it back, the contribution can be treated as though it were paid (and therefore eligible to tax relief) in the previous tax year.

I hope the above is helpful. If you have any further queries please do not hesitate to contact me.

Yours sincerely

A N Accountant

17 Stakeholder pensions

(a)   Maximum contributions

Tax year	Age at start of tax year	Basis year	%	Maximum contribution £
2004/05	42	2004/05	20	5,000
2005/06	43	2005/06	20	16,000
2006/07	44	2005/06	20	16,000
2007/08	45	2005/06	20	16,000
2008/09	46	2005/06	25	20,000
2009/10	47	2005/06	25	20,000
2010/11	48	2005/06	25	20,000
2011/12	49	2008/09	25	18,750

Note. The % depends on age at *start of the tax year of contribution* not on age at the start of the basis year.

(b)   **Personal pension contributions are paid net of basic rate tax**. This means that for a basic rate taxpayer tax relief is given at source and there is no need to take any further action.

Higher rate taxpayers obtain additional relief through their personal tax computation. The basic rate band is extended by the gross amount of the pension contribution.

18 Roger Thesaurus

(a)   **Income tax computation**

	Non-savings £	Savings (excl. dividend) £	Dividend £	Total £
Schedule D Case I	67,000			
Dividend (£900 × 100/90)			1,000	
Bank interest £1,197 × 100/80		1,496		
	67,000	1,496	1,000	
Less charges: copyright royalty	(6,000)			
STI	61,000	1,496	1,000	63,496
Less personal allowance	(4,745)			
	56,255	1,496	1,000	58,751

Tutorial note. In Unit 19 you will not be expected to compute Schedule D Case I income but you may, as here, be expected to include it in the income tax computation.

£

Tax on non-savings income
£2,020 × 10%	202
£29,380 × 22%	6,464
£15,000 (extended band) × 22%	3,300
£9,855 × 40%	3,942

Tax on savings (excl. dividend) income
£1,496 × 40%	598

Tax on dividend income
£1,000 × 32.5%	325
Tax liability	14,831
Less tax suffered on bank interest £1,496 × 20%	(299)
tax credit on dividends £1,000 × 10%	(100)
Tax payable	14,432

(b) As 1999/00 was the basis year, the maximum gross pension premium relievable in 2004/05 is 20% × £80,000, ie £16,000.

The basic rate band is extended by the gross amount of the premium actually paid, £15,000 (£11,700 × $^{100}/_{78}$).

The copyright royalty qualifies for tax relief as a charge on income. The royalty is paid gross.

Tutorial note. Note that the % for personal pension purposes depends on Mr Thesaurus' age at the **start** of 2004/05.

19 PAYE forms

(a) Following the end of each tax year, the employer must send the Revenue:

(i) by 19 May:

* **End of year Returns P14** (showing the same details as the P60);
* **Form P35** (summary of tax and NI deducted).

(ii) by 6 July:

* **Forms P11D** (benefits etc for directors and employees paid £8,500+ pa);
* **Forms P9D** (benefits etc for other employees).

(b) At the end of each tax year, the employer must provide each employee with a form P60. This shows total taxable emoluments for the year, tax deducted, code number, NI number and the employer's name and address. The P60 must be provided by 31 May following the year of assessment.

(c) When an employee leaves, a certificate on form P45 (particulars of Employee Leaving) must be prepared. This form shows the employee's code and details of his income and tax paid to date and is a four part form. One part is sent to the Revenue, and three parts handed to the employee. One of the parts (part 1A) is the employee's personal copy. If the employee takes up a new employment, he must hand the other two parts of the form P45 to the new employer. The new employer will fill in details of the new employment and send one part to the Revenue, retaining the other. The details on the form are used by the new employer to calculate the PAYE due on the next payday.

20 Frederick Fuse

Task 1

TAXABLE EARNINGS 2004/05

	£	£
Salary		41,000
Benefits:		
Car £14,000 × 25% (W1)	3,500	
Fuel £14,400 × 25% (W1)	3,600	
Private medical insurance	965	
Entertainment	3,000	
Home telephone: (£100 + £600)	700	
Computer (£10,000 × 20% × 4/12 – £500)	167	
		11,932
		52,932
Less: Claim for expenses wholly, exclusively and necessarily in the course of employment		
Telephone calls (50% × £600)	300	
Entertaining	2,900	
		(3,200)
Taxable earnings		49,732

Tutorial notes

1   The employee is taxed on the cost to the employer of providing the private medical insurance.

2   An employee is taxable of any amount reimbursed for expenses, such as in respect of entertaining or the use of a home telephone. However, he can then claim tax relief for any expense incurred wholly, exclusively and necessarily in the course of the employment. The rental of a home phone line cannot be the subject of such a claim although the charge for business calls can.

3   For assets made available for private use there is, in general, a taxable benefit of 20% per annum of the asset's market value when it was first made available. However, the first £500 of any such benefit calculated in respect of the private use of a computer is exempt from tax.

Working

1   *Car and fuel taxable percentage*
     CO_2 emissions = 195g/km (rounded down to nearest 5)
     Excess over baseline figure 195 – 145 = 50g/km
     Divide by × 5 = 10
     Taxable percentage = 15 + 10 = 25%

Task 2

	Non-savings £	Savings (excl dividend) £	Dividend £	Total £
Earnings (Part (a))	49,732			
Savings income:				
Dividends			3,700	
Buildings society interest		5,625		
ISA – exempt		0		
Bank interest		1,375		
National Savings Bank		95		
STI	49,732	7,095	3,700	60,527
Less: Personal allowance	(4,745)			
	44,987	7,095	3,700	55,782

Task 3

	£
Income tax on non-savings income	
£2,020 × 10%	202
£29,380 × 22%	6,464
£2,538 × 22% (extended basic rate band)	558
£11,049 × 40%	4,420
Income tax on savings (excl dividend) income	
£7,095 × 40%	2,838
Income tax on dividend income	
£3,700 × 32.5%	1,203
	15,685

Less: Tax credit on dividend income	370	
PAYE	13,600	
Savings income	1,400	
		(15,370)
Tax payable		315

Tutorial note 1. National Savings Bank interest is received gross.

Tutorial note 2. The basic rate band is extended by the gross amount of the personal pension contribution, £2,538, (£165 × 12 × 100/78).

Task 4

If Mr Fuse contributes £100 per month towards the private use of his car, the taxable value of the car benefit will be reduced by £100 a month.

There will be no reduction of the taxable value of the fuel benefit unless Mr Fuse pays the full cost of the private fuel. Therefore, if he contributes £10 a month towards the private fuel there will be no reduction in the taxable value of the fuel benefit.

21 The Benns

(a)   INCOME TAX COMPUTATION FOR MR BENN

	Non-savings £	Savings (excl dividends) £	Dividends £	Total £
Taxable earnings £(40,720 + 5,000)	45,720			
Building society interest × 100/80		400		
Dividends (given gross)			1,230	
Bank interest × 100/80		134		
STI	45,720	534	1,230	47,484
Less personal allowance	(4,745)	0	0	
Taxable income	40,975	534	1,230	42,739

Tutorial note. Interest arising on the ISA account is ignored as it is exempt.

(b)   Income tax

	£
Non-savings income	
£2,020 × 10%	202
£29,380 × 22%	6,464
£9,575 (W1) × 22%	2,107
Savings (excl dividend) income	
£534 (W1) × 20%	107
Dividend income	
£1,045 (W1) × 10%	104
£185 × 32.5%	60
	9,044

Tax liability

Working

1   **Basic rate band**

The basic rate band is extended by the gross amount of the pension contribution made by Mr Benn:

£8,700 × 100/78 = £11,154

(c)   INCOME TAX COMPUTATION FOR MRS BENN

	Non-savings £	Dividends £	Total £
Schedule D Case I	9,800		
Dividends (given gross)		100	
	9,800	100	
Less: Charge on income (£780 × 100/78)	(1,000)		
	8,800	100	8,900
Less personal allowance	(4,745)	0	
Taxable income	4,055	100	4,155

Tutorial note. Patent royalties are paid net of basic rate tax and so must be grossed up by multiplying $^{100}/_{78}$ in the income tax box.

		£
(d)	**Income tax liability**	
	Non-savings income	
	Starting rate band £2,020 × 10%	202
	Basic rate band: non-savings income £2,035 × 22%	448
	Dividend income	
	£100 × 10%	10
		660

Chapter 4 Investments and land

22 Tax rates

Tutorial note. A fairly simple explanation was appropriate, as the question clearly came from a layman.

Technicians & Co
14 Duke Street
Notown
NT4 5AZ

A Smith Esq
23 Charles Street
Anytown
AN1 4BQ

3 October 2004

Dear Anthony

Thank you for your letter of 1 October.

You are correct in your statement that dividends are received net of a 10% tax credit and building society interest is received net of 20% tax. However, although it may seem rather odd, there are special rules for taxing dividend and interest income which means that only higher rate taxpayers have to pay extra tax on of these types of income.

Any dividend income received must be grossed up by multiplying it by 100/90. The gross dividend is then included in the income tax computation and the gross amount is either taxed at 10% or at 32.5%. Higher rate taxpayers have to pay tax on dividend income at 32.5%. However, other taxpayers such as yourself, pay tax on dividend income at 10% which means that the tax liability is exactly matched by the 10% tax credit and there is no extra tax to pay.

Building society interest must be grossed up by multiplying it by 100/80. The gross amount is included in the income tax computation and is taxed at 10%, 20% or at 40%. Higher rate taxpayers pay tax at 40%, basic rate taxpayers pay tax at 20% and starting rate taxpayers pay tax at 10%. Again, for a basic rate taxpayer such as yourself this means that the tax liability is exactly matched by the tax deducted at source. A starting rate taxpayer would receive a tax repayment.

This may be best illustrated by the following example.

Suppose that four individuals, W, X, Y and Z each receive dividend income of £90 and building society interest of £80 (net). The other income of these four individuals is as follows:

Individual	Other income	Personal allowance	Marginal tax rate
	£	£	%
W	0	4,745	0
X	5,400	4,745	10
Y	15,000	4,745	22
Z	60,000	4,745	40

The tax positions of the four individuals are as follows.

W: a non-taxpayer

W cannot reclaim the tax credit of £10 attached to the dividend but he can reclaim the £20 tax suffered on the building society interest. Overall W gets £190 (£90 + £80 + £20) in his pocket.

X: a 10% taxpayer

X will have to pay tax at 10% on both his gross dividend income and his gross interest. The liability on the dividend income is exactly matched by the tax credit so there is no tax payable by X. However, there will be a repayment of the excess tax suffered on the building society interest. Overall X gets £180 (£90 + £80 + £10) in his pocket.

Y: a 22% taxpayer

Y will have to pay tax at 10% on his gross dividend income and tax at 20% on his gross interest. These liabilities are exactly matched by the tax credit/tax deducted at source so there is no tax to pay by Y. Overall Y gets £170 (£80 + £90) in his pocket.

Z: a 40% taxpayer

Z will have to pay tax at 32.5% on his gross dividend income and at 40% on his gross interest. Relief will be allowed for the tax credit/tax deducted at source

	Dividend £100	Interest £100
Gross income		
	£	£
Tax @ 32.5%/40%	32.50	40
Less: tax credit/suffered	(10.00)	(20)
Extra tax to pay	22.50	20

Overall Z will get £127.50 (£90 + £80 – £22.50 – £20) in his pocket.

I hope that this letter explains the position to you, even if it leaves you feeling that the rules are illogical!

Yours sincerely

Hilary Jones

Hilary Jones

23 Nitin

NITIN: SCHEDULE A INCOME

	£	£	£
First house			
Rent £8,000 × 9/12			6,000
Second house			
Rent £3,600 × 3		10,800	
Rent £21,000 × 1/3		7,000	
		17,800	
Less: water rates £390 × 6/12	195		
insurance £440 × 6/11	240		
interest £350,000 × 10% × 6/12	17,500		
repairs: capital	0		
furniture: in 2005/06	0		
		(17,935)	
			(135)
Schedule A income			5,865

Tutorial notes

1 Schedule A income is taxed on an accruals basis.

2 Tax relief will be available for the replacement furniture in 2005/06.

3 Profits and losses on Schedule A income are pooled, so the loss on the second house is set against the profit on the first house.

24 William Wiles

(a) (i) The houses qualify to be treated as a trade under the furnished holiday letting rules, because they were:

(1) **let furnished on a commercial basis with a view to the realisation of profits.**

(2) available for commercial letting to the public **for at least 140 days** during 2004/05 (294 days and 224 days respectively).

(3) **on average let for at least 70 days**. House 2 satisfies this test since the average for the two houses is 77 days. ([14 + 8 weeks] x 7 / 2

(4) **not occupied by the same person for more than 31 days for at least seven months** during 2004/05.

The tax advantages are that:

(1) **Relief for losses is available as if they were trading losses**, including the facility to set losses against other income. The usual Schedule A loss reliefs do not apply.

(2) **Capital allowances are available on furniture**.

(3) **The income qualifies as net relevant earnings for personal pension relief**.

(b) The Schedule A loss on the furnished holiday lets must be calculated separately to the Schedule A loss arising on the other accommodation.

Schedule A loss on furnished holiday lets:

	£	£
Rental income		
House 1 (14 × £375)		5,250
House 2 (8 × £340)		2,720
		7,970
Expenses		
Business rates (£730 + £590)	1,320	
Insurance (£310 + £330)	640	
Advertising (£545 + £225)	770	
Repairs	6,250	
Capital allowances		
House 1 (£5,200 × 50%)	2,600	
House 2 (£5,200 × 50%)	2,600	
Private use (re house 1)		
(£730 + £310 + £2,600) × 10/52	(700)	
		(13,480)
Schedule A loss		(5,510)

Schedule A loss on other lettings:

	£	£
Rental income		
House 3 (£8,600 × 3/12)		2,150
Expenses		
Loan interest	3,200	
Repairs	710	
Wear and tear allowance (£2,150 × 10%)	215	
		(4,125)
Schedule A loss		1,975

Tutorial note. No capital allowance available on lettings other that furnished holiday lettings. In Unit 19 you will not be expected to compute the amount of capital allowances but you may need to deduct capital allowances in arriving at net rental income, as here.

William can claim to have the Schedule A loss of £5,510 arising in respect of furnished holiday accommodation set off as if they were trading losses including the ability to set them off against his total income.

The Schedule A loss of £1,975 will be carried forward and set against the first available Schedule A profits.

Chapters 5 and 6 Capital gains tax

25 Oregon

(a) **The table**

	£
Proceeds	40,000
Less cost	(7,000)
	33,000
Less indexation allowance to April 1998	
0.789 × £7,000	(5,523)
Chargeable gain before taper relief	27,477

The table is a non-business asset which has been owned for seven years for taper relief purposes, so the taxable gain after taper relief is £20,608 (£27,477 × 75%)

Tutorial note. Non business assets qualify for an additional year for taper relief purposes if they were owned on 17 March 1998.

(b) **The picture**

	£
Proceeds	75,000
Less cost	(37,000)
	38,000
Less indexation allowance to April 1998	
1.047 × £37,000	(38,739)
	nil

The chargeable gain is nil. Indexation cannot convert a gain into a loss.

(c) **The land**

		£
Proceeds		120,000
Less expenses of sale		(2,500)
		117,500
Less:	cost	(57,000)
	expenditure in 2001	(4,000)
	expenditure in May 2003	(3,800)
		52,700

The chargeable gain before taper relief is £52,700. This is a non-business asset which has been held for five years, so the taxable gain after taper relief is £44,795 (£52,700 × 85%).

(d)

	£
Table (part (a))	20,608
Picture (part (b))	Nil
Land (part (c))	44,795
Chargeable gains	65,403
Less annual exemption	(8,200)
Taxable gains	57,203

(e)

    Capital gains tax liability £57,203 × 40%   **£22,881**

    Tutorial note. With income of £80,000, Oregon is clearly a higher rate tax payer and will, therefore, pay CGT at 40%.

26 John Lewis

(a)   JOHN LEWIS: TAXABLE GAINS

	£
Motor car: exempt asset	0
Gain on investment property (W1)	35,000
	35,000
Less allowable loss on part disposal (W2)	(300)
	34,700
Less loss brought forward (W3)	(1,500)
Net taxable gains before taper relief	33,200

(b)

Gain after taper relief (95%) (see note)	31,540
Less annual exemption	(8,200)
Taxable gains	23,340

Tutorial note 1. Taper relief reduces the gain on the investment property to 95% of the amount chargeable. There are three complete years of ownership post 5.4.1998.

Tutorial note 2. Taper relief applies to chargeable gains after deduction of any losses of the same tax year and any losses carried forward from earlier years.

(c)   (i)   CGT with income of £0,000

    The income will be partly covered by the personal allowance, with the rest £1,255 (£6,000 – £4,745) taxable at the starting rate of tax. £765 (£2,020 – £1,255) of the gains fall within the starting rate band and are taxable at 10%. The rest fall within the basic rate band, and are taxable at 20%.

    The capital gains tax liability will be as follows.

	£
£765 × 10%	76
£22,575 × 20%	4,515
	4,591

(ii)   CGT with income of £34,480

	£
Income	34,480
Less personal allowance	(4,745)
Taxable income	29,735
Basic rate limit	(31,400)
	(1,665)
Remaining basic rate band	
CGT: £1,665 × 20%	333
£21,675 £(23,340 – 1,665) × 40%	8,670
Capital gains tax liability	9,003

Workings

1   The disposal of the investment property

	£
Proceeds	60,000
Less cost	(25,000)
Gain before taper relief	35,000

2   The part disposal of the field

	£
Proceeds (£125,000 – £300)	124,700
Less probate value of part disposal $\dfrac{125,000}{125,000+375,000} \times £500,000$	(125,000)
Allowable loss	(300)

3   Losses brought forward

Year	Current year net gains £	Loss brought forward set off £	Annual exemption £
2002/03	7,000	0	7,700
2003/04	8,900	1,000	7,900
		1,000	
Loss brought forward at 6.4.02		2,500	
Loss brought forward to 2004/05		1,500	

27 Wyoming

(a) TAXABLE INCOME

	Non-savings £
Income	20,150
Less personal allowance	(4,745)
Taxable income	15,405

(b) INCOME TAX

	£
Non-savings income	
£2,020 × 10%	202
£13,385 × 22%	2,945
15,405	3,147

(c) CAPITAL GAINS AFTER TAPER RELIEF

	£
Gains	
Picture (75%)	10,875
Shares (75%)	15,000
	25,875
Less annual exemption	(8,200)
Taxable gains	17,675

The picture and the shares are both non-business assets which have been held for 7 years (including the additional year) so 75% of the gains are chargeable after taper relief.

Tutorial note. The motor car and the gilt edged securities are exempt assets so no allowable loss or chargeable gain arises on them.

(d) CAPITAL GAINS TAX

	£
£15,995 (£31,400 – £15,405) × 20%	3,199
£1,680 × 40%	672
17,675	3,871

28 Washington

Tutorial note. Losses carried back on death or carried forward during lifetime never waste the annual exemption.

Before Washington's death, the position would have been as follows.

	£
2001/02	
Gains	2,000
Less losses	(2,000)
Taxable gains	0
Losses carried forward	8,000
2002/03	
Gains	32,500
Less current year losses	(4,500)
	28,000
Less losses brought forward	(8,000)
	20,000
Less annual exemption	(7,700)
Taxable gains	12,300
2003/04	
Gains	10,100
Less losses	(2,000)
	8,100
Less annual exemption	(7,900)
Taxable gains	200

Following Washington's death, the position would be as follows.

	£
2004/05	
Gains	15,000
Less losses	(15,000)
Taxable gains	0
Losses to carry back	12,000

Year	Original taxable gains £	Losses brought back £	Final taxable gains £
2001/02	0	0	0
2002/03	12,300	11,800	500
2003/04	200	200	0
		12,000	

29 Alison Garry

Task 1

	£
Cottage 1	
Proceeds net of fees	92,082
Less cost	(41,000)
	51,082
Less indexation allowance to April 1998 0.917 × £41,000	(37,597)
Chargeable gain before taper relief	13,485

Task 2

	£
Cottage 2	
Proceeds net of fees £(85,000 – 850 – 1,500)	82,650
Less Cost	(30,000)
Enhancement expenditure (June 1983)	(10,000)
	42,650
Less indexation allowance to April 1998 (1.047 × £30,000)	(31,410)
£10,000 × 0.917	(9,170)
Chargeable gain before taper relief	2,070

Task 3

	£
Gains after taper relief £(13,485 + 2,070) × 75%	11,666
Less annual exemption	(8,200)
Taxable gains	3,466
CGT £3,466 × 40%	£1,386

Tutorial note: Both cottages had been owned for 7 years for taper relief purposes.

Chapter 7 Shares and securities

30 Eleanor

Post 6.4.98 acquisitions are treated as disposed of on a LIFO basis:

(i) 3.11.02 acquisition

	£
Proceeds (2,000/11,000) × £66,000)	12,000
Less: Cost	(12,800)
Allowable loss	(800)

(ii) 29.6.01 acquisition

	£
Proceeds (3,000/11,000 × £66,000)	18,000
Less: Cost	(17,500)
Gain	500

No taper relief as the shares had been owned for less that three years for taper relief purposes.

(iii) The FA 1985 pool

	Shares	Cost £	Indexed cost £
Acquisition 19.9.82	2,000	1,700	1,700
Indexation to April 1985			
0.158 × £1,700			269
Acquisition 17.1.85	2,000	6,000	6,000
Indexation to April 1985			
0.039 × £6,000			234
	4,000	7,700	8,203
Indexed rise to December 1985			
0.013 × £8,203			107
Acquisition 12.12.85	2,000	5,500	5,500
	6,000	13,200	13,810
Indexed rise to April 1998			
0.693 × £13,810			9,570
Value when pool closes (5.4.98)	6,000	13,200	23,380
Disposal 17.5.04	(6,000)	(13,200)	(23,380)
	0	0	0

	£
Proceeds $\dfrac{6,000}{11,000}$ × £66,000	36,000
Less cost	(13,200)
	22,800
Less indexation allowance £(23,380 − 13,200)	(10,180)
Chargeable gain before taper relief	12,620

The loss is first deducted from the gain of £500 as this does not qualify for taper relief. The balance of the loss, £300, is then deducted from the above gain before taper relief is applied.

There are seven complete years of ownership (including the additional year) post 5 April 1998 so the gain remaining after taper relief but before the annual exemption is £9,240 (75% (£12,620 − 300)).

Tutorial note. Losses should be set against gains where the largest percentage of the gain remains chargeable after taper relief.

31 Yvonne

The sale of Yvonne's shares is initially matched with the shares bought in the next 30 days.

	£
Proceeds (1,000/5,000)	4,600
Less: cost (28.3.05)	(4,400)
Chargeable gain	200

No taper relief.

Next the shares are matched with the post 6.4.98 acquisition.

	£
Proceeds (2,000/5,000)	9,200
Less: cost (19.9.02)	(5,000)
Gain	4,200

No taper relief due.

Finally the shares are matched with the FA1985 pool.

	No	Cost £	Indexed cost £
18.8.95	3,000	6,000	6,000
Index to April 1998			
£6,000 × 0.085			510
Pool at April 1998	3,000	6,000	6,510
Disposal. 13.3.05	(2,000)	(4,000)	(4,340)
Pool c/f	1,000	2,000	2,170

	£
	9,200
Disposal proceeds (2,000/5,000)	(4,000)
Less: cost	5,200
Less: indexation (4,340 − 4,000)	(340)
Gain before taper relief	4,860
Gain after taper relief (75%)	£3,645

Yvonne's total gain before the annual exemption is £8,045 (£3,645 + £4,200 + £200).

32 James Ramesty

(a) **Capital gains before taper relief**

Sale of holiday cottage

	£
Proceeds	160,000
Less: Legal fees	(2,000)
Estate agent's fees	(1,000)
	157,000
Less cost	(30,000)
	127,000
Less: Indexation allowance to April 1998 £30,000 × 0.883	
	(26,490)
Chargeable gain before taper relief	100,510

For taper relief purposes the holiday cottage was held for 7 years (including the additional year). This means that 75% of the gain remains chargeable after taper relief.

Sale of shares

The disposal of shares is initially matched with the post April 1998 acquisitions on a LIFO basis.

12 July 2002 acquisition

	£
Disposal proceeds ($\frac{1,000}{7,300} \times £41,010$)	5,618
Less: cost	(5,000)
Chargeable gain before taper relief	618

No taper relief is due as these shares have only been owned for two years for taper relief purposes.

7 June 2001 acquisition

	£
Disposal proceeds ($\frac{3,000}{7,300} \times £41,010$)	16,853
Less: cost	(15,000)
Gain before taper relief	1,853

For taper relief purposes, these shares have been owned for 3 years, so 95% of the gain will remain chargeable after taper relief (see below).

FA 1985 Pool shares

	No	Cost £	Indexed cost £
12.3.89	200	400	400
4.5.91			
£400 × 0.189			76
			476
Addition	2,000	10,000	10,000
Bonus issue	1,100	–	–
	3,300	10,400	10,476
5.4.98			
£10,476 × 0.218			2,284
Value when pool closes (5.4.98)	3,300	10,400	12,760
Less disposal (10.01.05)	(3,300)	(10,400)	(12,760)

	£
	18,539
Disposal proceeds ($\dfrac{3,300}{7,300}$ × £41,010)	
Less cost	(10,400)
	8,139
Less indexation (£12,760 – £10,400)	(2,360)
Chargeable gain before taper relief	5,779

For taper relief purposes, the share are a non business asset that has been held for 7 years (including the additional year). This means that 75% of the gain is chargeable after taper relief (see below).

Sale of car: Cars are exempt assets so no chargeable gain or allowable loss arises.

(b)   The losses brought forward should be allocated to the gains, where the highest amount of the gain remains chargeable after taper relief:

Shares		
12.7.02 Acquisition	618	
Less: loss brought forward	(618)	
Gain after taper relief		–
7.6.01 Acquisition	1,853	
Less: loss b/f (£1,000 – £618)	(382)	
	1,471	
Gain after taper relief (95%)		1,397
FA 1985 pool		
Gain after taper relief (75%)		4,334
Cottage (75%)		75,383
		81,114
Less: annual exemption		(8,200)
		72,914

(c)   Capital gains tax liability @ 40%   £29,166

33 Kay and Shirley

(a)

	£
Proceeds	31,600
Less: Part cost £40,000 × $\dfrac{31,600}{31,600 + 72,000}$	(12,201)
	19,399
Less: indexation to April 1998 £12,201 × 0.193	(2,355)
	17,044

Gain after taper relief £12,783 (75% × £17,044)

	£
Taxable gain	12,783
Less: Annual exemption	(8,200)
Chargeable gain	4,583

(b)   Shares are matched with post April 1998 acquisitions first:

Shares acquired November 2004

	No	Cost £
Bought	3,000	24,000
Bonus issue	1,500	–
	4,500	24,000

	£
Proceeds (4,500/7,000 × £56,000)	36,000
Less: cost	(24,000)
Gain	12,000

No taper relief due.

1985 Pool

	Number	Cost £	Indexed cost £
January 1997	4,000	18,000	18,000
April 1998 – Pool closes 0.053 × £18,000			954
	4,000	18,000	18,954
March 2001 rights issue	1,000	7,000	7,000
	5,000	25,000	25,954
January 2005			
Bonus issue	2,500	–	–
	7,500	25,000	25,954
March 2005			
Sale	(2,500)	(8,333)	(8,651)
C/f	5,000	16,667	17,303

	£
Proceeds $(56,000 \times \frac{2,500}{7,000})$	20,000
Less: cost	(8,333)
	11,667
Less: Indexation (£8,651 – £8,333)	(318)
	11,349

Gain after taper relief £8,512 (£11,349 × 75%)

Shirley's taxable gain before the annual exemption is £20,512 (£12,000 + £8,512).

Chapter 8 CGT: additional aspects

34 Michelle

	£
Proceeds	10,000
Less sales commission	(1,000)
Net proceeds	9,000
Less cost	(4,000)
Unindexed gain	5,000
Less indexation allowance to April 1998	
1.047 × £4,000	(4,188)
	812

The maximum gain is 5/3 × £(10,000 – 6,000) = £6,667.

The chargeable gain before taper relief is therefore £812.

The gain after taper relief is £609 (£812 × 75%)

Tutorial note. The gross proceeds are used in the formula for calculating the maximum gain on a chattel.

35 A cottage, shares and a chattel

(a) The cottage

	£	£
Proceeds £(100,000 – 800)		99,200
Cost	25,000	
expenditure 1.12.83	8,000	
		(33,000)
Unindexed gain		66,200
Less indexation allowance to April 1998		
1.047 × £25,000	26,175	
0.871 × £8,000	6,968	
		(33,143)
Gain before taper relief		33,057

The gain after taper relief is £24,793 (£33,057 × 75%).

Tutorial note 1. Enhancement expenditure is deductible if it is reflected in the state or nature of an asset at the time of disposal.

(b)   The disposal of shares in JVD Products plc

The shares are on a LIFO basis:

	£
2 August 2004 acquisition	
Proceeds (2,800/4,000 × £20,000)	14,000
Less: Cost	(13,900)
Gain	100

No taper relief

	£
10 March 2002 acquisition	
Proceeds (500/4,000 × £20,000)	2,500
Less: Cost	(800)
Gain	1,700

No taper relief

	£
6 June 2001 acquisition	
Proceeds (500/4,000 × £20,000)	2,500
Less: Cost	(400)
Gain before taper relief	2,100

The shares have been owned for three years so the gain after taper relief is £1,995 (£2,100 × 95%).

FA 1985 Pool

	£
Proceeds (200/4,000 × £20,000)	1,000
Less: Cost (200/2,000 × £1,500)	(150)
	850
Less: Indexation to April 1998	
0.036 × £150	(5)
Gain before taper relief	845

Gain after taper relief £634 (£845 × 75%)

The total chargeable gain on the sale of the shares is £4,429 (£100 + £1,700 + £1,995 + £634).

(c)   The oil painting

	£
Proceeds (market value)	7,000
Less cost	(10,000)
Loss	(3,000)

The loss on the disposal to John's sister, being on a disposal to a connected person, can only be set against a chargeable gain on a disposal to the same connected person while still connected. This loss must therefore be carried forward.

Tutorial note. A disposal to a connected person must be treated as though it were made at market value. Any loss arising can only be offset against gains made on disposal to the same connected person.

(d)   The tax liabilities

	Non-savings £
Salary/ STI	21,000
Less personal allowance	(4,745)
Taxable income	16,255

	£
Income tax on non-savings income	
£2,020 × 10%	202
£14,235 × 22%	3,132
Tax liability	3,334

	£
Gain on cottage	24,793
Gain on shares	4,429
	29,222
Less annual exemption	(8,200)
Taxable gains	21,022

Capital gains tax		£
£15,145	£(31,400 – 16,255) × 20%	3,029
£5,877	× 40%	2,351
21,022		5,380

36 Geoff Williams

		£	£
(i)	Ming vase		
	Proceeds	10,000	
	Less selling expenses	(500)	
		9,500	
	Less cost (£2,400 + £100)	(2,500)	
		7,000	
	Less indexation allowance to April 1998 0.171 × £2,500	(428)	
		6,572	
	Compared to:		
	Marginal relief (£10,000 − 6,000) × 5/3	6,666	
	Lowest gain taken		6,572
(ii)	Painting		
	Proceeds	20,000	
	Less cost $\dfrac{20,000}{20,000 + 90,000}$ × £40,000	(7,273)	
		12,727	
	Less indexation allowance to April 1998 0.596 × £7,273	(4,335)	
		8,392	
			8,392
(iii)	Picture - exempt as proceeds and cost < £6,000		Nil
	Gains before taper relief		14,964
	Gains after taper relief (6 April 1998 − 5 April 2004		
	= 6 years plus additional year = 7 years) 75% × £14,964		£11,223

37 Miss Wolf

(a) *The property*

	£
Proceeds	30,750
Less: cost	(6,383)
Unindexed gain	24,367
Less indexation allowance (January 1996 to April 1998)	
0.083 × £6,383	(530)
Gain before taper relief	23,837

Taper relief period is seven years (6.4.98 − 5.4.04 = 6 years plus additional year).

(b) *Painting*

	£
Proceeds	9,000
Less: costs of sale	(900)
	8,100
Less: cost	(2,200)
Gain	5,900

Gain restricted to 5/3 x £(9,000 – 6,000) = £5,000

Taper relief period is 10.9.00 to 9.9.03 = 3 years

(c)   *Summary*

The loss brought forward should be set against the gain on the painting as this has least taper relief.

	Non business	
	6 years	*3 years*
	£	£
Gains	23,837	5,000
Loss: loss b/f		(2,203)
Net gains	23,837	2,797
Taper relief percentages	75%	95%
	£	£
Gains after taper relief	17,878	2,657
Total gains		20,535
Less: annual exemption		(8,200)
		12,335
CGT £12,335 @ 40%		£4,934

38 Mr Fox

Gain on sale

	£
Proceeds	180,000
Less: cost	(50,000)
Unindexed gain	130,000
Less: indexation allowance	
0.703 x £50,000	(35,150)
Indexed gain	94,850

Principal private residence relief then applies to exempt part of the gain:

	Exempt years	Chargeable years
1.8.85 – 31.7.88 (actual occupation)	3	
1.8.88 – 31.7.92 (up to 4 yrs due to place of work	4	
– *not* employed abroad)		
1.8.92 – 31.7.93 (up to 3 years any other reason)	1	
1.8.93 – 31.1.94 (actual occupation)	½	
1.2.94 – 31.7.01 (note)		7½
1.8.01 – 31.7.04 (last 3 years)	3	
Totals	11½	7½

Gain exempt is 11 ½ out of 19 years x £94,850	£57,409
Gain left in charge £(94,850 – 57,409)	£37,441
Gain after taper relief (7 years)	
75% x £37,441	£28,081

Tutorial note. As Mr Fox did not return to live in the house, no part of the period 1.2.94 to 31.7.01 is exempt.

39 John Harley

John Harley – Gain on house

	£
Proceeds	120,000
Less: cost	(40,000)
Unindexed gain	80,000
Less: indexation allowance	
0.808 × £40,000	(32,320)
Indexed gain	47,680
Less: PPR exemption (W)	
179/(65 + 179) × 47,680	(34,978)
Gain left in charge	12,702
Gain after taper relief (6.4.98 – 5.4.04 = 6 years	
plus additional year = 7 years)	
£12,702 × 75%	9,527

Working

	Chargeable months	Exempt months
1.8.84 – 31.5.85 – actual residence		10
1.6.85 – 31.7.89 – employed abroad any period		50
1.8.89 – 31.7.93 – up to 4 years required to live elsewhere		48
1.8.93 – 31.10.95 – up to 3 years any reason		27
1.11.95 – 30.6.96 – actual residence		8
1.7.96 – 30.11.01 – absent	65	
1.12.01 – 30.11.04 – last 3 years ownership		36
Totals	65	179

No relief is given for any part of the last period of absence (eg rest of 3 years for any reason) as it is not followed by a period of actual residence.

40 Peter Robinson

Peter Robinson CGT payable 2004/05

Summary of gains

	£
Flat (W1)	Nil
Chandelier (W2)	2,500
Stamp (W3)	19,455
	21,955
Less: annual exemption	(8,200)
Taxable gains	13,755

CGT payable

£(31,400 − 27,500) = £3,900 × 20%	780
£(13,755 − 3,900) = £9,855 × 40%	3,942
CGT payable	4,722

1   The flat is Peter's principal private residence so no gain arises on its disposal.

2

	£
Proceeds	7,500
Less: cost	(4,000)
Gain	3,500
Cannot exceed £(7,500 − 6,000) × 5/3 =	2,500

Taper relief period less than 3 years so no taper relief available.

3

	£
Proceeds	20,000
Less: Cost	(545)
	19,455

Chapter 9 Administration

41 Mr Brown

(a)   **Returns**

Income tax returns must be submitted by 31 January following the tax year concerned. Thus an individual's return for 2004/05 must be delivered by 31 January 2006. However, if the notice requiring the return is served after 31 October following the tax year, the filing date becomes three months after the notice. Thus, if notice to deliver the return for 2004/05 were given, say, on 1 December 2005, it must be delivered by 28 February 2006.

Where a tax return is filed late a penalty of up to a maximum of £100 can be charged. The Commissioners may impose a further penalty of up to £60 for each day for which the return remains outstanding after the taxpayer is notified of the penalty, although it cannot be imposed after the failure had been remedied.

If no application is made by the Inspector to the Commissioners and the return is not filed within six months of the filing date, the taxpayer is liable to a further maximum penalty of £100 subject to a right of appeal on the grounds of reasonable excuse. If the failure continues after the first anniversary of the filing date and the return shows that there is an outstanding liability to tax, the taxpayer is liable to a penalty equal to that outstanding tax liability.

Any penalty will be limited to the amount of tax outstanding for the year and this will be mitigable.

As an alternative to completing their own calculation, the taxpayer can request Revenue assistance and submit a return by 30 September following the tax year (or, if later, two months from the date of the notice requiring delivery of a return). The Inspector must then raise an assessment in accordance with the information contained in the return and provide the taxpayer with a copy of the assessment.

Additionally, if a taxpayer is issued with one of the new Short Tax Returns, the Revenue will calculate tax provided the short tax return is submitted by 31 January following the tax year.

Payments of tax

Although an individual is not normally required to file a return until 31 January following the tax year, payments on account are required on 31 January in the tax year and on 31 July following it. These payments are required where an individual has either made a self-assessment or been assessed to tax following submission of his tax return for the previous tax year and the amount of the assessment exceeded the tax which was deducted at source: this excess is known as the relevant amount. Tax deducted at source includes PAYE, tax credits on dividends and income tax deducted or treated as paid. The taxpayer is required to pay 50% of the previous year's relevant amount on each of 31 January in the tax year and 31 July following it.

If the taxpayer believes that the current year's income tax and Class 4 NIC liability will be less than the previous year's amount, he may claim to reduce each payment on account may then be reduced to 50% of the amount which the taxpayer believes will be due. If the taxpayer fraudulently or negligently makes a false statement in connection with such a claim, he will be liable to a penalty equal to the amount of tax lost. Interest is charged on the amount by which payments on account are reduced if the reduced amount finally becomes payable. The interest runs from the due date of payment for the payments on account.

Income tax and Class 4 NICs due, in excess of the payments on account, together with the whole of any CGT, must be paid on 31 January in the following year.

Interest on overdue tax is charged on all unpaid tax from the due date. Where the balance of tax (due on 31 January following the year) is unpaid more than 28 days after the due date, a surcharge of 5% of the unpaid amount is also applied. If it remains unpaid more than six months after the due date, there is a further 5% surcharge. The surcharge carries interest from the date imposed to the date paid.

(b)   **Mr Brown**

Due dates of tax – 2004/05

Payments made	Paid	No claim to reduce payments on account	Due date
£		£	
4,500	28 February 2005	6,000	31 January 2005
4,500	14 August 2005	6,000	31 July 2005
4,000	13 March 2006	1,000	31 January 2006
13,000		13,000	

Interest due

Payments on account:

	£
£4,500 × 28/365 × 6.5%	22.44
£4,500 × 14/365 × 6.5%	11.22
£1,500 × 405/365 × 6.5%	108.18
£1,500 × 224/365 × 6.5%	59.84
Final payment:	
£1,000 × 40/365 × 6.5%	7.12
	208.80

42 John Jefferies

(a)   **John Jefferies – Taxable income 2004/05**

	Non-savings income	Savings (excl. dividends) income	Dividend income	Total income
	£	£	£	£
Salary	48,000			
Car benefit (W1)	5,580			
Car fuel (W1)	4,464			
Institute of Management	(140)			
Sports club – not allowable				
Taxable earnings	57,904			
Dividends 1,800 × 100/90			2,000	
NSB easy access a/c interest		300		
Schedule A rental (W2)	1,835			
STI	59,739	300	2,000	62,039
Less: PA	(4,745)			(4,745)
Taxable income	54,994	300	2,000	57,294

(b)   **John Jefferies – Income tax payable 2004/05**

	£
Non-saving income	
£2,020 @ 10%	202
£(31,400 – 2,020) = 29,380 @ 22%	6,464
£(390 × $^{100}/_{78}$) = 500 + 4,800 = 5,300 @ 22% (Gift aid and pension) (W3)	1,166
£(54,994 – 31,400 – 5,300) = 18,294 @ 40%	7,318
Savings income	
£300 @ 40%	120
Dividend income	
£2,000 @ 32.5%	650
Tax liability	15,920
Less: tax suffered	
dividend £2,000 @ 10%	(200)
Tax payable	15,720

Note.

1   Usually tax on salary and benefits would be collected through the PAYE system.

2   Interest on a national savings easy access account is recieved gross.

Workings

1 *Taxable percentage for car and fuel benefit*	£
List price	18,000

Taxable % = 225 – 145 = 80 g/km
Divide by 5 = 16
% = 15% + 16% = 31%

Car Benefit £18,000 × 31%	£5,580
Fuel Benefit £14,400 × 31%	£4,464

2

		£	£
Income from letting			5,400
Less:council tax		700	
water rates		350	
agents fees		600	
boiler repairs		350	(2,000)
			3,400
Less:wear and tear allowance			
10% × (5,400 – 700 – 350)			(435)
			2,965
Less:loss b/f			(1,130)
Assessable for 2004/05			1,835

Note. No deduction is allowable for the capital expenditure on the window frames. No specific allowance is given for the new furniture as this is covered by the wear and tear allowance.

3   Pension contribution £48,000 × 10% = £4,800

(c)

Tax Advisors
1 High Street
Anytown

Mr J Jefferies
2, Right Street
Anytown   [Date]

Dear Mr Jefferies

SELF ASSESSMENT

The self assessment system requires you to give details of your income to the Revenue on which your tax liability is then calculated.

(i)   *Time to keep information*

You should keep details of your employment income, bank interest, dividends, pension, gift aid payment and subscription payment for a year after 31 January following the end of the tax year ie until 31 January 2007.

Details of rental income and expenses should be kept for five years after 31 January following the end of the tax year ie until 31 January 2011.

(ii)   *Deadlines*

You must submit the return (and supplementary pages) by 30 September 2005 if you wish the Revenue to calculate your tax liability. However, if you wish to calculate your liability you have until 31 January 2006 to submit the return and your self assessment of tax.

(iii)   *Payment of tax*

The tax payable is due on 31 January 2006.

You may prefer to have your liability collected through your PAYE code. This will be done by the Revenue if the liability is less than £2,000 and your return is submitted by 30 September 2005 or shortly thereafter.

You may also be required to make payments on account of tax for 2005/06. These would be 50% of your tax payable for 2004/05. The instalments would be due on 31 January 2006 and 31 July 2006.

However, you are not required to make payments on account if the previous year's self assessment payment was reasonably small (ie less than £500 or 20% of total tax liability).

Please do not hesitate to contact me if you require any further information.

Yours sincerely

Tax Advisor

43 Kitty Bennett

Task 1

CALCULATION OF SCHEDULE A INCOME FOR 2004/05

	£	£
Rent accrued		
6.4.04 – 30.9.04		
£4,000 × 6/12		2,000
1.10.04 – 5.4.05		
£5,000 × 6/12		2,500
Less: Property management fees	800	
Interest	2,450	
Repairs	400	
		(3,650)
Schedule A income		850

Task 2

CALCULATION OF INVESTMENT INCOME 2004/05

	Received £	Gross £	Tax £
Dividends			
31.10.04	3,600	4,000	400
31.3.05	2,700	3,000	300
	6,300	7,000	700
Building society interest			
30.6.04	2,000	2,500	500
31.12.04	1,680	2,100	420
	3,680	4,600	920
Bank interest			
30.9.04	640	800	160
31.03.05	952	1,190	238
	1,592	1,990	398

Task 3

INCOME TAX COMPUTATION 2004/05

	Non-savings £	Savings (exc dividend) £	Dividend	Total £
Schedule D Case I	18,716			
Schedule A	850			
Dividends			7,000	
Building society interest		4,600		
Bank interest		1,990		
STI	19,566	6,590	7,000	33,156
Less personal allowance	(4,745)			
Taxable income	14,821	6,590	7,000	28,411

	£
Income tax on non-savings income	
£2,020 × 10%	202
£12,801 × 22%	2,816
Income tax on savings (excl dividend) income	1,318
£6,590 × 20%	
Income tax on dividend income	
£7,000 × 10%	700
	5,036
Tax liability	
Less: tax credit on dividends	(700)
Less: tax suffered on interest £6,590 × 20%	(1,318)
	3,018
Less payments made on account of 2004/05 tax liability	(1,000)
	2,018
Tax payable	

Task 4

Miss Kitty Bennett's income tax payable for 2004/05 after deducting tax suffered at source and the tax credit on dividends for 2004/05 is £3,018. Two payments on account of £500 each have been made in respect of this amount leaving a final payment of £2,018 due to be paid on 31 January 2006.

Two payments on account of Miss Bennett's 2005/06 income tax liability each of £1,509.00 must be made. These will be due for payment on 31 January 2006 and 31 July 2006.

You should have made the following entries.

Task 5

Supplementary – Land and property pages

Box 5.20: £4,500

Box 5.23: £4,500

Box 5.25: £400
Box 5.26: £2,450
Box 5.27: £800

Box 5.30: £3,650
Box 5.31: £850
Box 5.40: £850
Box 5.43: £850

44 Mr Watson

Task 1

CALCULATION OF TAXABLE EARNINGS FOR 2004/05

	£
Salary	30,250
Car benefit £15,850 × 18% (W) − £600	2,253
Fuel benefit 18% × £14,400	2,592
Medical insurance	656
Use of video £650 × 20%	130
Telephone £(125 + 595)	720
Travel	1,255
Entertaining	1,254
	39,110
Less: expenses claim	
Travel	(1,255)
Entertaining	(1,254)
Phone (£595 × 40%)	(238)
Taxable earnings	36,363

Workings

1 *Car and fuel taxable percentage*
CO_2 emissions = 160g/km
Above baseline 160 − 145 = 15g/km
Divide by 5 = 3
Taxable % = 15 + 3 = 18%

Task 2

SCHEDULES OF DIVIDEND AND INTEREST INCOME FOR 2004/05

	Received £	Gross £	Tax £
Building society interest			
30.6.04	4,768	5,960	1,192
31.12.04	4,888	6,110	1,222
Bank interest			
30.9.04	440	550	110
31.3.05	504	630	126
	10,600	13,250	2,650
Dividends			
31.10.04	1,800	2,000	200
31.3.05	900	1,000	100
	2,700	3,000	300

Task 3

INCOME TAX COMPUTATION 2004/05

	Non-savings £	Savings (excl dividend) £	Dividend £	Total £
Taxable earnings (Task 1)	36,363			
Dividends			3,000	
Bank and building society interest		13,250		
STI	36,363	13,250	3,000	52,613
Less personal allowance	(4,745)			
Taxable income	31,618	13,250	3,000	47,868

		£
Income tax on non savings income		
£2,020 × 10%		202
£29,380 × 22%		6,464
£218 × 40%		87
Income tax on savings (excl dividend) income		
£13,250 × 40%		5,300
Income tax on dividend income		
£3,000 × 32.5%		975
Tax liability		13,028
Less:	Tax credit on dividends	(300)
	PAYE	(9,059)
	Tax suffered on interest	(2,650)
Tax payable		1,019

Task 4

You should have made the following entries.

Supplementary – Employment pages

Box 1.8: £30,250
Box 1.11: £9,059

Box 1.16: £2,253
Box 1.17: £2,592
Box 1.21: £656
Box 1.22: £130
Box 1.23: £3,229

Box 1.32: £1,255
Box 1.35: £1,492

Task 5

You cannot, on the whole, choose your status as employed or self-employed. The Revenue consider several different factors in deciding your status, including the following.

    (a)   Indicators of employment

            (i)   You must accept further work when the current task is completed.

            (ii)   You have a right to further work.

            (iii)   You get paid holidays and sick pay.

            (iv)   You must obey normal office rules.

    (b)   Indicators of self-employment

            (i)   You provide your own equipment.

            (ii)   You can hire your own staff to help you.

            (iii)   You invest your own capital and can increase your profits by sound management.

Answers to Full Exam based Assessments

PRACTICE EXAM PAPER 1: ANSWERS

DO NOT TURN THIS PAGE UNTIL YOU HAVE COMPLETED THE EXAM

SECTION 1

ANSWERS (Task 1.1)

Taxable earnings

		£
Salary		41,000
Car benefit		
(£19,000 × 25%(W))	4,750	
Contribution towards private use of the car	(600)	
		4,150
Fuel benefit (£14,400 × 25%)		3,600
Private medical insurance		965
Entertainment	3,500	
Less claim for expenses incurred wholly, exclusively		
and necessarily in the course of employment	(3,500)	
		Nil
Asset made available for private use		
(£1,500 × 20% × 9/12)		225
Taxable earnings		49,940

Workings

1 **Taxable percentage for car and fuel benefit**

CO_2 emissions 195g/km (rounded down to nearest 5 below)
195 – 145 = 50g/km
Divided by 5 = 10
Taxable % = 15 + 10 = 25%

ANSWERS (Task 1.2)

Computation of Schedule A rental income

Property	1	2	3	4	Total
	£	£	£	£	£
Rental Income	4,000	3,000	2,000	6,500	15,500
Less allowable expenses:					
Management fees	400	300	200	650	1,550
Buildings Insurance	100	100	100	100	400
Contents Insurance	50	50	50	50	200
Cleaning	260	260	260	260	1,040
Repairs	100	250	nil	50	400
Council tax	450	350	200	350	1,350
Wear and tear allowance					
(10% rent-council tax)	355	265	180	615	1,415
	2,285	1,425	1,010	4,425	9,145

Total Schedule A income £9,145

Tutorial note The repairs expenditure on property 3 is not allowable as it is a capital item.

ANSWERS (Task 1.3)

Income for the year ended 5 April 2005

Inland Revenue

EMPLOYMENT

Fill in these boxes first

Name Jane Austen

Tax reference B452

If you want help, look up the box numbers in the Notes.

Details of employer

Employer's PAYE reference - may be shown under 'Inland Revenue office number and reference' on your P60 or 'PAYE reference' on your P45

1.1

1.2 Book Supplier Ltd

Employer's name

Date employment started
(only if between 6 April 2004 and 5 April 2005)

1.3 / /

Date employment finished
(only if between 6 April 2004 and 5 April 2005)

1.4 / /

Employer's address

1.5

Postcode

Tick box 1.6 if you were a director of the company
1.6 ✓

and, if so, tick box 1.7 if it was a close company
1.7

Income from employment

■ **Money** - see Notes, page EN3

Before tax

- Payments from P60 (or P45) **1.8** £ 41,000

- Payments not on P60, etc. - tips **1.9** £

  - other payments (excluding expenses entered below and lump sums and compensation payments or benefits entered overleaf) **1.10** £

Tax deducted

- **Tax deducted** in the UK from payments in boxes 1.8 to 1.10 **1.11** £15,000

■ **Benefits and expenses** - see Notes, pages EN3 to EN6. If any benefits connected with termination of employment were received, or enjoyed, after that termination and were from a **former** employer you need to complete Help Sheet IR204, available from the Orderline. Do not enter such benefits here.

	Amount			Amount
• Assets transferred/ payments made for you	**1.12** £		• Vans	**1.18** £
• Vouchers, credit cards and tokens	**1.13** £		• Interest-free and low-interest loans see Note for box 1.19, page EN5	**1.19** £
• Living accommodation	**1.14** £		*box 1.20 is not used*	
• Excess mileage allowances and passenger payments	**1.15** £		• Private medical or dental insurance	**1.21** £ 965
• Company cars	**1.16** £ 4,150		• Other benefits	**1.22** £ 225
• Fuel for company cars	**1.17** £ 3,600		• Expenses payments received and balancing charges	**1.23** £ 3,500

SA101

BS 12/04net

TAX RETURN ■ EMPLOYMENT: PAGE E1

Please turn over

BPP PROFESSIONAL EDUCATION

Income from employment continued

■ *Lump sums and compensation payments or benefits including such payments and benefits from a former employer*
Note that 'lump sums' here includes any contributions which your employer made to an unapproved retirement benefits scheme

You must read page EN6 of the Notes **before** filling in boxes 1.24 to 1.30

Reliefs

- £30,000 exception — **1.24** £
- Foreign service and disability — **1.25** £
- Retirement and death lump sums — **1.26** £

Taxable lump sums

- From box B of *Help Sheet IR204* — **1.27** £
- From box K of *Help Sheet IR204* — **1.28** £
- From box L of *Help Sheet IR204* — **1.29** £
- Tax deducted from payments in boxes 1.27 to 1.29 - *leave blank if this tax is included in the box 1.11 figure and tick box 1.30A.* — Tax deducted **1.30** £
- Tick this box if you have left box 1.30 blank because the tax is included in the box 1.11 figure — **1.30A**

■ *Foreign earnings not taxable in the UK in the year ended 5 April 2005 - see Notes, page EN6* — **1.31** £

■ *Expenses you incurred in doing your job - see Notes, pages EN7 to EN8*

- Travel and subsistence costs — **1.32** £
- Fixed deductions for expenses — **1.33** £
- Professional fees and subscriptions — **1.34** £
- Other expenses and capital allowances — **1.35** £ *3,500*
- Tick box 1.36 if the figure in box 1.32 includes travel between your home and a permanent workplace — **1.36**

■ *Seafarers' Earnings Deduction* — **1.37** £

■ *Foreign tax for which tax credit relief not claimed* — **1.38** £

Student Loans

■ *Student Loans repaid by deduction by employer - see Notes, page EN8* — **1.39** £

- Tick box 1.39A if your income is under Repayment of Teachers' Loans Scheme — **1.39A**

1.40 *Additional information*

*Now fill in any other supplementary Pages that apply to you.
Otherwise, go back to page 2 in your Tax Return and finish filling it in.*

BS 12/04net   TAX RETURN ■ EMPLOYMENT: PAGE E2

Income for the year ended 5 April 2005

Inland Revenue

LAND AND PROPERTY

Fill in these boxes first

Name

Jane Austen

Tax reference

B452

If you want help, look up the box numbers in the Notes.

Are you claiming Rent a Room relief for gross rents of £4,250 or less?
(Or £2,125 if the claim is shared?)

Read the Notes on page LN2 to find out
- whether you can claim Rent a Room relief; and
- how to claim relief for gross rents over £4,250

Yes

If 'Yes', tick box. If this is your only income from UK property, you have finished these Pages

Is your income from furnished holiday lettings?
If not applicable, please turn over and fill in Page L2 to give details of your property income

Yes

If 'Yes', tick box and fill in boxes 5.1 to 5.18 before completing Page L2

Furnished holiday lettings

- Income from furnished holiday lettings

5.1 £

■ *Expenses* (furnished holiday lettings only)

- Rent, rates, insurance, ground rents etc.   **5.2** £
- Repairs, maintenance and renewals   **5.3** £
- Finance charges, including interest   **5.4** £
- Legal and professional costs   **5.5** £
- Costs of services provided, including wages   **5.6** £
- Other expenses   **5.7** £

total of boxes 5.2 to 5.7
5.8 £

Net profit (put figures in brackets if a loss)

box 5.1 minus box 5.8
5.9 £

■ *Tax adjustments*

- Private use   **5.10** £
- Balancing charges   **5.11** £
- Capital allowances   **5.13** £

box 5.10 + box 5.11
5.12 £

- Tick box 5.13A if box 5.13 includes enhanced capital allowances for environmentally friendly expenditure   **5.13A**

Profit for the year (copy to box 5.19). If loss, enter '0' in box 5.14 and put the loss in box 5.15

boxes 5.9 + 5.12 minus box 5.13
5.14 £

Loss for the year (if you have entered '0' in box 5.14)

boxes 5.9 + 5.12 minus box 5.13
5.15 £

■ *Losses*

- Loss offset against 2004-05 total income   **5.16** £
- Loss carried back   **5.17** £   *see Notes, page LN4*
- Loss offset against other income from property (copy to box 5.38)   **5.18** £   *see Notes, page LN4*

SA105

BS 12/04net   TAX RETURN ■ LAND AND PROPERTY: PAGE L1   *Please turn over* ➡

Other property income

■ Income

		copy from box 5.14	
• Furnished holiday lettings profits	5.19 £		
• Rents and other income from land and property	5.20 £ 15,500	5.21 £	*(Tax deducted)*
• Chargeable premiums	5.22 £		
• Reverse premiums	5.22A £		boxes 5.19 + 5.20 + 5.22 + 5.22A 5.23 £ 15,500

■ Expenses (do not include figures you have already put in boxes 5.2 to 5.7 on Page L1)

• Rent, rates, insurance, ground rents etc.	5.24 £ 1,950
• Repairs, maintenance and renewals	5.25 £ 400
• Finance charges, including interest	5.26 £
• Legal and professional costs	5.27 £ 1,550
• Costs of services provided, including wages	5.28 £ 1,040
• Other expenses	5.29 £

total of boxes 5.24 to 5.29
5.30 £ 4,940

Net profit (put figures in brackets if a loss)

box 5.23 *minus* box 5.30
5.31 £ 10,560

■ Tax adjustments

• Private use	5.32 £
• Balancing charges	5.33 £

box 5.32 + box 5.33
5.34 £

• Rent a Room exempt amount	5.35 £
• Capital allowances	5.36 £
• Tick box 5.36A if box 5.36 includes a claim for 100% capital allowances for flats over shops	5.36A
• Tick box 5.36B if box 5.36 includes enhanced capital allowances for environmentally friendly expenditure	5.36B
• 10% wear and tear	5.37 £ 1,415
• Furnished holiday lettings losses (from box 5.18)	5.38 £

boxes 5.35 to box 5.38
5.39 £ 1,415

Adjusted profit (if loss enter '0' in box 5.40 and put the loss in box 5.41)

boxes 5.31 + 5.34 *minus* box 5.39
5.40 £ 9,145

Adjusted loss (if you have entered '0' in box 5.40)

boxes 5.31 + 5.34 *minus* box 5.39
5.41 £

• Loss brought forward from previous year

5.42 £

Profit for the year

box 5.40 *minus* box 5.42
5.43 £ 9,145

■ Losses etc

• Loss offset against total income (read the note on page LN8)	5.44 £
• Loss to carry forward to following year	5.45 £
• Tick box 5.46 if these Pages include details of property let jointly	5.46
• Tick box 5.47 if **all** property income ceased in the year to 5 April 2005 **and** you don't expect to receive such income again, in the year to 5 April 2006	5.47

*Now fill in any other supplementary Pages that apply to you.
Otherwise, go back to page 2 of your Tax Return and finish filling it in.* ➤

BS 12/04net   TAX RETURN ■ LAND AND PROPERTY: PAGE L2

BPP
PROFESSIONAL EDUCATION

ANSWERS (Task 1.4)

	Non-savings income £
Taxable earnings	49,940
Schedule A profits	9,145
	59,085
Less charges on income	–
Statutory total income	59,085
Less personal allowance	(4,745)
Taxable income	54,340

ANSWERS (Task 1.5)

	£
£2,020 × 10%	202.00
£29,380 × 22%	6,463.60
£22,940 × 40%	9,176.00
	15,841.60
Less tax suffered	(15,000.00)
Tax payable	841.60

Tutorial note. Tax is computed to the nearest pence. This was what the examiner did in the specimen paper and what would be required in practice.

SECTION 2

ANSWERS (Task 2.1)

1 Sale of property 1

	£
Sale proceeds	300,000
Less costs of sale	(1,500)
Less original cost	(125,000)
Unindexed gains	173,500
Less: indexation allowance to April 1998	
£125,000 × 1.047	(130,875)
Gain before taper relief	42,625

2 Sale of property 2

	£
Sale proceeds	100,200
Less costs of sale	(2,000)
Less original cost	(25,000)
Unindexed gain	73,200
Less indexation allowance to April 1998	
£25,000 × 0.124	(3,100)
Chargeable gain before taper relief	70,100

Both properties have been owned for seven years for taper relief purposes (including the additional year) so 75% of the gains remain chargeable after taper relief.

ANSWERS (Task 2.2)

	£	£
Property 1	42,625	
Less: Loss b/f	(10,000)	
		32,625
Property 2		70,100
Gains before taper relief		102,725
Gains after taper relief (75%)		77,044
Less: Annual exemption		(8,200)
Taxable gains		68,844

Tax payable £68,844 × 40% = £27,537.60

Tutorial note. As both gains attract the same rate of taper relief, it does not matter how the brought forward loss is offset.

ANSWERS (Task 2.3)

MOLE AND CO
CHARTERED ACCOUNTANTS
24 MAIN STREET
ANYTOWN
TELEPHONE (0116) 520 9345
TAX (0116) 520 9346

Jane Austen
Book Supplies Limited
121 High Street
Anytown

10 June 2005

Dear Mrs Austen

Self Assessment Income Tax Return and Tax Payable

I enclose copies of your income tax and capital gains tax computations for 2004/05, together with your completed Self Assessment Tax Return Form.

I would be grateful if you would look through the computation and the self assessment tax return, and if you are happy with them, please sign and date the self assessment tax return and return it to me for submission to the Revenue.

Your Tax computation shows that income tax of £841.60 and capital gains tax of £27,537.60 are due for 2004/05. The total due is £28,379.20. This should be paid to the Collector of Taxes on or before 31 January 2006. You should have received a payslip and prepaid envelope already, but if you need any assistance in making the payment, please do let me know.

If you have any queries, please do not hesitate to contact me.

Yours sincerely

Margaret Jones

Tax Department Manager

Mole and Co

PRACTICE EXAM PAPER 2: ANSWERS

DO NOT TURN THIS PAGE UNTIL YOU HAVE COMPLETED THE EXAM

SECTION 1

ANSWERS (Task 1.1)

Mr Smith – Taxable earnings

	£
Salary	40,000
Benefits (W1)	5,250
Taxable earnings	45,250

Working

1   **Benefits**

	£	£
Car parking space (exempt)		–
Reimbursed mileage allowance (15,000 × 50p)	7,500	
Less tax free: 10,000 × 40p	(4,000)	
5,000 × 25p	(1,250)	
Taxable amount		2,250
Home entertainment system		
£10,000 × 20%		2,000
Mobile phone (exempt)		–
Loan £20,000 × 5%		1,000
Subscription	225	
Less: allowance deduction	(225)	–
Homeworking costs		–
		5,250

Tutorial notes

1.   The provision of a parking space at or near work is an exempt benefit.

2.   The private use of a mobile phone is an exempt benefit

3.   The £104 paid by Mr Smith's employer towards his costs of working at home is an exempt benefit. Up to £104 per annum can be paid without supporting evidence

ANSWERS (Task 1.2)

Mr Smith – Investment income

Interest

	Net £	Tax £	Gross £
Exchequer Stock	1,600	400	2,000
Building society interest	960	240	1,200
	2,560	640	3,200

Dividends

	Net £	Tax £	Gross £
	720	80	800

ANSWERS (Task 1.3)

Mr Smith – Rental income

	£	£
Rental income		24,000
Less:		
Commission	2,400	
Advertising	250	
Repair	125	
Council tax	900	
Wear and Tear £(24,000 – 900) × 10%	2,310	
		(5,985)
Schedule A income		18,015

ANSWERS (Task 1.4)

Mr Smith – Income tax computation

	Non-savings £	Savings excl. dividend £	Dividend £	Total £
Taxable earnings (Task 1.1)	45,250			
Schedule A (Task 1.3)	18,015			
Interest (Task 1.2)		3,200		
Dividends (Task 1.2)			800	
	63,265	3,200	800	67,265
Less: Personal allowance	(4,745)			
	58,520	3,200	800	62,250

Income tax on non-savings income

	£
£2,020 × 10%	202.00
£29,380 × 22%	6,463.60
£7,000 (£2,000 + £5,000) (extended band) × 22%	1,540.00
£20,120 × 40%	8,048.00
	16,253.60

Income tax on savings (excl dividend) income

£3,200 × 40%	1,280.00

Income tax on dividend income

£800 × 32.5%	260.00
	17,793.60

Less:			
	Tax credit on dividend	80	
	PAYE	8,114	
	Tax suffered on building society interest	640	
			(8,834.00)
Tax payable			8,959.60

Tutorial note. The basic rate band is extended by the gross amount of the gift aid donation, £1,560 x 100/78 and the personal pension payments, £3,900 × $^{100}/_{78}$.

Tutorial note. Tax is computed to the nearest pence. This was what the examiner did in the specimen paper and what would be required in practice.

ANSWERS (Task 1.5)

Income for the year ended 5 April 2005

Inland Revenue

EMPLOYMENT

Name	**Tax reference**
Fill in these boxes first Robert Smith	

If you want help, look up the box numbers in the Notes.

Details of employer

Employer's PAYE reference - may be shown under 'Inland Revenue office number and reference' on your P60 or 'PAYE reference' on your P45

1.1

Employer's name

1.2 Global plc

Date employment started
(only if between 6 April 2004 and 5 April 2005)

1.3 / /

Date employment finished
(only if between 6 April 2004 and 5 April 2005)

1.4 / /

Employer's address

1.5

Postcode

Tick box 1.6 if you were a director of the company

1.6 ✓

and, if so, tick box 1.7 if it was a close company

1.7

Income from employment

■ **Money** - see Notes, page EN3

Before tax

● Payments from P60 (or P45)   **1.8** £ 40,000

● Payments not on P60, etc.   - tips   **1.9** £

    - other payments (excluding expenses entered below and lump sums and compensation payments or benefits entered overleaf)   **1.10** £

Tax deducted

● **Tax deducted** in the UK from payments in boxes 1.8 to 1.10   **1.11** £ 8,114

■ *Benefits and expenses - see Notes, pages EN3 to EN6. If any benefits connected with termination of employment were received, or enjoyed, after that termination and were from a **former** employer you need to complete Help Sheet IR204, available from the Orderline. Do not enter such benefits here.*

	Amount			Amount
● Assets transferred/ payments made for you	**1.12** £		● Vans	**1.18** £
● Vouchers, credit cards and tokens	**1.13** £		● Interest-free and low-interest loans *see Note for box 1.19, page EN5*	**1.19** £ 1,000
● Living accommodation	**1.14** £		box 1.20 is not used	
● Excess mileage allowances and passenger payments	**1.15** £ 2,250		● Private medical or dental insurance	**1.21** £
● Company cars	**1.16** £		● Other benefits	**1.22** £ 2,000
● Fuel for company cars	**1.17** £		● Expenses payments received and balancing charges	**1.23** £ 225

SA101

BS 12/04net   TAX RETURN ■ EMPLOYMENT: PAGE E1   *Please turn over*

Income from employment continued

■ *Lump sums and compensation payments or benefits including such payments and benefits from a former employer*
Note that 'lump sums' here includes any contributions which your employer made to an unapproved retirement benefits scheme

*You must read page EN6 of the Notes **before** filling in boxes 1.24 to 1.30*

Reliefs

- £30,000 exception **1.24** £

- Foreign service and disability **1.25** £

- Retirement and death lump sums **1.26** £

Taxable lump sums

- From box B of *Help Sheet IR204* **1.27** £

- From box K of *Help Sheet IR204* **1.28** £

- From box L of *Help Sheet IR204* **1.29** £

- Tax deducted from payments in boxes 1.27 to 1.29 - *leave blank if this tax is included in the box 1.11 figure and tick box 1.30A.* | Tax deducted **1.30** £

- Tick this box if you have left box 1.30 blank because the tax is included in the box 1.11 figure **1.30A**

■ *Foreign earnings not taxable in the UK in the year ended 5 April 2005 - see Notes, page EN6* **1.31** £

■ *Expenses you incurred in doing your job - see Notes, pages EN7 to EN8*

- Travel and subsistence costs **1.32** £

- Fixed deductions for expenses **1.33** £

- Professional fees and subscriptions **1.34** £

- Other expenses and capital allowances **1.35** £ 225

- Tick box 1.36 if the figure in box 1.32 includes travel between your home and a permanent workplace **1.36**

■ *Seafarers' Earnings Deduction* **1.37** £

■ *Foreign tax for which tax credit relief not claimed* **1.38** £

Student Loans

■ *Student Loans repaid by deduction by employer - see Notes, page EN8* **1.39** £

- Tick box 1.39A if your income is under Repayment of Teachers' Loans Scheme **1.39A**

1.40 *Additional information*

Now fill in any other supplementary Pages that apply to you.
Otherwise, go back to page 2 in your Tax Return and finish filling it in.

BS 12/04net   TAX RETURN ■ EMPLOYMENT: PAGE E2

PROFESSIONAL EDUCATION

Income for the year ended 5 April 2005

Inland Revenue

LAND AND PROPERTY

Name

Fill in these boxes first Robert Smith

Tax reference

If you want help, look up the box numbers in the Notes.

Are you claiming Rent a Room relief for gross rents of £4,250 or less?
(Or £2,125 if the claim is shared?)
Read the Notes on page LN2 to find out
- whether you can claim Rent a Room relief; and
- how to claim relief for gross rents over £4,250

Yes

If 'Yes', tick box. If this is your only income from UK property, you have finished these Pages

Is your income from furnished holiday lettings?
If not applicable, please turn over and fill in Page L2 to give details of your property income

Yes

If 'Yes', tick box and fill in boxes 5.1 to 5.18 before completing Page L2

Furnished holiday lettings

- Income from furnished holiday lettings | **5.1** £

■ *Expenses* (furnished holiday lettings only)

- Rent, rates, insurance, ground rents etc. | **5.2** £
- Repairs, maintenance and renewals | **5.3** £
- Finance charges, including interest | **5.4** £
- Legal and professional costs | **5.5** £
- Costs of services provided, including wages | **5.6** £
- Other expenses | **5.7** £

total of boxes 5.2 to 5.7
5.8 £

Net profit (put figures in brackets if a loss)

box 5.1 *minus* box 5.8
5.9 £

■ *Tax adjustments*

- Private use | **5.10** £
- Balancing charges | **5.11** £

box 5.10 + box 5.11
5.12 £

- Capital allowances | **5.13** £

- Tick box 5.13A if box 5.13 includes enhanced capital allowances for environmentally friendly expenditure | **5.13A**

Profit for the year (copy to box 5.19). If loss, enter '0' in box 5.14 and put the loss in box 5.15

boxes 5.9 + 5.12 *minus* box 5.13
5.14 £

Loss for the year (if you have entered '0' in box 5.14)

boxes 5.9 + 5.12 *minus* box 5.13
5.15 £

■ *Losses*

- Loss offset against 2004-05 total income | **5.16** £

- Loss carried back | see Notes, page LN4 **5.17** £

- Loss offset against other income from property (copy to box 5.38) | see Notes, page LN4 **5.18** £

SA105

BS 12/04net

TAX RETURN ■ LAND AND PROPERTY: PAGE L1

Please turn over

Other property income

■ Income

		copy from box 5.14
• Furnished holiday lettings profits	**5.19** £	
• Rents and other income from land and property	**5.20** £ 24,000	Tax deducted **5.21** £
• Chargeable premiums	**5.22** £	
• Reverse premiums	**5.22A** £	boxes 5.19 + 5.20 + 5.22 + 5.22A **5.23** £ 24,000

■ Expenses (do not include figures you have already put in boxes 5.2 to 5.7 on Page L1)

• Rent, rates, insurance, ground rents etc.	**5.24** £ 900
• Repairs, maintenance and renewals	**5.25** £ 125
• Finance charges, including interest	**5.26** £
• Legal and professional costs	**5.27** £
• Costs of services provided, including wages	**5.28** £
• Other expenses	**5.29** £ 2,650

total of boxes 5.24 to 5.29 **5.30** £ 3,675

Net profit (put figures in brackets if a loss)

box 5.23 minus box 5.30 **5.31** £ 20,325

■ Tax adjustments

• Private use	**5.32** £
• Balancing charges	**5.33** £

box 5.32 + box 5.33 **5.34** £

• Rent a Room exempt amount	**5.35** £
• Capital allowances	**5.36** £
• Tick box 5.36A if box 5.36 includes a claim for 100% capital allowances for flats over shops	**5.36A**
• Tick box 5.36B if box 5.36 includes enhanced capital allowances for environmentally friendly expenditure	**5.36B**
• 10% wear and tear	**5.37** £ 2,310
• Furnished holiday lettings losses (from box 5.18)	**5.38** £

boxes 5.35 to box 5.38 **5.39** £ 2,310

Adjusted profit (if loss enter '0' in box 5.40 and put the loss in box 5.41)

boxes 5.31 + 5.34 minus box 5.39 **5.40** £18,015

Adjusted loss (if you have entered '0' in box 5.40)

boxes 5.31 + 5.34 minus box 5.39 **5.41** £

• Loss brought forward from previous year	**5.42** £

Profit for the year

box 5.40 minus box 5.42 **5.43** £ 18,015

■ Losses etc

• Loss offset against total income (read the note on page LN8)	**5.44** £
• Loss to carry forward to following year	**5.45** £
• Tick box 5.46 if these Pages include details of property let jointly	**5.46**
• Tick box 5.47 if **all** property income ceased in the year to 5 April 2005 **and** you don't expect to receive such income again, in the year to 5 April 2006	**5.47**

Now fill in any other supplementary Pages that apply to you.
Otherwise, go back to page 2 of your Tax Return and finish filling it in.

BS 12/04net   TAX RETURN ■ LAND AND PROPERTY: PAGE L2

ANSWERS (Task 1.6)

If Mr Smith calculates his own tax liability the due date for submission of his 2004/05 return is 31 January 2006. If he were to wish the Revenue to calculate his tax liability, the due date for submission of the return would be 30 September 2005.

Payment dates

There are three due dates for the payment of tax:

(1)   31 January in the tax year

(2)   31 July following the tax year

(3)   31 January following the tax year

For any tax year a taxpayer must make payments on account of one half of the amount of tax that he had to pay under self assessment in the previous year. These payments on account are due in two equal instalments on the dates shown in (1) and (2) above. Mr Smith did not have to make payments on account of his 2004/05 tax. On 31 January 2006 he will have to pay £8,959.60 under self assessment. This is the balance of the tax he owes for 2004/05.

In addition he will have to make two payments on account of his 2005/06 tax, of £4,479.80; the first on 31 January 2006 and the second on 31 July 2006.

Confidentiality

The Revenue only correspond with those people whom a taxpayer has authorised to deal with his affairs. This ensures that confidentiality is maintained. Taxpayers must sign an authorisation allowing agents to deal with the Revenue on their behalf. The Revenue will not disclose details of a taxpayer's affairs to any other individual.

SECTION 2

ANSWERS (Task 2.1)

Mr Jones – Calculation of chargeable gains

Exchequer Stock

Any gain arising on the disposal of Exchequer Stock is exempt from capital gains tax, hence no chargeable gain arises.

Ordinary shares in Body Shack Enterprises plc

Post 6.4.98 acquisition

	£
Disposal proceeds ($\frac{10,000}{15,000} \times$ £24,000)	16,000
Less: cost	(9,000)
Chargeable gain before taper relief	7,000

No taper relief is due as the shares are a non-business asset held for one complete year only.

FA 1985 pool shares

	£
Disposal proceeds ($\frac{5,000}{15,000} \times$ £24,000)	8,000
Less: cost ($\frac{5,000}{15,000} \times$ £15,000)	(5,000)
	3,000
Less: Indexation £5,000 × 0.164	(820)
	2,180

Chargeable gain before taper relief.

The shares are a non-business asset that had been held for 7 years including the additional year.

∴ 75% of the net gain is chargeable after taper relief.

JOL plc ordinary shares

	£
Market value	50,000
Less: cost	(10,000)
	40,000
Less: Indexation £10,000 × 0.283	(2,830)
	37,170

The shares are a non-business asset that has been held for 7 years including the additional year. ∴ 75% of the net gain will be chargeable after taper relief.

Summary of gains

	£	£
Body Shack plc shares	7,000	
Less: Loss	(7,000)	–
Body Shack plc shares (FA 85 pool)	2,180	
Less: Loss	(2,180)	
		–
JOL plc Ordinary shares	37,170	
Less: Loss (£13,500 – £7,000 – £2,180)	(4,320)	
		32,850
		32,850
Gain after taper relief (75%)		24,638
Less: Annual exemption		(8,200)
Chargeable gain		16,438

Tutorial note. The capital loss brought forward is first set against the gains which attract the least amount of taper relief. (i.e. the gains where the highest percentage is chargeable after taper relief).

ANSWERS (Task 2.2)

Chargeable gain   £16,438

CGT @ 40% = £6,575.20

£6,575.20 is due for payment on 31 January 2006.

PRACTICE EXAM PAPER 3: ANSWERS

DO NOT TURN THIS PAGE UNTIL YOU HAVE COMPLETED THE EXAM

NOTE: THESE ANSWERS HAVE BEEN PREPARED BY
BPP PROFESSIONAL EDUCATION

SECTION 1

ANSWERS (Task 1.1)

	£
Car benefit (W1)	4,188
Fuel benefit (£14,400 × 24%)	3,456
Loan (£15,000 × (5% − 2%))	450
Entertainment	–
Pension	–
Taxable benefit	8,094

Tutorial notes

1   The company loan was available throughout 2004/05 so there is no need to time apportion it.

2   It is assumed that the reimbursement of the entertainment was a reimbursement of business expenditure.

3   There is no taxable benefit in respect of contributions made to an occupational pension scheme.

Workings

1   Car benefit

Excess of emission rating over baseline (175 (round down) − 145) = 30g/km

Divide by 5 = 6

Taxable % = 15% + 6% + 3%(diesel engine) = 24%

	£
24% × £21,200	5,088
Less contribution (£75 × 12)	(900)
	4,188

ANSWERS (Task 1.2)

	Non savings income £	Savings (excl. Dividend) income £	Dividends £	Total £
Salary	40,000			
Taxable benefits	8,094			
Dividends (× 100/90)			1,720	
Interest		–		
	48,094		1,720	49,814
Less: personal allowance	(4,745)	–		
Taxable income	43,349	–	1,720	45,069

Note Interest arising on an ISA account is tax free.

PROFESSIONAL EDUCATION

ANSWERS (Task 1.3)

Tax on non-savings income

	£
£2,020 × 10%	202.00
£29,380 × 22%	6,463.60
£11,949 × 40%	4,779.60
	11,445.20

Tax in dividend income

£1,720 × 32.5%	559.00
	12,004.20
Less: tax credit on dividend (£1,720 × 10%)	(172.00)
	11,832.20

ANSWERS (Task 1.4)

Provided Joanne is willing to compute her own tax, her tax return for 2004/05 must be submitted by the

(i)   31 January 2006
(ii)   3 months after a notice requiring the return was issued.

If Joanne wishes the Revenue to calculate her tax, her tax return must be submitted by 30 September 2005.

If Joanne submits her return during December 2005 she will have to calculate her own tax but there will be no penalties for late filing.

If Joanne submits her return during February 2006, she will have to calculate her own tax and she will be subject to a £100 penalty for the late filing of the return (assuming a notice requiring the return was issued by 31 October 2005).

ANSWERS (Task 1.5)

- Net rental income from the letting of property is assessed in a tax year on an accruals basis. This means the rental income due in a tax year is assessed in that year.

- Expenditure is deducted in computing net rental income in the year in which it is payable. In general, revenue expenditure is deductible if it is incurred wholly and exclusively for the letting business.

- Capital expenditure is not deductible. This means the cost of the furniture is not deductible. You may instead claim a wear and tear allowance in respect of the furniture. This is calculated as 10% (rent – water rates – council tax).

- Schedule A losses can be relieved against other Schedule A income in the same year. Alternatively losses can be carried forward to set against future Schedule A profits. They cannot be set against other types of income.

Tutorial note. The examiner has said that is it acceptable to answer a question like this using a bullet point list, as above. You will not lose any marks.

ANSWERS (Task 1.6)

Income for the year ended 5 April 2005

Inland Revenue

EMPLOYMENT

Fill in these boxes first

Name
Joanne Harper

Tax reference

If you want help, look up the box numbers in the Notes.

Details of employer

Employer's PAYE reference - may be shown under 'Inland Revenue office number and reference' on your P60 or 'PAYE reference' on your P45

1.1

Employer's name
1.2 Sunny Dials

Date employment started
(only if between 6 April 2004 and 5 April 2005)
1.3 / /

Employer's address
1.5

Date employment finished
(only if between 6 April 2004 and 5 April 2005)
1.4 / /

Postcode

Tick box 1.6 if you were a director of the company
1.6

and, if so, tick box 1.7 if it was a close company
1.7

Income from employment

■ *Money - see Notes, page EN3*

		Before tax
● Payments from P60 (or P45)		**1.8** £ 40,000
● Payments not on P60, etc. - tips		**1.9** £
- other payments (excluding expenses entered below and lump sums and compensation payments or benefits entered overleaf)		**1.10** £

Tax deducted
● **Tax deducted** in the UK from payments in boxes 1.8 to 1.10   **1.11** £

■ *Benefits and expenses - see Notes, pages EN3 to EN6. If any benefits connected with termination of employment were received, or enjoyed, after that termination and were from a **former** employer you need to complete Help Sheet IR204, available from the Orderline. Do not enter such benefits here.*

	Amount		Amount
● Assets transferred/ payments made for you	**1.12** £	● Vans	**1.18** £
● Vouchers, credit cards and tokens	**1.13** £	● Interest-free and low-interest loans see Note for box 1.19, page EN5	**1.19** £ 450
● Living accommodation	**1.14** £	*box 1.20 is not used*	
● Excess mileage allowances and passenger payments	**1.15** £	● Private medical or dental insurance	**1.21** £
● Company cars	**1.16** £ 4,188	● Other benefits	**1.22** £
● Fuel for company cars	**1.17** £ 3,456	● Expenses payments received and balancing charges	**1.23** £ 250

SA101

BS 12/04net

TAX RETURN ■ EMPLOYMENT: PAGE E1

Please turn over

BPP
PROFESSIONAL EDUCATION

Income from employment continued

■ *Lump sums and compensation payments or benefits including such payments and benefits from a former employer*
Note that 'lump sums' here includes any contributions which your employer made to an unapproved retirement benefits scheme

You must read page EN6 of the Notes before filling in boxes 1.24 to 1.30

Reliefs

- £30,000 exception — **1.24** £
- Foreign service and disability — **1.25** £
- Retirement and death lump sums — **1.26** £

Taxable lump sums

- From box B of *Help Sheet IR204* — **1.27** £
- From box K of *Help Sheet IR204* — **1.28** £
- From box L of *Help Sheet IR204* — **1.29** £
- Tax deducted from payments in boxes 1.27 to 1.29 - *leave blank if this tax is included in the box 1.11 figure and tick box 1.30A.* — Tax deducted **1.30** £
- Tick this box if you have left box 1.30 blank because the tax is included in the box 1.11 figure — **1.30A**

■ *Foreign earnings not taxable in the UK in the year ended 5 April 2005* - see Notes, page EN6 — **1.31** £

■ *Expenses you incurred in doing your job* - see Notes, pages EN7 to EN8

- Travel and subsistence costs — **1.32** £
- Fixed deductions for expenses — **1.33** £
- Professional fees and subscriptions — **1.34** £
- Other expenses and capital allowances — **1.35** £ *250*
- Tick box 1.36 if the figure in box 1.32 includes travel between your home and a permanent workplace — **1.36**

■ *Seafarers' Earnings Deduction* — **1.37** £

■ *Foreign tax for which tax credit relief not claimed* — **1.38** £

Student Loans

■ *Student Loans repaid by deduction by employer* - see Notes, page EN8 — **1.39** £

- Tick box 1.39A if your income is under Repayment of Teachers' Loans Scheme — **1.39A**

1.40 *Additional information*

*Now fill in any other supplementary Pages that apply to you.
Otherwise, go back to page 2 in your Tax Return and finish filling it in.*

BS 12/04net   TAX RETURN ■ EMPLOYMENT: PAGE E2

SECTION 2

ANSWERS (Task 2.1)

June 2002 acquisition

	£
Disposal ($^{500}/_{2,000}$ × £61,560)	15,390
Less: cost	(9,800)
Gain	5,590

No taper relief due as these shares have been held for less than three years.

FA 1985 pool

	No £	Cost £	Indexed cost £
July 1989	1,000	15,500	15,500
Indexation to August 1993			
			3,457
£15,500 × 0.223			18,957
Purchase	1,500	21,800	21,800
	2,500	37,300	40,757
Indexation to April 1995			
£40,757 × 0.054			2,201
			42,958
Rights issue	500	5,000	5,000
	3,000	42,300	47,958
Indexation to April 1998			
£47,958 × 0.091			4,364
	3,000	42,300	52,322
Less May 2000 disposal	(800)	(11,280)	(13,952)
Less March 2005 disposal	(1,500)	(21,150)	(26,161)
Balance c/f	700	9,870	12,209

	£
Disposal ($^{1,500}/_{2,000}$ × £61,560)	46,170
Less: cost ($^{1,500}/_{3,000}$ × £42,300)	(21,150)
	25,020
Less: Indexation (£52,322 – £42,300) × $\dfrac{1,500}{3,000}$	(5,011)
Gain	20,009

The shares are a non-business asset that have been held for seven years including the bonus year. 75% of this is chargeable after taper relief.

ANSWERS (Task 2.2)

The gain arising on disposal of the antique table is **EXEMPT**.

Note The table is a chattel sold for GROSS PROCEEDS of £6,000 or less.

ANSWERS (Task 2.3)

	£
Proceeds	101,000
Less: cost £50,000 × $\dfrac{101,000}{101,000+25,000}$	(40,079)
	60,921
Less indexation £40,079 × 0.361	(14,469)
Gain before taper relief	46,452

ANSWERS (Task 2.4)

	75% Gain chargeable	100% Gain chargeable
	£	£
Gain on land	46,452	
FA 1985 pool shares	20,009	
June 2001 acquisition		5,590
	66,461	5,590
Less : loss b/f	(14,410)	(5,590)
Net gains	52,051	–

Gains chargeable after taper relief

	£
£52,051 × 75% =	39,038
Less Annual Exemption	(8,200)
Taxable gain	30,838

Tutorial note. The loss is initially allocated to the gain that attracts the least amount of taper relief, (ie where 100% of the gain is chargeable).

ANSWERS (Task 2.5)

	Savings (exclu. divided) income	Dividend income £	
Dividend (× 100/90)		8,500	
Bank interest (× 100/80)	900		
	900	8,500	9,400
Less: personal allowance	(900)	(3,845)	
Taxable income	–	4,655	4,655

Income tax liability

Dividend income

£4,655 × 10% = £465

Capital gains tax liability

	£
£26,745 × 20%	5,349.00
£4,093 × 40%	1,637.20
	6,986.20

ANSWERS (Task 2.6)

Thank you for your query. You need not be concerned that your tax affairs will not remain private. The firm of Accountants that you use are bound by the ethical guidelines of confidentiality. This means that they may not disclose any details of your affairs to a third party without your consent.

PRACTICE EXAM PAPER 4: ANSWERS

DO NOT TURN THIS PAGE UNTIL YOU HAVE COMPLETED THE EXAM

**NOTE: THESE ANSWERS HAVE BEEN PREPARED BY
BPP PROFESSIONAL EDUCATION**

SECTION 1

ANSWERS (Task 1.1)

	£
Car (£28,600 × 22% (W1))	6,292
Fuel (£14,400 × 22% (W1))	3,168
Loan £20,000 × (5% − 2.5%)(Note)	500
	9,960

Workings

1   **Taxable percentage for car and fuel benefit**
    Emission rating rounded down to the nearest 5 below = 180g/km.
    Amount over baseline figure 180 − 145 = 35g/km
    Divided by 5 = 7
    Taxable percentage = 15% + 7% = 22%

Tutorial note Take care when you read the dates; the loan was available for the whole of the tax year.

ANSWERS (Task 1.2)

	Non-savings £	Savings £	Dividend £	Total £
Salary	18,500			
Less pension @ 5%	(925)			
	17,575			
Less annual subscription	(250)			
	17,325			
Benefits (task 1.1)	9,960			
BSI (gross)		5,200		
Dividends (gross)	–	–	6,000	
	27,285	5,200	6,000	38,485
Less PA	(4,745)			
Total	22,540	5,200	6,000	33,740

Tutorial note. Contributions to an employer's pension scheme are deducted in arriving at taxable income. In contrast, contributions to a personal pension plan are not deducted in computing taxable income. The figure on the P60 issued to Phil Bright will be £(18,500 − 925) = £17,575.

ANSWERS (Task 1.3)

	£
Tax on non-savings income	
£2,020 × 10%	202.00
£20,520 × 22%	4,514.40
£22,540	
Tax on savings income	
£5,200 × 20%	1,040.00
Tax on dividend income	
£3,660 × 10%	366.00
£2,340 × 32.5%	760.50
£6,000	6,882.90

	£	
Less tax deducted at source		
Dividends	600	
BSI	1,040	(1,640.00)
Net tax liability		5,242.90

ANSWERS (Task 1.4)

Protecting client confidentiality is crucial. Under no circumstances should the details of a person's tax situation be discussed with another person. You should politely, but firmly, explain to Beryl that you cannot comply with her request, although you would be happy to assist her individually.

ANSWERS (Task 1.5)

Income for the year ended 5 April 2005

Inland **Revenue**

EMPLOYMENT

Fill in these boxes first

Name

Tax reference

If you want help, look up the box numbers in the Notes.

Details of employer

Employer's PAYE reference - may be shown under 'Inland Revenue office number and reference' on your P60 or 'PAYE reference' on your P45

1.1

Employer's name

1.2

Date employment started
(only if between 6 April 2004 and 5 April 2005)

1.3 / /

Date employment finished
(only if between 6 April 2004 and 5 April 2005)

1.4 / /

Employer's address

1.5

Postcode

Tick box 1.6 if you were a director of the company

1.6

and, if so, tick box 1.7 if it was a close company

1.7

Income from employment

■ *Money - see Notes, page EN3*

Before tax

● Payments from P60 (or P45) **1.8** £ *18,500*

● Payments not on P60, etc. - tips **1.9** £

- other payments (excluding expenses entered below and lump sums and compensation payments or benefits entered overleaf) **1.10** £

Tax deducted

● Tax deducted in the UK from payments in boxes 1.8 to 1.10 **1.11** £

■ *Benefits and expenses - see Notes, pages EN3 to EN6. If any benefits connected with termination of employment were received, or enjoyed, after that termination and were from a **former** employer you need to complete Help Sheet IR204, available from the Orderline. Do not enter such benefits here.*

Amount

● Assets transferred/ payments made for you **1.12** £

● Vouchers, credit cards and tokens **1.13** £

● Living accommodation **1.14** £

● Excess mileage allowances and passenger payments **1.15** £

● Company cars **1.16** £ *6,292*

● Fuel for company cars **1.17** £ *3,168*

Amount

● Vans **1.18** £

● Interest-free and low-interest loans see Note for box 1.19, page EN5 **1.19** £ *500*

box 1.20 is not used

● Private medical or dental insurance **1.21** £

● Other benefits **1.22** £

● Expenses payments received and balancing charges **1.23** £

SA101

BS 12/04net

TAX RETURN ■ EMPLOYMENT: PAGE E1

Please turn over

Income from employment continued

■ *Lump sums and compensation payments or benefits including such payments and benefits from a former employer*
Note that 'lump sums' here includes any contributions which your employer made to an unapproved retirement benefits scheme

You must read page EN6 of the Notes before filling in boxes 1.24 to 1.30

Reliefs

- £30,000 exception   **1.24** £
- Foreign service and disability   **1.25** £
- Retirement and death lump sums   **1.26** £

Taxable lump sums

- From box B of *Help Sheet IR204*   **1.27** £
- From box K of *Help Sheet IR204*   **1.28** £
- From box L of *Help Sheet IR204*   **1.29** £
- Tax deducted from payments in boxes 1.27 to 1.29 - *leave blank if this tax is included in the box 1.11 figure and tick box 1.30A.*   Tax deducted   **1.30** £
- Tick this box if you have left box 1.30 blank because the tax is included in the box 1.11 figure   **1.30A**

■ *Foreign earnings not taxable in the UK in the year ended 5 April 2005* - see Notes, page EN6   **1.31** £

■ *Expenses you incurred in doing your job* - see Notes, pages EN7 to EN8

- Travel and subsistence costs   **1.32** £
- Fixed deductions for expenses   **1.33** £
- Professional fees and subscriptions   **1.34** £ 250
- Other expenses and capital allowances   **1.35** £
- Tick box 1.36 if the figure in box 1.32 includes travel between your home and a permanent workplace   **1.36**

■ *Seafarers' Earnings Deduction*   **1.37** £

■ *Foreign tax for which tax credit relief not claimed*   **1.38** £

Student Loans

■ *Student Loans repaid by deduction by employer* - see Notes, page EN8   **1.39** £

- Tick box 1.39A if your income is under Repayment of Teachers' Loans Scheme   **1.39A**

1.40 *Additional information*

Now fill in any other supplementary Pages that apply to you.
Otherwise, go back to page 2 in your Tax Return and finish filling it in.

SECTION 2

ANSWERS (Task 2.1)

	No	Cost £	Indexed cost £
April 1986 – purchase	300	3,000	3,000
IA to May 1990 (£3,000 × 0.224)			672
			3,672
Purchase	500	8,500	8,500
	800	11,500	12,172
June 1992 – bonus issue	160		
	960		
IA to April 1995 (£12,172 × 0.181)			2,203
			14,375
Purchase	1,000	16,000	16,000
	1,960	27,500	30,375
IA to April 1998 (£30,375 × 0.091)			2,764
			33,139
March 2001 – disposal	(400)	(5,612)	(6,763)
	1,560	21,888	26,376
January 2005 – disposal	(1,560)	(21,888)	(26,376)

	£
Proceeds	45,000
Cost	(21,888)
	23,112
IA (26,376 – 21,888)	(4,488)
Chargeable gain before taper relief	18,624

For taper relief purposes the shares have been owned for 7 years. The gain after taper relief is £13,968 (£18,624 × 75%)

ANSWERS (Task 2.2)

There is no taxable gain or allowable loss as a car is exempt from CGT.

ANSWERS (Task 2.3)

	£
Proceeds	71,000
Less: cost	
£80,000 × $\dfrac{71{,}000}{71{,}000 + 95{,}000}$	(34,217)
	36,783
IA (£34,217 × 0.062)	(2,121)
Chargeable gain before Taper relief	34,662

For taper relief purposes the land has been owned for seven years (including the additional year) so 75% of the gain is chargeable after taper relief – £25,997

ANSWERS (Task 2.4)

	£
Rent receivable (£4,800 – £500)	4,300
Loss b/fwd	(1,600)
Net Schedule A income	2,700

Tutorial note. Rental income is taxable on an accruals basis.

ANSWERS (Task 2.5)

INCOME	£
Schedule A (task 2.4)	2,700
Less PA (restricted)	(2,700)
Taxable income	–

	Total
GAINS	£
Gain on shares (task 2.1)	13,968
Gain on car (task 2.2)	0
Gain on land (task 2.3)	25,997
	39,965
Annual exemption	(8,200)
	31,765

Capital gains tax payable:	
	£
£2,020 × 10%	202.00
£29,380 × 20%	5,876.00
£365 × 40%	146.00
	6,224.00

MEMO

To: Jeanette Alsop

From: Accounting Technician

Date: 1 June 2005

Ref: Late declaration of income

It is always important, when you are dealing with the Revenue, to be as honest as possible. I would therefore recommend that you make a late declaration of income, so that the Revenue has the full picture of your income for 2003/04.

The Revenue will view your mis-declaration as being a submission of an incorrect tax return. Normally, the penalty for this is a charge of up to 100% of the amount of tax underpaid as a result of the incorrect return.

Once the building society interest is taken into account, you will be a 40% taxpayer so you will have made an underpayment of tax. You will therefore need to pay both the underpayment and the penalty.

PART G

Lecturers' Resource
Pack Activities

Note to Students

The answers to these activities and assessments are provided to your lecturers, who will distribute them in class.

If you are not on a classroom based course, a copy of the answers can be obtained from Customer Services on 020 8740 2211 or e-mail publishing @bpp.com.

Note to Lecturers

The answers to these activities and assessments are included in the Lecturers' Resource Pack, provided free to colleges.

If your college has not received the Lecturers' Resource Pack, please contact Customer Services on 020 8740 2211 or e-mail publishing @bpp.com.

Lecturers'
Practice Activities

1 Mary

Mary, a single 24 year old, has business profits of £14,000. She also receives building society interest of £6,400 net, dividends of £1,800 (net), and pays a charge of £2,500 (gross) each year.

Task

Calculate how much cash will she have available to spend in 2004/05? Ignore national insurance.

2 Tom Tulliver

Tom Tulliver has been appointed sales director of Pembridge plc. In addition to a basic salary of £50,000 he has been offered a comprehensive benefits package. The proposed deal is as follows.

(a) The company will provide him with a new 1,400 cc motor car which together with accessories will cost £19,500. The car emits CO_2 of 245g/km. Petrol for private use will be provided but Mr Tulliver must make a contribution of £400 per year towards its cost.

(b) A loan of £5,200 interest free will be made to him on appointment and need only be repaid on his leaving the company. This will be used by Mr Tulliver to purchase a boat.

(c) He has a choice of meals in the company canteen, which is open to all staff free of charge or luncheon vouchers worth £5 per day, an amount equivalent to the normal cost of the meals. He has decided to accept the luncheon vouchers. The normal working year is 200 working days.

(d) His son, aged three, is presently attending a private nursery; this costs £2,000 per year. Pembridge has offered to give his son a free place in their own day nursery at their offices. Mr Tulliver would like to continue the existing arrangement and for Pembridge to continue paying the fees to the existing nursery.

Mr Tulliver's appointment will date from 1 April 2005 and he wishes to examine his tax position before the start of the fiscal year 2005/06.

Tasks

(a) Calculate the taxable benefits arising from Mr Tulliver's employment package as it stands.

(b) Advise him of any changes you consider that he should make to maximise the tax efficiency of the proposed package.

Notes

(a) The official rate of interest should be taken to be 5%.
(b) Use benefit rules for 2004/05 throughout.

3 Simon Harris

During the tax year 2004/05 Simon Harris had the following income:

	£
Salary	28,000
UK dividends (cash amount)	1,800
Building society interest (cash amount)	1,744
Rental income (amount due)	6,000
National savings bank easy access account interest (cash amount)	30

He works for a large UK company and was provided with the following benefits:

- A petrol engined motor car with a list price of £10,667. The CO_2 emissions of the car was 160 g/km. The company paid for all petrol.

- An average outstanding loan of £8,000 to help purchase his main residence. The company charged him a flat rate of 2.75% interest. Simon had no other loans from any source.

- Medical insurance. The company paid £575. A similar scheme would have cost Simon £650 if he had obtained the cover himself.

Tasks

(a) Calculate the income tax payable by Simon for the year 2004/05.

(b) How will the company notify the Revenue of the benefits provided to Simon, and by what date must this be done?

(c) How will the company notify the Revenue of the total pay paid to and the total tax deducted from Simon for the year? By what date must this be done?

Assume the official rate of interest is 5%.

4 Albert

Albert owns a lock-up shop which he had let for some years to Jim at a rent of £2,400 a year payable on the first of each month in advance. The tenancy terminated on 30 June 2004 and the premises remained vacant until 1 October 2004.

On 1 October 2004 Albert let the shop to Jean a rent of £10,400 a year payable quarterly in advance.

Expenditure on repairs incurred by Albert (who was responsible for all repairs) during the year ended 5 April 2005 was as follows.

	£
Period to 30 June 2004	700
1 October 2004 to 5 April 2005	650

Task

Compute Albert's Schedule A income for 2004/05.

5 Joe Joseph

(i)   In the tax year 2004/05 Joe Joseph realised a net capital gain after taper relief (but before the annual exemption) of £12,300. His total taxable income for that year was £29,600.

Task

Calculate the capital gains tax payable.

(ii)   Jim made disposals of non-business assets during 2004/05 resulting in a gain before taper relief of £12,000 and a loss of £3,000. The asset sold at a gain had been purchased in 1990. He has unrelieved losses brought forward of £6,000.

Tasks

(a)   What is Jim's taxable gain after taper relief and the annual exemption?
(b)   What is his loss left unrelieved at the end of 2004/05?

6 Thomas More

In the year to 5 April 2005, Thomas More made the following disposals.

(a)   A flat in a house that he had purchased on 31 March 1982 for £40,000. The house had never been occupied as his main residence and had been consistently let during his period of ownership. The property had been converted into two flats in September 1985 at a cost of £18,000. The flat was sold for £71,000 on 1 December 2004 and out of this legal fees of £2,000 were paid. It was agreed that the value of the other flat was £65,000 in December 2004.

(b)   An investment property which cost £60,000 in December 1990 and which was sold for £160,000 in December 2004.

Tasks

(a)   Calculate the chargeable gain arising on the sale of the flat, after taper relief if applicable.

(b)   Calculate the chargeable gain arising on the sale of the investment property, after taper relief, if applicable.

Assume indexation factors

March 1982 to April 1998	1.047
September 1985 to April 1998	0.704
December 1990 to April 1998	0.252

7 Cecelia

Cecelia acquired 2,500 shares in Black plc on 6 October 1989 for £4,000 and another 2,500 shares for £16,000 on 1 June 2000. She sold the shares on 26 June 2004 for £39,000. The shares are not a business asset for taper relief purposes.

Cecelia's sold no other assets during 2004/05.

Task

Calculate the chargeable gain, after taper relief if applicable, arising on the disposal of the shares.

Assume indexation factors

October 1989 to April 1998   0.384

8 Cubist

Cubist bought and sold three paintings as follows.

Painting	Date bought	Purchase price £	Date sold	Selling price £
A	31.10.89	2,500	4.6.04	7,200
B	16.5.99	7,000	6.8.04	4,800
C	25.6.00	4,000	1.2.05	6,300

All selling prices are shown net of 10% commission paid to the auctioneer. Cubist did not make any other disposals in 2004/05.

Task

Compute Cubist's net chargeable gain for 2004/05 after taper relief but before the annual exemption.

Assume indexation factor

October 1989 to April 1998   0.384

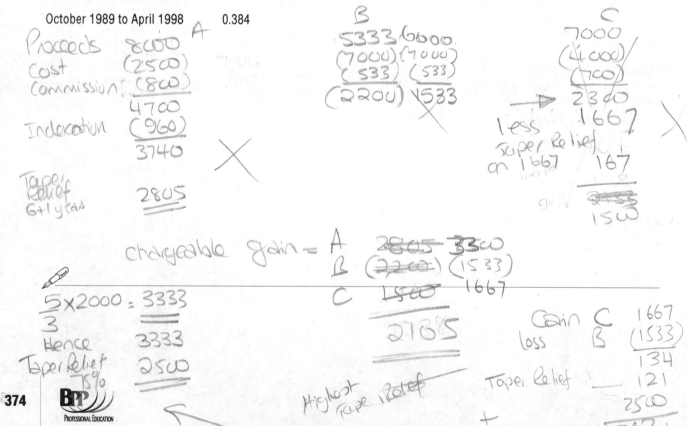

BPP
PROFESSIONAL EDUCATION

9 John Hood

John Hood made the following disposals of assets during the tax year 2004/05.

(i)   16 July 2004, 2,000 shares in ABC plc were given to his son in reward for him passing his accounting examinations. These were the only shares held by John and had cost him £3,000 in September 1999. The shares were valued at £9,200 on the 16 July 2004.

(ii)   19 August 2004. A house was sold for £640,000. This had cost John £66,000 in August 1985. John had lived in the house from August 1985 to August 1996. Thereafter he had lived in a second house he had bought as his principal private residence. The house was let from August 1996 to August 2004.

John was a 40% taxpayer for income tax purposes. None of the assets were business assets for taper relief.

The Revenue had issued a tax return to John on 6 June 2004. This was not the new short tax return.

Tasks

(a)   Calculate John Hood's chargeable gains for 2004/05.

(b)   Calculate the capital gains tax payable.

(c)   State when payment of the tax is due.

(d)   By what date(s) must John return his self assessment form for 2004/05 to the Revenue?

(e)   What penalties may be imposed by the Revenue if John misses the deadline for submitting his tax return?

Assume indexation factors

August 1985 – April 1998   0.703

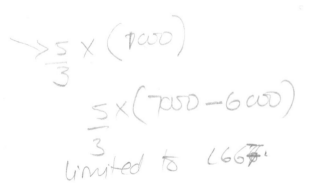

$$\rightarrow \frac{5}{3} \times (7000)$$

$$\frac{5}{3} \times (7000 - 6000)$$

limited to ∠66~~7~~:

Lecturers' Practice Exam

LECTURERS' PRACTICE EXAM

TECHNICIAN STAGE – NVQ4

UNIT 19

Preparing Personal Taxation Computations

Time allowed – 3 hours plus 15 minutes' reading time.

DO NOT OPEN THIS PAPER UNTIL YOU ARE READY TO START UNDER TIMED CONDITIONS

INSTRUCTIONS

This examination paper is in TWO sections.

You have to show competence in BOTH sections.

You should therefore attempt and aim to complete EVERY task in EACH section.

You should spend about 100 minutes on Section 1 and 80 minutes on Section 2.

COVERAGE OF THE PERFORMANCE CRITERIA

The following performance criteria are covered in this practice exam.

Element	PC Coverage
19.1	**Calculate income from employment**
A	Prepare accurate computations of emoluments including benefits
B	List allowable expenses and deductions.
D	Make computations and submissions in accordance with current tax law and take account of current Revenue practice
G	Maintain client confidentiality at all times
19.2	**Calculate property and investment income**
A	Prepare schedules of dividends and interest received on shares and securities
B	Prepare schedules of property income and determine profits and losses
E	Record relevant details of property and investment income accurately and legibly in the tax return
F	Make computations and submissions are made in accordance with current tax law and take account of current Revenue practice
I	Maintain client confidentiality at all times
19.3	**Prepare income tax computations**
A	List general income, savings income and dividend income and check for completeness
B	Calculate and deduct charges and personal allowances
C	Calculate income tax payable
E	Make computations and submissions in accordance with current tax law and take account of current Revenue practice
H	Maintain client confidentiality at all times
19.4	**Prepare capital gains tax computations**
A	Identify and value disposed of chargeable personal assets
B	Identify shares disposed of by individuals
C	Calculate chargeable gains and allowable losses
D	Apply reliefs and exemptions correctly
E	Calculate capital gains tax payable
G	Make computations and submissions in accordance with current tax law and take account of current Revenue practice
I	Maintain client confidentiality at all times

SECTION 1

Data

You went to a meeting held on 19 September 2005 with Mrs Joan Davis, whose husband, Albert, died suddenly on 31 March 2005.

Mrs Davis has asked that we sort out both her and her late husband's tax position for 2004/05. She has supplied the following information.

Mr Albert Davis – deceased – personal details

Income for 2004/05

Employment with Vanhire Ltd	– salary – £14,250, PAYE tax deducted £2,085.
	– benefits – Petrol engined car with CO_2 emissions 197g/km. List price of car £16,800. Capital contributions towards the original cost of the car were £800. In 2004/05 £600 was paid towards the private use of the car. Vanhire Ltd paid for all petrol.

Vanhire Ltd paid other expenses of £460 which relate to a training course which Albert was required to attend by Vanhire Ltd.

Albert was also provided with a TV and video system for use at home. The original cost of this was £1,200.

Task 1.1

Calculate the taxable earnings of Mr Albert Davis for 2004/05.

Mrs Albert Davis

Income for 2004/05

(i)   Pension from old employers ICD plc £7,035 gross (tax deducted £1,945)

(ii)   State retirement pension £3,926

(iii)   **Statement of Rental Income and Expenditure**

Letting of furnished properties	14 West Crescent		Harbour Cottage	
	£	£	£	£
Rental income receivable		5,400		4,000
Less: Legal fees re tenancy agreement	800		–	
Insurance	300		300	
Decoration	240		460	
Repairs	2,800		1,900	
Council Tax	410	(4,550)	290	(2,950)
Surplus for year		850		1,050

Notes

(1)   Both properties were fully let all year and are fully furnished.

(2)   Repairs comprise:

14 West Crescent – installation of central heating £2,800
Harbour Cottage – repairs to roof damaged during storm £1,900

(3)   Joan claims wear and tear allowance instead of the renewals basis.

(iv) **Statement of Savings Income**

	£
Interest on Halifax Building Society account	
Amount credited – on 31 December 2004	720
– on 31 December 2005 – estimated	800
Interest on HSBC bank deposit account	
Amount credited – on 30 June 2004	300
– on 31 December 2004	260
– on 30 June 2005	340
Interest on National Savings Bank easy access account	
Amount credited – on 31 December 2004	130

(v) **Statement of Dividend Income**

	£
Dividends on Interweb plc shares purchased in 2004	
Cheques received – on 19 July 2004	280
– on 3 December 2004	350
– on 4 May 2005	400

(vi) Miscellaneous income – Since her retirement, Joan has sold flowers and bouquets on a part time basis. It has been agreed with the Revenue to treat this income as assessable under Schedule D Case I. The amount assessable for 2004/2005 has been agreed as £2,800.

Payments for 2004/05

Cheque for £250 to NSPCC – a charity – under the gift aid scheme
Cheque for £300 to BUPA for private medical care

Task 1.2

Calculate the Schedule A rental income for 2004/05.

Task 1.3

Prepare schedules showing taxable interest and dividend income for 2004/05.

Task 1.4

Prepare an income tax computation for 2004/05.

Task 1.5

Complete the extract from Mrs Davis' tax return for the year ended 5 April 2005.

Task 1.6

State the dates by which Mrs Davis' tax return for 2004/05 should be submitted. Assume that Mrs Davis does not receive the Short Tax return form.

SECTION 2

Data

In 2004/05 Mrs Davis sold a number of assets in anticipation of moving house in early 2006. She has supplied the following information on these sales.

		£
(i)	*Antique bookcase* – gross proceeds 15.5.04	6,900
	Auctioneer's fee	510
	Cost on 31.3.01	200
(ii)	*Antique clock* – proceeds 4.9.04	7,200
	Cost on 31.3.1982	3,000
(iii)	*Harbour Cottage* – proceeds 29.3.05	81,000
	Cost on 15.3.03	40,000
(iv)	*8,000 shares on Speculate plc* – proceeds 15.12.04	48,000

Joan had bought 3,000 shares in April 1988 for £6,000 and a further 7,000 shares on 3 June 2003 for £28,000. A bonus issue had been made of one for two in June 2004. These shares are a non-business asset for taper relief purposes.

Joan has unrelieved capital losses of £50,000 at 6 April 2004.

Task 2.1

Calculate the capital gains on the disposals in 2004/05.

Task 2.2

Calculate the capital gains tax payable. ✂

Albert's nephew, Rodney Davis, understands that he is a beneficiary in Albert's will. He has left a message on our answerphone asking if we will send him a letter setting out Albert's average annual income and a list of his assets.

Task 2.3

Draft a letter replying to Rodney for me to review.

Cost 6900
      200
      ‾‾‾‾
      6700
Act   510
      ‾‾‾‾
      6190

900 × 5/3

      1500
      ‾‾‾‾
Taper 90%

Antique Clock   7200
                3000
               ‾‾‾‾
                4200   Exempt under 6k.

Harb Cottage   81,000
               40,000
              ‾‾‾‾‾‾
               41,000   95% Taper

shares. 8,000 48,000 £6·00

BPP
PROFESSIONAL EDUCATION

Income for the year ended 5 April 2005

Inland Revenue

LAND AND PROPERTY

Name

Tax reference

Fill in these boxes first

If you want help, look up the box numbers in the Notes.

Are you claiming Rent a Room relief for gross rents of £4,250 or less?
(Or £2,125 If the claim is shared?)
Read the Notes on page LN2 to find out
- whether you can claim Rent a Room relief; and
- how to claim relief for gross rents over £4,250

Yes ☐

If 'Yes', tick box. If this is your only income from UK property, you have finished these Pages

Is your income from furnished holiday lettings?
If not applicable, please turn over and fill in Page L2 to give details of your property income

Yes ☐

If 'Yes', tick box and fill in boxes 5.1 to 5.18 before completing Page L2

Furnished holiday lettings

- Income from furnished holiday lettings

5.1 £

- *Expenses* (furnished holiday lettings only)

- Rent, rates, insurance, ground rents etc.   **5.2** £
- Repairs, maintenance and renewals   **5.3** £
- Finance charges, including interest   **5.4** £
- Legal and professional costs   **5.5** £
- Costs of services provided, including wages   **5.6** £
- Other expenses   **5.7** £

total of boxes 5.2 to 5.7
5.8 £

Net profit (put figures in brackets if a loss)

box 5.1 *minus* box 5.8
5.9 £

- *Tax adjustments*

- Private use   **5.10** £
- Balancing charges   **5.11** £

box 5.10 + box 5.11
5.12 £

- Capital allowances   **5.13** £

- Tick box 5.13A if box 5.13 includes enhanced capital allowances for environmentally friendly expenditure   **5.13A** ☐

Profit for the year (copy to box 5.19). If loss, enter '0' in box 5.14 and put the loss in box 5.15

boxes 5.9 + 5.12 *minus* box 5.13
5.14 £

Loss for the year (if you have entered '0' in box 5.14)

boxes 5.9 + 5.12 *minus* box 5.13
5.15 £

- *Losses*

- Loss offset against 2004-05 total income   **5.16** £

see Notes, page LN4
- Loss carried back   **5.17** £

see Notes, page LN4
- Loss offset against other income from property (copy to box 5.38)   **5.18** £

SA105

BS 12/04net

TAX RETURN ■ LAND AND PROPERTY: PAGE L1

Please turn over ▶

Other property income

■ Income

	copy from box 5.14	
● Furnished holiday lettings profits	**5.19** £	

		Tax deducted
● Rents and other income from land and property	**5.20** £	**5.21** £
● Chargeable premiums	**5.22** £	
● Reverse premiums	**5.22A** £	boxes 5.19 + 5.20 + 5.22 + 5.22A **5.23** £

■ Expenses (do not include figures you have already put in boxes 5.2 to 5.7 on Page L1)

● Rent, rates, insurance, ground rents etc.	**5.24** £	
● Repairs, maintenance and renewals	**5.25** £	
● Finance charges, including interest	**5.26** £	
● Legal and professional costs	**5.27** £	
● Costs of services provided, including wages	**5.28** £	
● Other expenses	**5.29** £	total of boxes 5.24 to 5.29 **5.30** £

Net profit (put figures in brackets if a loss)   box 5.23 *minus* box 5.30 **5.31** £

■ Tax adjustments

● Private use	**5.32** £	
● Balancing charges	**5.33** £	box 5.32 + box 5.33 **5.34** £
● Rent a Room exempt amount	**5.35** £	
● Capital allowances	**5.36** £	
● Tick box 5.36A if box 5.36 includes a claim for 100% capital allowances for flats over shops	**5.36A**	
● Tick box 5.36B if box 5.36 includes enhanced capital allowances for environmentally friendly expenditure	**5.36B**	
● 10% wear and tear	**5.37** £	
● Furnished holiday lettings losses (from box 5.18)	**5.38** £	boxes 5.35 to box 5.38 **5.39** £

Adjusted profit (if loss enter '0' in box 5.40 and put the loss in box 5.41)   boxes 5.31 + 5.34 *minus* box 5.39 **5.40** £

Adjusted loss (if you have entered '0' in box 5.40)   boxes 5.31 + 5.34 *minus* box 5.39 **5.41** £

● Loss brought forward from previous year	**5.42** £

Profit for the year   box 5.40 *minus* box 5.42 **5.43** £

■ Losses etc

● Loss offset against total income (read the note on page LN8)	**5.44** £	
● Loss to carry forward to following year	**5.45** £	
● Tick box 5.46 if these Pages include details of property let jointly	**5.46**	
● Tick box 5.47 if **all** property income ceased in the year to 5 April 2005 **and** you don't expect to receive such income again, in the year to 5 April 2006	**5.47**	

Now fill in any other supplementary Pages that apply to you.
Otherwise, go back to page 2 of your Tax Return and finish filling it in.

BS 12/04net   TAX RETURN ■ LAND AND PROPERTY: PAGE L2

TAXATION TABLES

Capital gains tax

Annual exemption £8,200

Indexation factors

March 1982 - April 1998 1.047

Income tax

Allowances	£
Personal allowance	4,745

Rates of income tax

Taxed @ 10%	First £2,020
Taxed @ 22%	Next £29,380
Taxed @ 40%	The balance

Car fuel benefit

Set figure £14,400

Car benefit

Baseline CO_2 emissions   145 g/km

Official rate of interest   5%

Index

AAT Order

To BPP Professional Education, Aldine Place, London W12 8AW

Tel: 020 8740 2211. Fax: 020 8740 1184

E-mail: Publishing@bpp.com Web:www.bpp.com

Mr/Mrs/Ms (Full name)

Daytime delivery address

Postcode

Daytime Tel

E-mail

	5/04 Texts	5/04 Kits	Special offer	8/04 Passcards	Success CDs
FOUNDATION (£14.95 except as indicated)				Foundation	
Units 1 & 2 Receipts and Payments	☐	☐	Foundation Sage Bookeeping and Excel Spreadsheets CD-ROM free if ordering all Foundation Text and Kits, including Units 21 and 22/23 ☐	£6.95 ☐	£14.95 ☐
Unit 3 Ledger Balances and Initial Trial Balance	☐ (Combined Text & Kit)				
Unit 4 Supplying Information for Mgmt Control	☐ (Combined Text & Kit)				
Unit 21 Working with Computers (£9.95)	☐				
Unit 22/23 Healthy Workplace/Personal Effectiveness (£9.95)	☐				
Sage and Excel for Foundation (Workbook with CD-ROM £9.95)	☐				
INTERMEDIATE (£9.95 except as indicated)					
Unit 5 Financial Records and Accounts	☐	☐		£5.95 ☐	£14.95 ☐
Unit 6/7 Costs and Reports (Combined Text £14.95)	☐			£5.95 ☐	
Unit 6 Costs and Revenues		☐			£14.95 ☐
Unit 7 Reports and Returns		☐			
TECHNICIAN (£9.95 except as indicated)					
Unit 8/9 Core Managing Performance and Controlling Resources	☐	☐		£5.95 ☐	£14.95 ☐
Spreadsheets for Technician (Workbook with CD-ROM)	☐		Spreadsheets for Technicians CD-ROM free if take Unit 8/9 Text and Kit ☐		
Unit 10 Core Managing Systems and People (£14.95)	☐ (Combined Text & Kit)			£5.95 ☐	£14.95 ☐
Unit 11 Option Financial Statements (A/c Practice)	☐	☐		£5.95 ☐	
Unit 12 Option Financial Statements (Central Govnmt)	☐	☐		£5.95 ☐	
Unit 15 Option Cash Management and Credit Control	☐	☐		£5.95 ☐	
Unit 17 Option Implementing Audit Procedures	☐	☐		£5.95 ☐	
Unit 18 Option Business Tax FA04 (8/04) (£14.95)	☐ (Combined Text & Kit)			£5.95 ☐	
Unit 19 Option Personal Tax FA04 (8/04) (£14.95)	☐ (Combined Text & Kit)			£5.95 ☐	
TECHNICIAN 2003 (£9.95)					
Unit 18 Option Business Tax FA03 (8/03 Text & Kit)	☐	☐			
Unit 19 Option Personal Tax FA03 (8/03 Text & Kit)	☐	☐			
SUBTOTAL	£	£	£	£	£

TOTAL FOR PRODUCTS £ ☐

POSTAGE & PACKING

Texts/Kits	First	Each extra	
UK	£3.00	£3.00	☐ £
Europe*	£6.00	£4.00	☐ £
Rest of world	£20.00	£10.00	☐ £
Passcards			
UK	£2.00	£1.00	☐ £
Europe*	£3.00	£2.00	☐ £
Rest of world	£8.00	£8.00	☐ £
Success CDs			
UK	£2.00	£1.00	☐ £
Europe*	£3.00	£2.00	☐ £
Rest of world	£8.00	£8.00	☐ £

TOTAL FOR POSTAGE & PACKING £ ☐

(Max £12 Texts/Kits/Passcards - deliveries in UK)

Grand Total (Cheques to *BPP Professional Education*)

I enclose a cheque for (incl. Postage) ☐ £

Or charge to Access/Visa/Switch

Card Number ☐☐☐☐ ☐☐☐☐ ☐☐☐☐ ☐☐☐☐   CV2 No ☐☐☐ last 3 digits on signature strip

Expiry date ☐☐☐☐   Start Date ☐☐☐☐

Issue Number (Switch Only) ☐☐

Signature _____

We aim to deliver to all UK addresses inside 5 working days; a signature will be required. Orders to all EU addresses should be delivered within 6 working days. All other orders to overseas addresses should be delivered within 8 working days. * Europe includes the Republic of Ireland and the Channel Islands.

AAT Order

To BPP Professional Education, Aldine Place, London W12 8AW
Tel: 020 8740 2211. Fax: 020 8740 1184
E-mail: Publishing@bpp.com Web:www.bpp.com

Mr/Mrs/Ms (Full name)

Daytime delivery address

Postcode

Daytime Tel   E-mail

OTHER MATERIAL FOR AAT STUDENTS

	8/04 Texts	3/03 Text	3/04 Text

FOUNDATION (£5.95)

Basic Maths and English ☐

INTERMEDIATE (£5.95)

Basic Bookkeeping (for students exempt from Foundation) ☐

FOR ALL STUDENTS (£5.95)

Building Your Portfolio (old standards) ☐

Building Your Portfolio (new standards) ☐

Basic Costing ☐

AAT PAYROLL

	Finance Act 2004 8/04	Finance Act 2003 9/03
	December 2004 and June 2005 assessments	June 2004 exams only

Special offer Take Text and Kit together £44.95 ☐   **Special offer** Take Text and Kit together £44.95 ☐

☐   ☐
☐   ☐

For assessments in 2005   For assessments in 2004

☐   ☐
☐   ☐

LEVEL 2 Text (£29.95) ☐   £

LEVEL 2 Kit (£19.95) ☐

LEVEL 3 Text (£29.95) ☐   £

LEVEL 3 Kit (£19.95)

SUBTOTAL £

TOTAL FOR PRODUCTS £

POSTAGE & PACKING

Texts/Kits	First	Each extra	
UK	£3.00	£3.00	£
Europe*	£6.00	£4.00	£
Rest of world	£20.00	£10.00	£
Passcards			
UK	£2.00	£1.00	£
Europe*	£3.00	£2.00	£
Rest of world	£8.00	£8.00	£
Tapes			
UK	£2.00	£1.00	£
Europe*	£3.00	£2.00	£
Rest of world	£8.00	£8.00	£

TOTAL FOR POSTAGE & PACKING £
(Max £12 Texts/Kits/Passcards - deliveries in UK)

Grand Total (Cheques to *BPP Professional Education*)

I enclose a cheque for (incl. Postage) £

Or charge to Access/Visa/Switch

Card Number   CV2 No   last 3 digits on signature strip

Expiry date   Start Date

Issue Number (Switch Only)

Signature

We aim to deliver to all UK addresses inside 5 working days; a signature will be required. Orders to all EU addresses should be delivered within 6 working days. All other orders to overseas addresses should be delivered within 8 working days. * Europe includes the Republic of Ireland and the Channel Islands.

Review Form & Free Prize Draw – Unit 19 Preparing Personal Taxation Computations (8/04)

All original review forms from the entire BPP range, completed with genuine comments, will be entered into one of two draws on 31 January 2005 and 31 July 2005. The names on the first four forms picked out on each occasion will be sent a cheque for £50.

Name: _____   Address: _____

_____

_____

How have you used this Combined Text and Kit?
(Tick one box only)

☐ Home study (book only)

☐ On a course: college _____

☐ With 'correspondence' package

☐ Other _____

Why did you decide to purchase this Interactive Text? *(Tick one box only)*

☐ Have used BPP Texts in the past

☐ Recommendation by friend/colleague

☐ Recommendation by a lecturer at college

☐ Saw advertising

☐ Other _____

During the past six months do you recall seeing/receiving any of the following?
(Tick as many boxes as are relevant)

☐ Our advertisement in *Accounting Technician* magazine

☐ Our advertisement in *Pass*

☐ Our brochure with a letter through the post

Which (if any) aspects of our advertising do you find useful?
(Tick as many boxes as are relevant)

☐ Prices and publication dates of new editions

☐ Information on Interactive Text content

☐ Facility to order books off-the-page

☐ None of the above

Your ratings, comments and suggestions would be appreciated on the following areas

	Very useful	Useful	Not useful
Introduction	☐	☐	☐
Chapter contents lists	☐	☐	☐
Examples	☐	☐	☐
Activities and answers	☐	☐	☐
Key learning points	☐	☐	☐
Quick quizzes and answers	☐	☐	☐
Activity checklist	☐	☐	☐

	Excellent	Good	Adequate	Poor
Overall opinion of this Text	☐	☐	☐	☐

Do you intend to continue using BPP Interactive Texts/Assessment Kits?   ☐ Yes   ☐ No

Please note any further comments and suggestions/errors on the reverse of this page.

The BPP author of this edition can be e-mailed at: suedexter@bpp.com

Please return this form to: Janice Ross, BPP Professional Education, FREEPOST, London, W12 8BR

Review Form & Free Prize Draw (continued)

Please note any further comments and suggestions/errors below

Free Prize Draw Rules

1   Closing date for 31 January 2005 draw is 31 December 2004. Closing date for 31 July 2005 draw is 30 June 2005.

2   Restricted to entries with UK and Eire addresses only. BPP employees, their families and business associates are excluded.

3   No purchase necessary. Entry forms are available upon request from BPP Professional Education. No more than one entry per title, per person. Draw restricted to persons aged 16 and over.

4   Winners will be notified by post and receive their cheques not later than 6 weeks after the relevant draw date.

5   The decision of the promoter in all matters is final and binding. No correspondence will be entered into.